The Reminiscences of

VICE ADMIRAL BERNARD L. AUSTIN

U. S. Navy, Retired

U. S. Naval Institute
Annapolis, Maryland
1971

Preface

This manuscript is the result of a series of tape-recorded interviews with Vice Admiral Bernard L. Austin, USN (Ret.) at his home in Rockville, Maryland, commencing in August, 1969, and continuing into January, 1971. These interviews were conducted by Commander Paul L. Hopper, USNR (Ret.) for the Oral History Office in the U. S. Naval Institute.

Only minor emendations and corrections have been made to the text by Admiral Austin. The reader is asked, therefore, to bear in mind that he is reading a transcript of the spoken word rather than the written one.

VICE ADMIRAL BERNARD L. AUSTIN, UNITED STATES NAVY, RETIRED

Bernard Lige Austin was born in Wagener, South Carolina, on December 15, 1902, son of Elijah Andrew and Loula Ola (Gantt) Austin. He attended The Citadel, Military College of South Carolina, in Charleston, before his appointment to the U. S. Naval Academy from the Second District of his native state in 1920. While a Midshipman he was a member of the Lucky Bag Staff. Graduated and commission Ensign in June 1924, he subsequently advanced in rank to that of Rear Admiral to date from September 1, 1951, having served in the temporary rank of Commodore from December 12, 1944, to October 29, 1945. He was promoted to the rank of Vice Admiral, to date from February 8, 1956.

After graduation from the Naval Academy in 1924, he was assigned to the Bureau of Ordnance, Navy Department, Washington, D. C., for temporary duty under instruction at the Naval Gun Factory, Navy Yard, Washington; the Naval Proving Ground, Dahlgren, Virginia, and Naval Powder Factory, Indian Head, Maryland. Completing his instruction in August 1924, he joined the USS NEW YORK, in which he served for two years. Between July and December 1926, he had instruction at the Naval Torpedo Station, Newport, Rhode Island, and the ensuing six months had submarine training aboard the USS CHEWINK, station ship at the Submarine Base, New London, Connecticut. In July 1927 he joined the submarine R-10, based on Pearl Harbor, T. H., and in June 1929 was transferred to the submarine R-6, in which he served until May 1931.

The three succeeding years he was an instructor in the Department of Electrical Engineering and Physics at the Naval Academy and, returning to sea in May 1934, he commanded the USS R-11 until June 1937, then for six months he served as Executive Officer of the USS POTOMAC. In December 1937 he became Press Relations Officer, Navy Department, and remained in that assignment until August 1940, when he was sent to the American Embassy, London, England, as a Special Naval Observer. He commanded the USS WOOLSEY from February 12 to December 1942, and for meritorious achievement as Commanding Officer of the USS WOOLSEY, during operations against enemy forces off the Coast of North Africa, on November 16, 1942, was awarded the Bronze Star Medal with Combat "V." The citation follows in part:

"...While patrolling the entrance to Casablanca Harbor in company with the USS SWANSON and the USS QUICK, Lieutenant Commander Austin contacted an enemy submarine and, by skillful direction of the offensive weapons of his ship, launched vigorous underwater attacks against the hostile vessel. Closely cooperating with the two accompanying destroyers, he contributed materially to the destruction of the enemy submarine before she could carry out an attack on any friendly ship..."

V. Adm. B. L. Austin, USN, Ret.   Page 2

After fitting out the USS FOOTE, he assumed command of that destroyer upon her commissioning, December 22, 1942, and in May 1943 became Commander Destroyer Division 46. For services in that command in the Solomon Islands area, he was awarded the Navy Cross and a Gold Star in lieu of the Second Navy Cross, with citations which follow, in part:

Navy Cross: "For extraordinary heroism as Commander, Destroyer Division FORTY-SIX, attached to Destroyer Squadron TWENTY THREE, during a night engagement with six enemy Japanese warships off Bougainville, British Solomon Islands, on November 24-25, 1943...(He) fought his division with resolute courage and daring aggressiveness, frequently risking his own personal safety to press home vigorous unrelenting attacks upon Japanese surface forces...to contribute materially to the crushing defeat imposed upon the enemy in the sinking of four ships and the serious damaging of two others. An expert seaman and tactician, (he) retired his forces from the engagement without loss or damage..."

Gold Star in lieu of Second Navy Cross: "For extraordinary heroism as Commander Destroyer Division FORTY-SIX, in action against enemy Japanese forces in the Solomon Islands on the night of November 1-2, 1943. With his Task Force engaging a Japanese surface force of superior fire power, (he) hurled the full fighting strength of his ship against the enemy and, by his inspiring leadership and skilled combat tactics, aided his Task Force in sinking five hostile warships, in damaging four others and in completely routing the enemy, thereby contributing materially to the successful establishment of our beachhead on Bougainville Island..."

He also has the Ribbon for, and facsimile of the Presidential Unit Citation to Destroyer Squadron TWENTY-THREE for "extraordinary heroism in action against enemy Japanese forces during the Solomon Islands Campaign from November 1, 1943 to February 23, 1944..." The citation concluded with: "The brilliant and heroic record achieved by Destroyer Squadron TWENTY-THREE is a distinctive tribute to the valiant fighting spirit of the individual units in this indomitable combat group and of each skilled and courageous ship's company."

In December 1943 he reported as Commander, Destroyer Squadron FOURTEEN, with additional duty as Commander Destroyer Division TWENTY-SEVEN. On April 15, 1944, he was transferred to duty as Assistant Chief of Staff for Operations and Training on the Staff of the Commander Destroyers, Pacific Fleet. On June 9, 1944, he became Assistant Chief of Staff for Administration to the Commander in Chief, Pacific Fleet and Pacific Ocean Areas. He was awarded the Legion of Merit "For exceptionally meritorious conduct... (in that assignment) from June 9, 1944 to September 1, 1945...during the Marianas, Iwo Jima and Okinawa Campaigns and the occupation of Japan..."

On October 25, 1945 he was ordered to duty in the Office of the Chief of Naval Operations, Navy Department, and in December of the same year was assigned duty as Navy Secretary of the State-War-Navy Coordinating Committee. Completing the course at the National War College, Washington, D. C., in June 1947, he was detached to duty as Assistant to the Assistant Chief of Naval Operations for Politico-Military Affairs, Navy Departmennnt, and served in that capacity until October 1949.

After a year's special duty in England, in January 1950 he was designated Commander Service Squadron ONE, and in July was sent to the Western Pacific to organize and command Service Squadron THREE. For his contribution to the war effort in Korea, he was awarded the Distinguished Service Medal. In May 1951 he became Assistant Director, International Affairs Division, Office of the Chief of Naval Operations, and from February 1952 to March 1954 served as Director of that Division. He then reported as Commander Cruiser Division TWO, and in April 1955 joined the staff of the Supreme Allied Commander, Europe.

On March 15, 1956, he reported, in the rank of Vice Admiral, as Director of the Joint Staff Office, Joint Chiefs of Staff, Washington, D. C. On May 5, 1958 he assumed command of the SECOND Fleet with additional duty as Commander Strike Fleet, Atlantic. He was Deputy Chief of Naval Operations (Plans and Policy), Navy Department, from March 1959 until July 1960, when he became President of the Naval War College, Newport, Rhode Island. "For exceptionally meritorious service...(in that capacity), from July 1960 to July 1964..." he was awarded a Gold Star in lieu of the Second Distinguished Service Medal. The citation further states in part:

"An inspiring leader and educator, Vice Admiral Austin drew upon his great wealth of wisdom and experience in a dedicated effort to enrich the postgraduate education of students at the Naval War College in the field of maritime strategy and its relationship to overall national and allied objectives and strategy. Among his numerous achievements during this period were he sursuance of an optimum use of the Navy Electronic Warfare Simulator to achieve maximum attainment of its full potential for advancement of the art of war gaming; his substantial contributions to the cause of international understanding and cooperation through his contacts with senior foreign officers attending the Naval Command Course, and the many foreign officers and civilian dignitaries who visit Newport; his revitalization of the Naval War College leadership in the study of fundamentals of warfare and maritime strategy by directing the War College staff to research and present each year a series of lectures on sea power and maritime strategy; and his acute awareness of the importance of interservice cooperation and understanding by promoting these ends at every opportunity. Through these and many other achievements, Vice Admiral Austin rendered outstanding and distinguished service to his country..."

On August 1, 1964 he was transferred to the Retired List, but continued to serve on active duty as Chairman of the Inter-American Defense Board, Washington, D. C. He was awarded a Gold Star in lieu of the Third Distinguished Service Medal and cited as follows:

V. Adm. B. L. Austin, USN, Ret.   Page 4

"For exceptionally meritorious service...from August 1964 through June 1967. As Chairman of this international military organization consisting of twenty American Republics, Vice Admiral Austin has gained the confidence and respect of his associates and has been highly successful in furthering United States national policy and security interests. Guiding the board to a new sense of unity and purpose, he has attained outstanding cooperation, among the military forces of the hemisphere, in support of Inter-American Defense Board policies formulated with a view toward solving the complex problems of the defense and security of the Western Hemisphere. Through his outstanding leadership, (he) has fostered the need for a better understanding of the requirement for unity among the countries of the Western Hemisphere, thus contributing to the maintenance of world peace and security..."

He was assigned to the Bureau of Naval Personnel, Navy Department, during the period August to October 17, 1967, when he was released from active duty. Ordered to return to active duty, he served from June to August 15, 1968 as Senior Naval Officer in connection with the investigation of the disappearance of the USS SCORPION (SS(N)-589), attached to the Staff of the Commander in Chief, U. S. Atlantic Fleet and in November 1968 again returned to active duty to serve in the same capacity until December 14, 1968.

In addition to the Navy Cross with Gold Star in lieu of a Second Navy Cross, the Distinguished Service Medal with two Gold Stars, the Legion of Merit, the Bronze Star Medal with Combat "V," and the Ribbon for the Presidential Unit Citation to Destroyer Division TWENTY-THREE, Vice Admiral Austin has the American Defense Service Medal, Fleet Clasp; European-African-Middle Eastern Campaign Medal; Asiatic-Pacific Campaign Medal; the World War II Victory Medal; Navy Occupation Service Medal, Europe Clasp; National Defense Service Medal with bronze star; Korean Service Medal; United Nations Service Medal; Navy Expeditionary Medal (Cuba). He also has the Peruvian Cross of Naval Merit (Grand Officer) Distintivo Blanco and the Korean Presidential Unit Citation Badge.

Vice Admiral Austin and his wife, the former Isabella Murray Leith of Springfield, Massachusetts, officially reside at 420 Oakland Avenue, Rock Hill, South Carolina.

Navy Office of Information
Internal Relations Division (OI-430)
11 March 1969

DECLARATION OF TRUST

The undersigned does hereby appoint and designate as his (her) Trustee herein, the Secretary-Treasurer and Publisher of the United States Naval Institute to perform and discharge the following duties, powers, and privileges in connection with the possession and use of a certain taped interview between the undersigned and the Oral History Department of the United States Naval Institute.

1. Classification of Transcript.

   ( )a. If classified OPEN, the transcript(s) may be read or the recording(s) audited by the qualified personnel upon presentation of proper credentials, as determined by the Secretary-Treasurer of the U. S. Naval Institute.

   (✓)b. If classified PERMISSION REQUIRED TO CITE OR QUOTE, the user will be required to obtain permission in writing from the interviewee prior to quoting or citing from either the transcript(s) or the recording(s).

   ( )c. If classified PERMISSION REQUIRED, permission must be obtained in writing from the interviewee before the transcribed interview(s) can be examined or the tape recording(s) audited.

   ( )d. If classified CLOSED, the transcribed interview(s) and the tape recording(s) will be sealed until a time specified by the interviewee. This may be until the death of the interviewee or for any specified number of years.

2. It is expressly understood that in giving this authorization, I am in no way precluded from placing such restrictions as I may desire upon use of the interview at any time during my lifetime, nor does this authorization in any way affect my rights to the copyright of my literary expressions that may be contained in the interview.

Witness my hand and seal this 3rd day of May 1971.

Bernard L. Austin

I hereby accept and consent to the foregoing Declaration of Trust and the powers therein conferred upon me as Trustee:

R. E. Bowsher Jr.

Interview #1

Interview with Vice Admiral
    Bernard L. Austin

by Paul L. Hopper

Washington, D. C.

August 22, 1969

Mr. Hopper: After graduation from the Naval Academy in 1924 Admiral, known affectionately among his associates as Count Austin, has had a very distinguished and varied naval career.

Admiral Austin: I was born in a small town in South Carolina, Wagener, population roughly 1,000. I went through graded school in Wagener, and remember that we had all of four in our graduating class, three boys and one girl. I finished high school at Wagener also in the new brick school house, which replaced the old frame building that I'd been through in the lower grades. I was then 15 years old.

My father had indicated that I could choose my college, and that then he expected me to do my part making good there when I made the choice. I considered many colleges from Harvard all the way down to Presbyterian College of South Carolina. I finally settled upon the Citadel, probably because one of the Citadel graduates was the President of our local bank. He had been a very good friend to me as a young boy on many occasions. In fact, he tried to get my father to let me go in his bank as an employee; with the idea of training me in the banking business.

My first pair of long trousers were put on the morning I left on the train to go to the Citadel. When I got to the Citadel, the age matter had been accepted by the authorities. They made an exception to the regular rule about admissions. Shortly thereafter, this became a problem for the administrative authorities of the school because the entire student body of the Citadel was inducted into the U. S. Army as a member of the student Army Training Corps.

Q: Was that before the ROTC was set up as such?

Austin: I really couldn't say, but I think it was.

One day the Colonel in charge of the unit at the Citadel, sent for me and advised me that I was causing him a lot of trouble. I expressed regret at this and asked what I could do about it. He said, "There isn't anything you can do about it, because it's a matter of your age. We're not allowed to have anybody in the student Army Training Corps at the age of 15. You're the only one in the school that poses this problem. You've paid your tuition fees, and we can't very well have a separate school for you. We want you to cooperate with us a little. We'll let you stay in the student Army Training Corps, but we won't carry you on the rolls. You won't get any pay, and you'll have to pay for your own equipment."

Austin - 3

I thought that over, and he gave me an estimate of how much it would cost me. I figured that probably I could raise that amount extra. So, I agreed to be in the Army, but not in the Army.

Recently at a dinner given by one of my very good friends in the Army, Clyde Edleman, for General Westmoreland; General Westmoreland in his remarks referred to me as the only one at the dinner who was not really an Army person. He pointed out that I had defected, after going to the Citadel as he had done; and had gone in the Navy. When he made so much of this defection on my part to the Navy, the host asked me to get up and say a few words. I reminded General Westmoreland that on the surface I may appear as an outsider, but that I had been in the Army before he, because he went to the Citadel at a later date than I. He was quick on the trigger, and he said, "Oh, yes, you were in that student Army Training Corps, weren't you?" I didn't tell him the story about my being in, but not in. I let him think that I had preceeded him as a member of the U. S. Army.

At the Citadel, I became very good friends with a history professor there, a Captain Williams. I had never really liked history as a student in high school, but this man taught it in such a fascinating way. He made it make sense. It wasn't just a combination of dates, and times, and places, and names of prominent participants. He traced the undercurrents of history. At the end of the first term under him, he sent for me one night and asked if I had ever taught history. I said, "No, Captain I've never taught history." He said, "I've just finished correcting your paper. You have gotten every point that I tried to get across to that class this term. I've never corrected such a paper before." I said, "It was just interesting, sir, so I guess I just remembered it."

So, near the end of my second year at the Citadel; I received a letter from Mr. Byrnes, who was then the Congressman from our district in South Carolina, saying that he had spoken to my father and asked him if I would be allowed to accept an appointment to Annapolis. My father had replied that that would be entirely up to me. That's why he was writing to me direct.

I took this letter to my good friend, Captain Williams and asked for his advice. He and I had previously been discussing the probabilty of my shifting from the Citadel to the University of Virginia to study law. The University of Virginia was Captain Williams alma mater before he went abroad to study at various places. We had just about decided that that was what I was going to do.

So, we were discussing the pros and cons of this offer from Mr. Byrnes for my going to Annapolis instead; and had about arrived at the decision that we would tell Mr. Byrnes, "No," When one of the other Captains on the faculty came in,

He was the mathematics professor. It just happened that I was standing number one in mathematics in my class, so when Captain Hare heard that I was about to consider going to the Naval Academy, he said, "There's only one answer. You turn it down. You stay right here."

Captain Williams told him that even if I didn't go to the Naval Academy, I probably wouldn't come back to the Citadel next year. Then they had an argument which was not exactly friendly. Captain Williams was accused of not having the interest of the good Citadel at heart, and that sort of thing.

I went home on my summer's leave from the Citadel. My father and I were over in Aiken, our county seat, where Mr. Byrnes lived; and we ran in to him on the street.

He jumped on me with great vim and vigor. He was not lacking in eloquence anyway. So, when he finished telling me how the Naval Academy took a young boy in, measured every muscle in his body, gave him the necessary exercise to bring it up to par, and how the cirriculum was wonderfully interesting and broad –– he had just been on the board of visitors, so he was well informed. I was impressed. During this eloquent explanation of why I should have accepted, intead of turning down his appointment; he had said that he had already given the appointment to another boy. When I could break in with a word, I said, "Mr. Byrnes, why do you want to make me so unhappy, if you've given the appointment away? I'd never even thought of going to Annapolis, until I got your letter. I did give it serious consideration, sir. I went and discussed it with my best friend on the faculty at the Citadel. Frankly after hearing you, I think I've probably made a big mistake. Why do you want to make me feel so badly about it? I'd thought a little about going to West Point maybe, but I'd never thought about Annapolis until I got your letter. If I'd known then what I know now, I probably would have said, yes."

At that, he pointed his finger at me, and said, "Will you go, if I get you another appointment?" I said, "Yes, sir, I would."

This was a Saturday. The next day, I had the family car out with a few of my friends in it and when I passed the house my father waved me down with a telegram. It was from Mr. Byrnes. The telegram read, as best I remember, "Have appointment for you either West Point or Annapolis. Which do you accept?"

About ten days later, I was in Annapolis. And in a suit of the most poorly fitted white works that you could imagine, and a very ungainly-looking young midshipman.

Q: Did you have to take a qualifying examination?

Austin: No, or I couldn't have gotten in that quickly. My

Austin - 7

credits from the Citadel were accepted. So, I went in on what they called a certificate, instead of an examination.

As a young boy, I wanted to engage in some lucrative activity. This caused, I recall, a very definite argument between my father and my mother. My mother was more sympathetic towards my desires than my father, because what I wanted to start out doing, was deliver papers. My father said, no, he didn't want his boy delivering papers. As very often happens in arguments between man and wife, my mother won. And I delivered papers.

Later on, I got my father to agree to let me be the agent for the steam laundry in Columbia, South Carolina. In those days people wore stiff collars, and the housewife couldn't do the stiff collars quite as well as the steam laundry could do them. So, I became the agent in our little town for the steam laundry.

As years went on, I employed one of my contemporaries as an assistant in my paper and laundry business. His name was Asa Godbold. Asa was a good assistant, he was a hard worker. When I went off to college, I turned over my laundry and paper business to him on a commission basis. He was to keep the books, and he was to take half of the net profits, and I was to get the other half.

After about a year and a half at the Citadel receiving these monthly checks from Asa, my conscience got the better of me. I decided that Asa had adequately paid for my share of the business. So, I wrote him a letter and told him that hereafter, all the profits would be kept and none would be sent to me.

One of the things that I loved as a youngster was hunting. I had several young friends who also liked to hunt. I got my first shotgun as the result, shall we say of marksmanship.

I didn't pose as any great marksman, but I was out one day with my father and some of his friends. They had been dove shooting, and they were waiting for a car to pick them up. They were shooting shell boxes off of a post.

I asked if I could take a turn. My father looked at me and said, "Why, son the gun would kick you down." I said, "Not if I hold it tight enough." He said, "Alright if you want to try. If you knock that shell box off of that post over yonder with one shot, I'll give you a shotgun of your own." When he said it like that, I took about the best aim in shooting in my life. Sure enough, I knocked the shell box off. He lived up to his word, and bought me a nice little 20 guage shotgun.

One day, one of my friends and I were out shooting in a cornfield. We shot a bird and it fell. We went over to pick it up. One of our contemporaries a chap named Spurgen who had been a little bit of a trouble maker at school, who once before had shot me in the neck with a bb rifle; came over to claim the bird. We advised him that we thought it was our bird, and he advised us that he knew it was his bird. He grabbed the bird and started away. Whereupon we did what sometimes young people will do, we ganged up on him. We took the bird, and proceeded on our way. We hadn't gotten far enough, before we heard a bang behind us; and Spurgeon had shot us with his shotgun.

If we hadn't had on pretty thick hunting coats, we probably would have been more endangered than we were. As it happened, we had to take a few shot out of our backs after we got home; but none had gone in far enough to damage any organs. After that, Spurgeon was not our favorite companion on shooting expeditions.

Speaking of the rare luck and marksmanship of shooting a shell box off with a shotgun, I later at the Naval Academy was an instructor in Physics there for three years. One day after we'd finished our tote - up of the marks at the office; some bachelors who were in the same committee as I, asked me to join them for lunch out at their country place, just out of Annapolis.

So, we went out and we had a nice lunch. After lunch I saw one of them wink to one of the others, He said, "Now, Count, we always do a little shooting after lunch." So, they threw up the window - this was in the wintertime. They said, "You're our guest, you take the first shot. You see those bottles and cans on that row out there on the shelf, those are our targets." I said, "What's your most difficult target?" They exchanged some glances, and said, "You see that apple tree out there?" I said, "Yes." They said, "You see the crotch on the right hand side?" I said, "Yes." They said, "Do you see that cigarette in that crotch?" I said, "If you say that's a cigarette; I see something that looks like a little stick or something in there." They said, "That's a cigarette." I said, "That's your most difficult target?" They said, "Yes."

So, I took the 22 rifle. Without having the faintest idea that I would come anywhere near the cigarette, I shot and the cigarette went into a thousand pieces. They said, "Oh, now try --". And they pointed out another difficult target. I said, "No boys. I never waste my time with anything but the most difficult target." So, I got away with it.

Q: Well, you must have been a very good shot, count, even at that.

Austin: I'd been shooting ever since I was a little boy. I have qualified as an expert rifleman in the Navy, but I'm not that good. That was just a miracle.

Austin - 11

I used to like to go fishing when I was boy. Even when I was a very small boy, my father and mother would let me go down to a farm which she'd inherited from her family on the old Edisto River. There're two Edistos, north and south. This was north Edisto. There was a fine old colored man who was kept there, not so much because he was a good farmer, but because he was a good fisherman. He was a very dependable man. So, the family felt that if old William was going to be around keeping an eye on us; we'd be all right. I had to take a friend with me; I wasn't allowed to camp out there on the bank of the river alone.

My main partner in those fishing expeditions was a fellow named Louie Brodie. Louie and I were avid fisherman. We'd go down, and we'd do our darnest to catch our own food. We'd do a little shooting too. But, whenever we didn't have any fresh food; old William always just happened to have caught some. He had them in a wire trap around the corner, I'm sure. We never went hungry.

Q: You must have had a delightful boyhood.

Austin: It was a pleasant boyhood, yes. It was a small town type of boyhood, where everybody knew everybody else. I'm sure we had problems there, as any small town would have; but I don't think it was quite a 'Peyton Place'. It was a fairly law-abiding little town, although somebody'd shoot it up now and then.

My father was Mayor for quite a while and very often had to intercede when somebody did want to shoot it up, and the policemen happened to be conveniently out of town.

It was a pleasant little community. We used to go over to Columbia and Augusta for the more citified pleasures of life, such as seeing The Birth of A Nation and the plays that would travel to the hinterland in those days.

Q: I had occasion to see a re-run of The Birth of A Nation.

Austin: It's quite a film, yes. At that time, it was something that was almost as impressive to a youngster as seeing a television program of a man walking on the moon to youngsters of today. Because they expect so much today; and they just say, "Well he's walking on the moon." They saw that in a movie ten years ago.

Q: Could you say a little bit about your school there, you went to high school there?

Austin: Yes. My father was quite interested in the local school, because he did have children in school. He, through his own personal efforts did a lot of the recruiting to bringing good teachers there. We had pretty good little school for a small community. I don't think I could have stood as well as I did at the Citadel, if I hadn't had pretty good schooling.

One of the teachers that my father brought in was a Miss Phillips. She had come from the little town of Springfield, not very far from Wagener. Miss Phillips was a maiden lady of, shall we say, about 35 or more years when he brought her there to teach in our school. She was an excellent teacher, and she had agreed to tutor me as necessary in return for being allowed to board at our home.

So Miss Phillips had quite a little bit to do with seeing that I did the things in the curriculum that weren't as attractive to me as the others, as well as the ones that I liked to do. Math was always easy for me, and I had no difficulty with subjects related to English literature. Some of the other subjects that were required I could have done without, as far as I was concerned, but not as far as Miss Phillips was concerned.

As a matter of fact I used to read quite a bit as a boy. We had electric lights in our little town toward the end of high school days of my stay there. The electric light company consisted of a diesel engine and one generator. The young man who operated it was named McCabe. McCabe usually got sleepy around eleven o'clock, although he was not supposed to turn off the lights until 12; sometimes they went off a little earlier.

So, I kept candles in my room so that I could keep reading after the lights went off; if it were an interesting book that I was reading. I remember one that I was reading one night, just at the point where it was getting really interesting, it was Ivanhoe; so I finished it that night by candle light. It probably didn't do my eyes much good, but I never had too much trouble with my eyes.

My family were not happy at my reading too late at night that way, so I sort of had to mask the candle light from going out under the crack of the door; or else I got told to put them out and go to bed.

Q: Did you take part in sports Admiral, to any extent in high school? Or, did you have time?

Austin: Yes, I liked sports. As a young boy, I had typhoid fever; and when I went off to college I weighed 94 pounds. Although I played football, I couldn't do much at any sport that required too much heft, and size. I was pretty good at basketball though. I made the first team in basketball, because there agility is a little bit more rewarded than in football.

Q: In those days, they didn't think always of basketball players as having to be at least six feet --

Austin: No. As a matter of fact, when I got to the Naval Academy, having been on the first team in my little home town I thought maybe I could make the team at the Naval Academy. So, I went out for basketball. I weighed more than 94 pounds then; I weighed about 115.

One day, shortly after I went out for basketball, the coach came over to me. He said, "Son, you're fast, you're eager, you're earnest; but you simply just aren't big enough to be a basketball player. Go on out for something else."

There was a friend of mine from South Carolina named Calhoun, who was in my class at the Academy. He came around and wanted me to go out with him for boxing. I wasn't too keen to go out for boxing, but it looked like it was the only way to get him to go; so I went out with him for boxing.

He was a very intent young fellow. We were sparring one day and I was nursing a slightly bent nose from a previous bout a few days back. I said, "Allston be careful of that nose of mine, will you?" "Oh sure, I won't hit you on the nose." It wasn't long after that, I evidently was too open and he forgot; and bango, right on the nose.

So, the doctor looked me over, and he said, "Son, I don't know whether it's your ability as a boxer, or what. You've got the nearest to a broken nose that I've ever seen.

It isn't broken, but how about giving up boxing?" So, I did boxing in class bouts and that sort of thing after that. But I gave up the varsity stuff, because evidently the doctor thought it was better for my nose, with my ability to close the entrance to the other fellow.

I went out for fencing and gym; sports that you could do without having too much avoirdupois. I made my class numerals in fencing. I was on the gym team of the class. I was never exactly a Buzz Bories or anything like that, because I didn't have the weight for many of the competitive sports. I evidently didn't have the skill as a boxer, because there of course you only fight against your own weight. I was letting too many through; and the doctor very seriously advised me to stop it. I let the nose have a chance.

As you probably know, at the Naval Academy, those Midshipmen who have nothing to do with girls are called Red Mikes. I wasn't a Red Mike because I did like to go to the dances, and as we called it, 'drag' a girl to the various events at the Academy.

Early in my career there, I conceived that a young officer might have considerable demands made on his time by his profession. I therefore, in typical youthful zeal, developed this theory; that no young naval officer should get married until he was at least a senior Lieutenant and able to support a wife properly. I would take my closest friends aside when I saw them dragging the same girl in quick succession a number of times; and ~~them~~ tell them about my theory. Evidentally it worked better for them than it did for me.

When I married about a year after graduation, my friends stopped in a jewelry shop in Honolulu, purchased a silver loving cup, and appropriately reminded me of my theories which I did not keep. Somehow, my wife never cherished that loving cup. I found it in the attic once, and now I don't know where it is.

Of course, in those days, the pay of an Ensign, married, was $183 a month. It wasn't easy to live in dignity and a reasonable amount of comfort on $183 a month even in those days.

My wife and I during a short period ashore, at Norfolk with the Scouting Fleet Landing Force, found that we could spend a very limited amount for entertainment. We budgeted very closely and were able to go out one night a week to a little restaurant called Parks, I believe on Grandy Street where we could get a satisfying meal for 75¢. Then we would go to the movies, which in those days were about 25¢. So, for $1 a piece a week, which added up roughly to $8 a month out of that $183; we got our recreation.

While a plebe at the Academy, I was assigned to a table which fortunately had very fine first classman, and for the most part very fine second classman at it.

Austin - 18

One of the amusing incidents occured one night with one of the second classman who was not the most popular of his class, either with his contemporaries or those of us in the lowly plebe state. His name was Weiser, and of course he was nicknamed 'Bud'. He enjoyed hazing the plebes and at our table one of the other plebes was named Bush, Stone Elkin Bush.

Stony was a descendant of Francis Scott Key, and by some means he had inherited a little of the poetic ability of his ancestor. But Stone was very modest about his poetic ability. In fact, I don't think that very many of his contemporaries ever knew that he was a poet. He kept his poems in a strong box in his room, and one day he showed them to me. I frankly thought they were pretty good. I'd written a poem or two myself in my lifetime, and had a little knowledge of the various meters in poetry. I thought he was not bad.

Not very many people knew of his poetic ability until this particular night, when Bud Weiser banged on the table in his accustomed uncouth manner and demanded that Bush come down with a limerick.

Bush was sitting on the one inch of his chair allowed to a plebe, on the front edge, braced up. So, without batting an eye, but looking Bud Weiser in the eye, Bush came down with the following limerick:

"The man sitting near by, Sir,

By the name of Bud Weiser,

Of his entire class

Is the biggest jack ass

And this I maintain is no lie, sir."

Bud Weiser was not pleased with this poetic display, and he turned his thumb down and told Bush to go under the table. Which was customary punishment for a plebe who had not pleased his seniors at the table. But Bud Weiser's classmates thought this was wonderful.

So, they decreed that not only should Mr. Bush not go under the table; but some one should go under the table and that should be Bud Weiser. So, Bud Weiser went under the table for a period of one week. And Stone Elkin Bush carried on for this period, which meant that he could sit on the whole chair and be normal and relaxed at his meal.

Some people have been interested in knowing how I came by the nickname of 'Count'. Very complimentary stories have been told about the origin of this nickname, but actually it was very simple.

One of the first classman at this table one night banged on the table, pointed to me, and addressed all of my classmates at the table; and he said, "From now on you plebes call him 'Count". And so, I have been going by that nickname ever since.

When first married, my wife was not too keen about it. She tried to get away from it. She would be at parties where my contemporaries were present, she would say something about me and call me by a name other than Count; and they'd say,

Austin - 20

"Oh, you mean Count, Don't you?" So, she finally gave up. I still go by that name among my contemporaries, and friends.

One of my pleasant duties at the Academy was as the sub-editor of our Lucky Bag for those members of the class who had departed from our ranks since entrance. Our class was, as I recall, about 850 strong. We graduated 525. So, there were a good many that I had to get the information on, and see that they were appropriately mentioned in the Lucky Bag. This task was quite pleasant, and at times, a little trying.

There are, of course, some parents who are more doting than others. When I communicated with some of the parents about what we could put in the Lucky Bag about their son, they were not always too happy with the length of the description of their son's stay at the Academy. So, it took a little diplomacy to keep everybody happy and still stay within my budget of numbers of pages in the Lucky Bag. It did give me the opportunity to establish somewhat of a writing acquaintance, at least, with many of my classmates that I'd never met while at the Academy. Some of these had departed early in plebe year. With the size class that we had, one didn't get to know everyone in his class.

Q: You had boys dropping out all along the way?

Austin: All along the way. The largest number left after the first term examinations in plebe year. Those are the ones who probably were not adequately prepared by previous schooling for the course. Strangely enough a good many of them failed English. The most of course failed math, because math is something that if you don't get the building blocks at the bottom, you're kind of floored when you get to something like calculus or trigonometry or spherical geometry, or something of that sort. So the attrition was largely at the end of the first term as plebes, but it did continue all the way through.

Q: I suppose the organization of the Academy studies is based on the supposition that there will be considerable attrition during the first year.

Austin: Yes. The experience has been studied, of course. I'm not too familiar with the latest figures, but I do believe that nowadays the entrance requirements insure a little better level of, shall we say, probability of staying than in previous years.

Of course youngster year, that's the second year, physics used to be one of the difficult subjects. The course is not too difficult, I taught it for three years. If a youngster came there without previous high school physics, he had no trouble picking it up if he had the proper mathematical background and if he really started getting each assignment as it came. Because in physics, too, there's a certain building block process.

I used to enjoy taking extra instruction assignments with the youngster in physics. Those that were on the verge of failing would come for extra instruction. I found, for example, that where you had a smaller number to deal with you could size up your pupil and you could get a better estimate of how to get over to him something that he was having difficulty with.

I remember one day - I had a football player who was an enormous chap. We were trying to get over to him the principle that F is equal to MA (force is equal to mass times accleration). I used his football experience to get this over to him. I said, "Now you know that if a fellow with lots of mass comes at you slowly, he doesn't hurt you very much if you're carrying the ball. But if he comes at you fast, the same mass but a little faster, multiply the mass times the accleration; you're going to feel a terrifice force; aren't you?" It was delightful to see the light of comphrension dawn in his eyes, that had been stupefied by these physical formulas.

This process can be used on not just football players. You can take any student and find out what he knows, and then build on that. When you have many in a class, you can't give this personal tutoring much. So, I used to enjoy the sessions with the poor chaps who were frightened to death that they were going to fail. Some did, of course, Some just couldn't get physical concepts.

Q: Some minds, I think, have difficulty in comphrending some concepts; and yet they can learn other concepts that are difficult.

Austin: That's right, yes.

Q: I recall when I was in mining engineering school that one of the courses I had to take was crystalography. I just had a miserable time with crystalography. It was so much to learn, all the different crystal systems.

Austin: Yes.

Q: I made a passing grade, but it was one of the hardest courses I ever had to take.

Austin: I think it's easier at the Academy now for a Midshipman to avoid those things which he is just not able to hoist aboard. You have more elective courses there now. But in the days when I was teaching there, there were no electives. The course was iron-bound and you took it, and you passed it or else.

This is why, frankly, so many of them got frightened. They knew it would be a great disappointment to them, not only to themselves but to their parents, if they got sent home. So, the nearer they got to failing the higher the panic factor became, and frankly the more difficult for them to succeed. This was why it was a real pleasure to see that you had helped some of the chaps get out of the panic stage, and into the hopeful stage again.

Q: Not only that, Admiral, but I should think that that experience probably served you well with the years ahead in furthering your capabilities as a communicator with people.

Austin: I think you're right. I think that the quicker any young man can learn to communicate with other men, the better off he'll be prepared to face whatever it is he faces in life.

When I was a boy delivering newspapers, I learned a great deal about human nature; just as a paper boy. For example -- we had one very pompous individual in the town. He complained more about the time that he got his newspaper than anybody else. He was what I think most people would term a four flusher. He dressed well, he put on quite a front, he demanded a great deal; but he never paid his paper boy. There was always an excuse - he only had a twenty dollar bill.

I'd say, "I'll change a twenty dollar bill." He'd say, "No, I I I I I've got to use that tomorrow."

Q: Did you continue to deliver him papers?

Austin: No, I finally discontinued it. But he got into me for quite a bill. You see, I was just learning about human nature.

I think that there are many things that a youngster can pick up about dealing with other human beings and communicating with them; if he isn't kept too much in cotton batting. This is one reason why I think it's a good idea for a boy to go to some public school, as we term it in this country, rather than entirely private school. I think the private schools, full and by, very often are much better to prepare a boy for college and all that sort of thing; but they miss a little of the full spectrum of human relationship.

Q: Give and take.

Austin: A little give and take, yes.

Q: Would you like to comment some on June Week, and the ceremonies, and so on? It seems to me that that's a feature of the Academy life that everyone looks back upon with a great deal of pleasure and excitement.

Austin: By my June Week, I had no one and only girl to invite. So, I don't look back on June Week with any great feeling of nostalgia or pleasant memories or anything. To me it was just the termination of four years of very interesting, but very definitely hard work. I felt that it was the beginning of a new phase of life because as a young officer I'd have a chance to do some of those things that I felt that if they'd only give me the chance, I could do.

I shall never forget the feeling when I went to my first ship, the USS NEW YORK. Before I got there, I felt that I could run the Navy much better than anybody else if they'd just only give me the chance. Of course, when you get aboard ship and they begin to throw a little responsibility on you; you realize that it's not quite as easy as you thought it was. I don't think that's untypical of youth at all. I think it's not regretable that youth feels it can do more, than it probably can.

It is a sobering thought when a youth has to realize that though he may have learned a great deal, the more he learns the more he realizes he doesn't know. That was my experience when I got aboard ship. I realized quite readily that the Captain had had a lot more experience than I'd had. And maybe he didn't run the ship perfectly, but he probably ran it better than even I could have run it.

Q: I think it's wonderful that you had that realization early, Admiral, because I think often times youth doesn't have it. It takes many years of experience and maturity to arrive at that realization.

Austin: I think one of my good breaks in the Navy was getting command at a very young age. I was a junior Lieutenant and Executive Officer of a submarine in Honolulu. My commanding officer went to the hospital for his annual physical, and they kept him.

So, the division commander called me up and told me that I would be the acting commanding officer until my Captain got back. My Captain didn't get back until after I'd taken the ship through it's torpedo and gunnery year.

The division commander was impressed with our results and recommended to the Bureau of Personnel that I be assigned as the Captain of the ship. The Bureau of Personnel didn't agree with that. Unfortunately, the division commander had called me up and practically told me that I was going to be the Captain, by proper assignment. So, he was very ambarrassed to call me up and show me the letter back from the Bureau of Personnel. They took the view that no officer, junior to a senior Lieutenant should command a submarine at that time. I was not a senior Lieutenant by quite a bit.

Q: It would have been different during the war time.

Austin - 28

Austin: Yes, they would probably have advanced you in rank during war time.

It gave me the experience whether I was assigned as the Captain of the ship by due process or not. I remember - there was an old Chief Petty Officer on board, named Dorn, who was the Chief of the boat. That's a term in submarines to indicate the senior Petty Officer of the ship. He is the Executive Officer's number one contact with all the rest of the crew, and he is sort of the man who runs the ship for the Exec by delegated authority; to the extent that he runs it, of course.

Chief Dorn was quite an able Chief. He had been in this particular type of boat for many years. He had helped commission one of the R-boats.

When I went down to take the ship out for the first time as acting Captain, we were going out on manouevrs. Two divisions were going out together, there were ten boats in each division. The R-boats in those days normally only had three officers on board. With the Captain gone, that meant I had only one officer left; so I had to use Dorn as a watch stander.

I and the other officer kept the bridge during the manoeuvre part of the day, and then we would turn over to Dorn for a trick at being officer of the deck while we could catch a little sleep. Dorn had the watch, and it was about midnight. I was awakened suddenly by the messenger. He said, Dorn would like me on the bridge, emergency. So, I got to the bridge just in time to see looming up ahead, the counter

Austin - 29

of a tremendous size ship. Poor Dorn didn't know what to do evidentally. As soon as I saw what I saw, I backed emergency and just passed under the stern of the ship. If I had been two seconds later, even backing two second later emergency; we would have still hit the rudder or the screws. We just skimed by.

Q: That was a close shave.

Austin: So, when we got back to port after these manoeuvres; Dorn came up to the ship's office and said, "Sir, could I talk to you a little bit?" I said, "Yes, Dorn, sit down." He said, "Sir, you know when we aaw you mount the bridge to take us out we thought you were pretty young. Now, sir, you've qualified. We know that we don't have anything to worry about." So, I got qualified by Dorn, if not by the Bureau of Personnel.

Q: Which was more satisfying to you anyway.

Austin: He was closer to the picture.

Q: I notice Admiral that after you left the Academy, you were assigned to the Navy Yard in Washington. I suspect that was somewhat of a new experience for you, you hadn't had much contact with the national capitol before, had you?

Would you like to comment on that period a bit?

Austin: I wasn't assigned to the Navy Yard. Frankly, I don't know just which duty you are referring to there, because I was never assigned to the Yard, except during the period right after graduation.

I was given a sort of a tour under the Bureau of Ordnance; which included short stays at the Naval Gun Factory at the old Washington Navy Yard, and the Naval Proving Grounds at Dahlgren, and the Naval Powder Factory at Indian Head.

During this period, we were used - that is the young Ensigns in the same catagory as I - in the calibration of the guns of the new battleship WEST VIRGINIA.

They used different color dyes for the shells; and we sat on the banks of the river and took what they call rake observations of these splashes. In this way, you can plot where the splashes are with respect to the target. This gives them the data for computing the pattern of a salvo from the ship's battery. It also gives individual data, due to the individual colors for the different guns of the ship. They were calibrating the big guns of that battleship at that time.

While sitting on the banks of the Potomac for day after day is not of itself unpleasant - it was balmy summertime, we were coolly dressed - but there was one little unpleasant facet to this which I'm sure that not only I, but all the rest remember.

Austin - 31

From time to time, we would sit on logs and although I should have know better, having done a bit of camping as a youngster; we didn't realize that we were just getting the most wonderful case of chiggers or redbugs or whatever you want to call them, that you can imagine. So, when we got back to Indian Head after this exercise, the sick bay was full of young Ensigns just peppered all over with red bumps and most uncomfortable.

Q: You were not married then, were you?

Austin: No, I was not married then. As a matter of fact, it was during a short visit to Washington that I met my wife. She was a guest at the home of a friend of hers over in Virginia. At that time, I was living in a fraternity house on R Street.

One of my best friends at this fraternity house was a young instructor at George Washington. He stuttered a bit. One Sunday he came into my room, I was reading a book, and he said, "C C Count wouldn't you like to g g go out into V V Virginia with me, and meet some V V Very lovely friends of mine?" I said, "Dark, I'd love to meet your friends. I'm sure that I'd enjoy it, but this is an interesting book. I kind of wanted to finish it today." We discussed whether I should go, or shouldn't go for a bit. Finally Dark said,

"C C Count, there's a l l lovely g g girl out there, I would l l like you to meet." My resistance had been worn down by this time, so I finally went with Dark.

As we approached, they were all playing croquet on the front lawn. I had played croquet quite a bit as a boy back home, and thought I was fairly good. But when they gave me a ball and a mallet, somehow I never got beyond the middle wicket going out; 'cause my eyes were on this little blue-eyed girl. That's Mrs. Austin. She's the one that caused me to forget all about my very well-founded theories about young officers not getting married until becoming a senior Lieutenant.

Q: Would you like to discuss your first assignement Admiral, with the NEW YORK?

Austin: I enjoyed my first assignment in the NEW YORK, because I was assigned to what they call the fire control division. I was one of the plotting room officers, with additional duties as range finder, and optical officer. Which gave me, shall we say, an opportunity to have some contact with all of the batteries of the ship. They all used optics or depended on the range finder one way or another.

During the inventory of my optical equipment, I found an old German range finder of the stereoscopic type. So, I broke it out and tried it out; and it was in excellent condition. It had been properly stored, and everything.

We were not having any luck in our anti-aircraft practices. The ship stood very well in gunnery, except for anti-aircraft practices. We had just never hit a sleeve towed past the ship.

My roommate, who was also one of the plotting room j.o.'s, and I devised a fire control system based around this old stereoscopic range finder. We set it up back aft, where you had a little room aft of number five turret. It consisted of a big drawing board, we had curves on it, we had different colors for different zones; and it was a rather crude fire control system. But with the help of a sextant and a stop watch and this range finder, we were able to knock down the next sleeve which was towed by on our anti-aircraft practice.

Of course, most people thought that was just a piece of luck. A certain amount of luck always enters into these things. Actually, it wasn't; because we consistently, after that, did pretty well on all of our anti-aircraft practices.

The system that we devised, of course, would certainly not produce any good results today; because your targets are so much faster and your range differentials are so much greater. But for the rather rudimentary type of practice that we had in those days, we had it boxed in. We could be pretty sure of hitting with the anti-aircraft guns that were mounted on top of the boat crane, on each side. Up to that time, everyone had said those cranes vibrate so much, you'll never hit anything with those little pop guns. No one had ever taken them very seriously.

My roommate and I were a little proud of our rather crude fire control system.

Q: The Captain must have been pleased.

Austin: Oh, he was, oh yes. He was quite pleased. As a matter of fact, both my roommate and I became fairly fair-haired boys of the Captain. As a result, it was a little hard to get off the ship.

I tried several times to get to schools that I wanted to go to. Each time, the Captain would say, "Not until after the next gunnery season." The next gunnery season always seemed to be in the offing.

We had a very interesting gunnery officer at that time. His name was Commander Virgil J. Dixon. He was an old bachelor, and he wore very prominent black moustachios. He really looked fierce.

Each time on the eve of a gunnery practice, Commander Dixon would send for me. I would knock and I'd be admitted. He would look up and he'd say, "Will we hit on the first salvo?" I'd say, "Yes, Commander we'll straddle on the first salvo." "That's all I want to know."

He did pretty well as a gunnery officer, because he did depend on other people to the degree that he had confidence in them. He didn't know too much about gunnery when he came to the job as illustrated by this little anecdote.

They said that the first day that he became gunnery officer, he'd been an engineer before that, he went up into the conning tower. All of the turrets and stations reported ready. His assistant said, "Sir, all have reported ready." Not knowing what to do, Commander Dixon sent out over his sound-powered phone to all stations, "All magazines load and lock."

That was something he had a hard time living down, but he did turn out to be a good gunnery officer. He knew how to use the talent of the officers under him. Yes, he was a good boss, and everybody recognized him as such.

This reminds me of an amusing little incident that took place while I was actually a Midshipman going through the Panama Canal.

The gunnery officer of this particular ship had been very hard on the band master that was aboard for the Midshipmen's cruise. He just seemed to take delight in picking on the band master. We were all at quarters, of course, going through the Canal, ship shape and everything. The gunnery officer was berating the band master because one of his bandmen's shoes weren't shined well enough or something. Just about that time, a messenger came dashing up and said, "Sir, one of the five-inch guns on the starboard side has just been carried away." The poor band master was saved from further wrath on the part of the gunnery officer; he had more important things to worry about by that time.

The gun hadn't been properly trained in, and going through the Canal we'd gotten too close on that side. Its muzzle came up against the side of the canal and it just lifted off the foundation. So, he had something then to worry about other than a shoe shine of a bandsman.

Q: Would the gunnery officer normally have much to say about the band master?

Austin: No. While at quarters, his sort of top-side quarters station was back on the quarter-deck there where the band was paraded. So, he somehow always found something to berate this poor band master about.

The Midshipmen had noticed this. It was quite a - not a joke - but it was something that caused all of the Midshipmen to sort of snicker when they heard the messenger report to the gunnery officer, while bawling out the band master about the shoe shine, report to him that one of his five-inch guns was having trouble.

Q: They were probably sympathetic towards him.

Austin: Yes, that's right. They thought he was overdoing it.

This is a thing that I think works in more ways than most people realize - that if anyone is too much of a tyrant, or too unappreciative of the practical factors surrounding a situation; those of his mess mates, contemporaries, his juniors, and his seniors evaluate. This goes in to what's know as his service reputation. I'm sure you know all about that. It's a matter that a fellow can get a bad service reputation very quickly if he isn't a little considerate of other people and of the practical factors that enter into a situation.

Q: I think that's more true perhaps of service life now than it used to be.

Austin: Very much so. When I first entered the service, people in higher ranks got away with things that they wouldn't last very long today doing. There just wasn't the feeling that one could speak out against those things in those days, but it's changed quite a bit.

Q: After leaving the NEW YORK, you went to Torpedo School I believe; didn't you?

Austin: Yes, I went to Torpedo School in Newport. That's a six months course. Our first daughter was born while we were in Newport at that school.

You were required to write a thesis on some subject while there. One day a lecturer on the Mark eleven torpedo pointed out that the torpedo was a fine torpedo, but by placing the elliptical head on it to get the speed they had sacrificed a certain amount of explosive effect, because the elliptical head had placed the center of gravity of the explosive charge further from the skin of the ship.

In my studies there at the Torpedo School, I had run across a formula. It was an empirical formula developed down at Indian Head, which indicated that even an inch made a heck of a lot of difference in the explosive effect of a given amount of charge.

So after this lecture I was talking to one of my classmates at the school there, named T. Woolsey Johnson, Jr., and I said, "Woolsey, I know what I'm going to write about for our thesis." He said, "So do I." I said, "Did you get the idea from this talk?" He said, "Yes. That explosive effect of that warhead - I think I know how to restore it." I said, "I do too. What's your idea?" He told me, and I said,"Mine's the same thing. Let's work on it together." So we did.

We ran into mathematical problems that we found his father very helpful on, because his father was in the math department as a civilian instructor at the Naval Academy.

The head of the school was Commander M. O. Carlson, he got quite interested in our project. The head of the torpedo station also became quite interested. Commander Carlson excused us from all firings and everything else that we found that we needed to be excused from in order to get along with this project. To make a long story short, we designed a warhead which we thought would increase the explosive effect of the Mark eleven warhead by some magnitude of three. We submitted this.

We got commended by the head of the torpedo station at that time. Then about a year later, I had a secret letter delivered to me which was from the Chief of the Bureau of Ordnance. The subject was our warhead design, Johnson's and mine. The letter was about a page and a half long, but you could sum it up in a very few words. "You young fellows have shown considerable knowledge of the subject, but remember the Bureau of Ordnance is the fount of all knowledge." It suggested that perhaps when it came time for me to take a postgraduate course, if I would apply for an ordnance postgraduate course, I might learn enough to begin to design warhead for the Bureau of Ordnance.

Q: What persuaded you initially to become interested in submarines?

Austin: Actually, I didn't become interested in them until I got orders to go to Submarine School. Toward the end of the torpedo course, my roommate and I had both been given an indication that we would be sent to specific destroyers in the same division as the torpedo officers; which was very pleasing to us.

We had been together on the NEW YORK, and we had kept our relationship up there at Newport. So, we looked forward with pleasure to being in the same divisions, similar jobs, and friendly competition. Then, out of the blue, came orders.

This was right at the end of the torpedo school. The class standings were already out, and we were just sort of waiting for graduation. The top five in the class were ordered to submarine school. That caught both my roommate and me.

He was down in Washington not long after that. He stopped by to see our old Captain, Captain David Theleen; who was then the Aide to the Secretary of the Navy. He had known him personally as a little boy, and so he just stopped in to pay his respects.

The Captain said, "How do you and Austin like your orders to submarine school?" Pat said, "We don't, Captain." So, the Captain said, "I think you should be pleased with them." Pat told him about our already being lined up to go as torpedo officers of these two destroyers, and how we were both keen to follow up what we'd learned at torpedo school. And that

Austin - 41

going to submarines just didn't seem to be necessarily following that up. Captain Theleen told him that he would be willing to intercede and get our orders re-considered if we both indicated we didn't want to go, but that he would recommend that we go. Because he said, "You'll never get command of a combatant earlier than in submarines."

Q: That's what I wanted.

Austin: When Pat came back and told me what Captain Theleen had said, I said, "As far as I'm concerned, it's all right with me. He's got more knowledge and judgement in these things than we have." So, we both went to submarine school, from torpedo school.

Q: I should think you would have an opportunity of obtaining command of a ship at an earlier age in submarines.

Austin: Yes.

Q: Are there any incidents or anecdotes about people which you would like to recall that happened during that time?

Austin: During the submarine period?

Q: Yes.

Austin: A most unusual situation developed while I was in my first sea cruise in submarines. As I previously stated I did not get permanent command of the ship that I got temporary command of, by the accident of my Captain's going to the hospital. They found that he had ulcers, I hoped that I hadn't given them to him. He came back, and I was called up by the division commander one day and told that he was going to transfer me to another ship in the division. I was a little surprised at this. I thought I was getting along all right on my ship. I didn't know why I was being transferred, so I asked him.

I said, "Is this because my commanding officer is displeased with me, or anything?" He said, "Oh, no, Bob thinks the world of you. But I've got a situation on the R-6 that I'm not happy about. What I'm going to tell you, you've got to keep to yourself. They're sending a commanding officer to that ship against my wishes. I do not consider him able to command. He's been in submarines a long time, but I don't consider him able to command a submarine. I am sending you there as the Executive Officer to protect that ship and that crew. If you ever have to do it, you can take over. But keep this to yourself."

The man who came was a delightful person. Socially, he was a very personable individual. He was a very admirable fellow in many ways. But he simply did not react in a manner that would inspire confidence.

The first time that this became quite obvious to me was when we were going out the channel and he was conning the ship. A barge that was being used in dredging had gotten a little athwart the channel and he just kept going right for the barge as if it were going to get out of his way. All of a sudden, I decided I'd better speak up, and I said, "Captain, don't you want to give left rudder?" He said, as he looked at me, "You think we're going to hit it?" I said, "Yes sir." So, we gave left rudder and she just scraped down it's corner by doing so.

Then a little later, we were out on a manoeuvre; a submerged manoeuvre of a whole division of submarines. We were operating in a very unsafe way actually, even if every one did what he was intended to do. We were operating at the same depth, same horizontal plane; and we were conducting close order formation changes in this one level. We were a middle boat, we had a boat on each side of us. The oscilator signal came for a simultaneous turn to the right. Now, if everybody turns to the right, it's all right; but if one fellow turns to the left, you're in trouble. So, the Captain said, "Left full rudder." I said, "Captain, you mean right full rudder, sir." He looked at me and said, "Right full rudder. Count, you're right as usual; but some day you're going to be wrong and I'm going to cut your throat from ear to ear."

Austin - 44

I don't believe the division commander; though he had done something very unorthodox in telling me, a junior, that I was his representative for that ship; was too far wrong. Because this fellow just didn't react quickly enough and accurately enough to be the Captain of the submarine.

Q: When a junior decides that he must take over command from a senior, it involves quite a risk for him; from the standpoint of responsibility.

Austin: Oh, yes. Usually, even though his judgement may prove to have been better than that of his Captain's, it's not justifiable for him to be a one man judge as to whose judgement is better. Presumably the more mature and more experienced officer has the better judgement. So, unless the person who is relieved by the junior is found to be psychiatrically unsound, the junior's in a tough spot.

Q: I was thinking about the novel and the motion picture, Cain Mutiny.

Austin: Yes.

Q: You were in submarines four years then Admiral, weren't you, or so before you --- had a change of duty?

Austin: I was four years the first time before I went ashore. Then I was in command of a boat up at New London for three years after that. I had seven years at sea in submarines.

Q: You probably met my old friend, Captain Thorp, somewhere.

Austin: Oh, yes, Pinkie Thorp. Pinkie was out in Honolulu the same time that I'm talking about. Pinkie would know the person that was the commanding officer of this ship.

I didn't mention the name purposely, because he was a very fine individual.

Q: Did he continue in the service?

Austin: No, he failed in selection. He was a Lieutenant Commander then, and he never got selected above that.

Q: I worked with Pinkie Thorp over in the Munitions Board first, and then the Assistant Secretary of Defense.

Austin: Yes, I've known Pinkie for all these years. I run in to him once in a while at the Army-Navy Club.

Q: Awfully nice chap.

Austin: Yes, he is. Typical Vermonter.

Austin - 46

Q: Before we get to your next duty, which was shore duty at Annapolis; can you think of any thing particular during those first four years in submarines that you'd like to cover by way of personalities or incidents?

Austin: I'd only been out in this assignment for a very short time, in fact when I arrived there the ship was in the Navy Yard undergoing a very extensive overhaul. The housings for the Nelsico engines in the R-boats had been made of bronze. They developed cracks, and of course cracked housings don't conduce toward very good alignment of engines. So, the alteration had been approved and we were one of the first ships to get it; to replace these bronze housings by steel housings.

The Captain took me over to the Navy Yard, and he showed me one pile of parts. He said, "That's your starboard engine." He showed me another pile of parts and he said, "That's your port engine." He gave me the date that we would be operating. He said, "I don't want to be late."

Frankly, I looked at those piles; that looked like two piles of junk; and I wondered if I'd ever be able to make engines out of that. But, we got put back together. We were at the stage of testing the main ballast tanks.

As the engineer officer, that was one of my duties to view the tests and approve them for the ship or not. So, during the test of the number two main ballast tank; I had my head down in what we call the sump tank in the engine room. It's a tank that sits down in the main ballast tank.

When they got the pressure up to 44 pounds on the ballast tank, the sump tank took on the aspects of a needle shower. These little needles of water started coming out all around.

I told the quarterman in charge of the test that I thought something had to be done to correct this. There was no use to go ahead with the test. If it leaked like that at 44, it would certainly leak more at 88. He said, "That's nothing. You know you seldom go down deep enough to get that much pressure on your ballast tanks anyway. Furthermore, all it means is a teeny bit of salt water in your oil. That can be taken out by the separator. It's nothing to worry about. I assure you. I've done many of these."

I said, "Yes, but I don't want to run my engines on a combination of salt water and lub oil." Not being able to convince him, I went to his immediate superior and talked to him. He wasn't anymore sympathetic with my view, than his quarterman was. So, I finally got all the way up to the manager of the yard. He wouldn't listen to me either.

So, I went over and I told my Captain the story. I told him what I had observed and what I had done as a result. I handed him a letter which I had written for his signature, pointing out why the ship would not be operationally ready on such and such a date unless this were corrected. Also, requesting a full power trial at sea before we would accept the overall job.

The Captain said, "You think we need to do this?" I said, "I've tried to talk to them over there. They don't listen too good. I think if you just have this in your right hand as an ace in the hole, if the manager of the yard won't talk turkey with you; it might be helpful."

So, we went over and the manager of the yard told my Captain, "Ensign Austin here is just fresh out of sub school. He's a perfectionist. My people tell me that what he's observed there on that test is nothing to worry about. That's just a dump tank. It isn't that important." My Captain knew enough about submarines to know that this was no dump tank. He knew what the sump tank was. He said, "Sir, that's not a dump tank. That's the tank that's really the service lubricating oil tank for the engines."

The manager of the yard looked at his advisor there and he said, "You didn't tell me that." The fellow started quibbling, so the manager blew him down. He said, "Now you tried to put something over on me. I agree with the Ensign. We shouldn't try to run the engines on a combination of lub oil and salt water. It's not good practice. You get that fixed."

When the Captain and I got down to the ship, they were swarming on the ship going down both hatches just like wasps going into their holes at a wasp nest. They fixed it.

Q: I suppose there was a tendency to be less precise in yard work in the early years.

Austin: I think the main trouble here is the trouble that we still have with us. That is - when they get hard pressed to meet a deadline date to get a ship ready for sea, they try to take a few short cuts. I think we still have that with us.

Q: The Commanding Officer, as the to-be Commanding Officer, of a ship under overhaul or a new ship getting ready to be commissioned, who presumably is watching construction or overhaul daily and hour by hour, if he finds things wrong, and he goes to the manager of the yard who gnerally is an officer superior to himself - isn't he really in a sort of a delicate position?

Austin: Oh yes, you are. But you always have recourse to some one who is very much senior to the manager, even to the Commandant of District. I'll cite you a little experience of mine during World War II.

I came in to the Navy Yard, New York. I was on a brand new ship down from Bath, Maine. We had limited time to get ready for sea and get going.

I had a young supply officer assigned to me. I had him up in the cabin with me and I discussed the importance of getting aboard all of our spares. Particularly was I interested in getting the electronic spares on board, because I knew

Austin - 50

we were going to the South Pacific. I couldn't tell him that, but I knew it. I had had word from contemporaries of mine in the South Pacific that they were desperately short on electronic spares down there. So, I didn't intend to go out there short on electronic spares right fresh from the source of supply.

He came to me one day and said, "Captain I'm not having any luck getting our electronic spares. All I get is a run around and get told to just keep yourself calm, they'll be aboard." I suggested to him what to do. That he might suggest to the supply officer that he get on the phone and check as to whether or not the spares had been shipped yet. To put a tracer on them if they had been shipped, and hadn't arrived in a reasonable time. So, he did all this, and he came back and reported to me, that he had done it.

Time got shorter and shorter. About four days before we were due to sail, I decided I would have to take things in my own hands. I went up and I saw the supply officer of the yard. He gave me quite a brush-off. He said, "Oh, it's not anything for you to worry about. We'll have your spares on board. Don't you worry about them." I said, "Are they in the yard now?" "No", he said, "They aren't." I said, "If they're not here now, what have you done to get them here before I sail?" He said, "That's my business." I said, "It's my business also." He hummed and he hawed, and he admitted he hadn't phoned, he hadn't wired, he hadn't even written a letter. He just was trusting they'd get there. If they didn't get there, it was just going to be my bad luck.

I told him, "Unless you take action immediately, I'll be back up to see you tomorrow, I'm going to have to report that my ship will not be ready for sea on the date that we're supposed to go to sea. And I'm going to have to lay it on the line why."

I went up the next day, and I got the same sort of brush-off. Then, I went back to my ship and I addressed a message to Cominch - CNO, Admiral King. I laid it on the line.

Not many hours later, I was in the Commandant's office, with a very irate Admiral walking up and down and wanting to know; why the hell I'd done what I'd done. I said, "Admiral I'm the Captain of that ship. I felt it my duty to do what I did." He said, "Why didn't you come to see me before you went to Ernie King?" I said, "Admiral, I did try to get to see you but you were a busy man. In the first place, I assumed that you would not be able to do much more than your staff had been able to do. I felt that my boss, on the operational side, should know that I'm not going to be able to carry out my orders unless something is done about it." He said, "Ernie King's been on the phone here giving me hell."

Q: That was hell from a pretty high source in those days.

Austin - 52

Austin: It was. They found that the spares had been shipped in plenty of time, but they had gone into a rail yard and had been parked in a car in Philadelphia. So, they trucked those parts up to the ship, right away quick. And everything was all hunkey-dorey.

We got under way with our spares on board. When I got to the South Pacific, my fellow destroyer people were very happy to see me; because I had more electronic spares than the tender had at that time.

Q: You could share.

Austin: I could share, and it was well that I insisted on getting those spares on board.

Q: I'm sure it was.

You've been talking for quite a while now --

Austin: I think that's a pretty good session, don't you?

Interview # 3
(# 1 and # 2 marked as # 1)

Vice Admiral Bernard L. Austin
Washington, D. C.

by Paul L. Hopper
September 19, 1969

Mr. Hopper: Admiral Austin, as we finished up our last interview, it seems to me that we had gotten around to the stage of your career where you were about to assume command of the President's yacht. Would you like to comment on that?

Admiral Austin: As I pointed out in our last interview, I had orders to the Naval War College as a student and was quite reluctant to have those orders changed. But, on the advise of my highly esteemed senior, and Commander of my submarine division; I bowed to the new orders and reported as the Executive Officer of the POTOMAC, and as the prospective relief for the Commanding Officer.

During the interval between my selection and being ordered to the POTOMAC, the Presidential aide had changed. The one who had been a part in my selection was replaced by a Captain Woodson. Captain Woodson was a very proper gentleman. We had many early morning walks on the deck together during the early months of my service in the POTOMAC. At no time during these walks or other contacts, did he indicate anything other than that I would in time relieve the Commanding Officer as the new Captain of the ship.

However, months passed. I became a little, shall we say, less certain than I had been when I arrived on board that I would in fact ever become the Commanding Officer of the ship.

One day, about six months after I reported aboard, having thought this thing over quite a bit, I went to the Captain; and told him that I didn't like to seem impatient to speed him on his way, but it appeared that I was going to do a cruise as Exec of the ship instead of in Command of it; And that I had not come with that in mind. He acted a little sheepish, but finally admitted to me that the new Presidential aide had said to him, that he did not intend to have a married man relieve the Commanding Officer of the ship.

I, being a married man, pointed out that I, therefore, felt that I was entitled to ask for other duty. The Captain was a little reluctant to give his permission for my doing so, but finally did.

I went up to the Bureau of Personnel. There I found that they were very much embarrassed. It seems that the point of my being married had been brought up at the time of my nomination to the President. The Chief of the Bureau, had in fact, had a personal connection with the clearing of my nomiation; and had specifically pointed out my married status, But, that the President had waived that, And that the previous Presidential aide had raised no point of order about my being married. And so, the Chief of Bureau was embarrassed, that he had ordered me away from a duty that I had wanted; and to a duty that was not panning out as had been planned.

So, I was told that I would be handed orders, then and there; to report to the Chief of Naval Operations, Admiral Leahy, as the Press Relations Officer of the Navy Department. And, that I was not to tell either Captain Woodson or my Commanding Officer about these orders until I had reported to Admiral Leahy.

I pointed out that unless normal procedures were waived, it would be necessary for me to tell my Commanding Officer in order for him to be able to sign the detachment endorsement on my orders. This waiver was granted – rather the instructions to me were changed so that the normal procedures for detachment could be followed.

I reported to Admiral Leahy, as the Press Relations Officer. In due time, Captain Woodson was made the Judge Advocate General of the Navy by the President's express order.

As Judge Advocate General of the Navy, then Admiral Woodson – because the office carried with it a promotion to flag rank – had access to the legislative program of the Navy. In those days, very few people had access to the future legislative program of the service.

One day, Admiral Leahy called me down and expressed great concern that the legislative program of the Navy had appeared

Austin - 56

in the WASHINGTON POST of that morning. He said, "I know that you didn't give this out. I want you to find out who did and report him to me."

I, of course, said, "Aye, aye, sir," and left with the full appreciation that I had a difficult task to perform. I went to see Captain Wilkinson, who was the Plans Officer in the Bureau of Personnel, and who had been most understanding and helpful to me as a young Press Relations Officer.

Captain Wilkinson said, "No, I didn't give any information on the legislative program. Not very many people have access to the whole program. Perhaps somebody in the Judge Advocate General's office might have talked to the press. I suggest you try there."

I went around to the Deputy Judge Advocate General's office and told him that I would like to inquire as to whether or not anyone in the Judge Advocate General's office, who did have access to the legislative program, had recently talked to a member of the press.

I could tell that the Deputy Judge Advocate was not happy with my request, and I could tell that he was trying to give me a brush-off. But, I was not being brushed-off too easily. After some time time discussing the matter with the Deputy, Admiral Woodson called from his adjacent office and said for me to come in.

Austin - 57

I went in and Admiral Woodson said, "I am the guilty party. I gave the legislative program to Jack Norris. I know I did wrong. He kept badgering me so much that I finally just reached in the middle drawer and pulled it out and gave it to him, to get rid of him. I can assure you, it won't ever happen again."

Q: This was curious behavior on the part of a responsible naval officer.

Austin: It was. So, I went back to Admiral Leahy. I said, "Admiral, I know who gave out the information which appeared in the POST on the Navy's legislative program for next year. Admiral, he will never do such an indiscrete thing again. I have been given this assurance by him. I don't think you want me to tell you the name of the person involved."

Admiral Leahy was a wonderful man to work for. He looked at me for a few minutes. He said, "Are you certain that he will remember this and that he's had his lesson?" I said, "Yes, sir, I think I'm certain enough to assure you that it won't happen in that particular office again." He said, "All right, don't tell me."

Q: He was a very understanding person.

Austin: He was indeed. I might tell you another little interesting story about Admiral Leahy.

I received a request from the United Press representative in Washington, at a time before World War II when things were heating up. He wanted an Admiral to write a by-line story for United Press on the prospects of war.

I assured him that no Admiral on active duty in his right mind would undertake to do such. He said, "How about Admiral Woodward up in New York? He's been making some speeches that indicate that we'd better get our ducks in a row. Frankly it's some of those speeches that have caused my boses to put the bee on me to get such a by-line story written." I said, "The Admiral wouldn't do such a thing." He kept badgering me, and like Admiral Woodson, I got a little weak-kneeded as he kept twisting my arm. He said, "Wouldn't you just ask him? If you just ask him, and he says no, I'll shut up." I said, "All right."

I immediately put in a phone call to Admiral Woodward, who was then the Commandant of the district up in New York. Admiral Woodward came on the phone, and I told him the request. He said, "I can't write a story like that. You know that." I said, "Yes, I do, sir. I had to have it from you." He said, "You've got a lot of my speeches down there on the shelf. If it would help this young fellow at all, he can take any of my speeches, and he can quote from them."

I should have known better, but I made available to the correspondent all of the speeches that I had on file from Admiral Woodward. He did a masterful job of taking out of context a sentence here in one speech, and a sentence there in another, so that the next morning when I went to breakfast I was confronted with the front page of the POST big headlines which said, "Admiral predicts war." And Admiral Woodward's picture covering half of the front page.

My spirits were not exhilarated as I read this masterful juxtaposing of unrelated sentences taken out of context and put together in a very effective way. So I went to the Navy Department that morning with a heavy heart. I hadn't been in the job very long, or I would have been more experienced.

I went directly down to Admiral Leahy's office. I said, "Admiral, have you seen the POST this morning?" He looked up and said, "Yes, I've seen it." I said, "Sir, I feel it's entirely my fault that that happened. I should have known better than to make available all the speeches that we had and tell the man that he could quote from all of them as if he had made an interview with Admiral Woodward." Admiral Leahy said, "Don't feel too badly about it. Go back to your office and write a letter of reprimand to Woodward and have it ready for me to sign. I'll be called by several senators (and he named them) as soon as they get to their offices. When Mr. Hull gets to his office, he will be very perturbed. I think I can handle all this. In a way, you know, this may just be a blessing in disguise. It will jar lots more people than the senators and Mr. Hull. I'm not sure that it won't be in our country's best interest to have people shocked a little bit, by having the POST say that an Admiral is predicting war. Now, I want you to write a personal letter to Admiral Woodward and tell him that I have told you to tell him to disregard the letter of reprimand that I will send him, and to tear it up. Tell him that we have no carbon copies of it back here."

That is an indication of how broad a mind, and how kind a heart Admiral Leahy had. He was a wonderful man to work with.

Q: I' like for you to relate anything further in the way of your contacts with Admiral Leahy that you think would be of interest. I would suspect that somewhere along the line --

Austin: I'll tell you of another incident, where I think he showed great understanding. When the SQUALUS sank off Portsmouth, my first inquiry from the press came during the lunch hour. I went down to Admiral Leahy's office and asked if he were in, and he wasn't. He was up in the cafeteria eating his lunch.

I went up and went to the table where he was eating with a couple of his friends, and asked him if he had any information regarding the sinking of the SQUALUS.

He said, "Yes. I received a phone call just before I left my office to come up here for lunch. It's unfortunately true." I said, "Can I tell the press?" He said, "Yes, you can." He said, "How do you want to handle this? The last time we had a submarine sink, we had a very bad press, and partly it was deserved. Because when the press couldn't get any help from any other source, they hired a tugboat and went out where the attempted salvage of the S-4 was in progress. The officer in charge on the scene turned the firehose on them. They came back and wrote the stories in a not unfriendly way. How do you propose to handle this one?"

I said, "Admiral, I would like to take a course about 180° from that. I would like to answer every question straightforwardly and honestly, regardless of how it may seem to hurt, at the time. I think in the long run, we will come out a lot better than if we start trying to cover up anything or trying to tell half-truths and delude the public. I think there is a tremendous national interest in this sort of disaster. I don't think we ought to interpose ourselves between the public, and what can, without giving away any real secrets, be given to them." He said, "You have my permission to do so."

Austin - 62

I said, "Now, I'd like to understand, sir. Can I allow the press to put their microphones directly to their radio stations in my office, in order to give hot off the griddle reports?" He said, "You can do anything you want. You have my carte blanc. You handle it. I have confidence that you know how."

So, I went back to my office. I answered the question affirmatively. Of course, I began to get many other questions quite rapidly. It wasn't long before about 40 or 50 press people were in my office, making various and sundry requests about setting up microphones and bringing in photographers and so forth. I played it as I indicated to Admiral Leahy that I would.

There were about 40 or 50 people around my desk, asking questions as fast as I could answer them. Radio messages from the scene were coming in. We had given them an immediate phone call and told them what we were going to do; That we would handle the press on the thing in Washington and for them to just keep feeding us all the information. So, I was getting a continuous stream of messages and answering questions as fast as I could. I'd been doing this for about five hours. I was beginning to get a little hoarse.

Q: Quite a bit weary by that time.

Austin: I hadn't had any lunch because it caught me at the lunch hour. Everyone was being very considerate.

They were taking their turns, they'd hold up their hands, and I'd recognize them in turn. Everythings was going very nicely until a Mr. Kluckhorn, New York TIMES; elbowed his way through the crowd, planked his fist down on the desk in front of me in a very beligerant manner and asked me a question.

I said, "Mr. Kluckholm, you're not the only representative of the press who has questions that he'd like to have answered. The rest of the press are taking their turns. If you'll do so, I'll answer your question. But, I'm not going to let you come in here and get at the head of the cue."

He did not react in a docile and pleased way. He shook his finger in my face and said, "Young man, I will report you to the Secretary of the Navy, he personally and immediately; if you don't answer my question now."

I said, "Mr. Kluckholm, the Secretary's office is out that door and to the right. I you want to go report me to him, that will help you get there. But, I'm not going to answer your question out of turn."

He went out the door very much in a huff and started towards the Secretary's office, but on the way he passed the CNO's office. So, he went in there instead of going on to the Secretary's office.

Admiral Denfeld, who was then Captain Denfeld, was Admiral Leahy's senior aide and administrative assistant. Captain Denfeld received him and asked him what he could do for him. Kluckholm, I guess in an unfriendly and belligerent manner, demanded to see Admiral Leahy.

According to the report of what happened, given to me later by the junior aide, Captain Denfeld told Kluckholm that he would have to tell him what he wished to see Admiral Leahy about before he would work him into Admiral Leahy's schedule. The aide said that Kluckholm got very belligerent, and said that he wanted to report the Press Relations Officer for failure to perform his duty.

Captain Denfeld had been down to my office, off and on, during the afternoon. He had stood in the back, I guess, to see how things were going and to give Admiral Leahy a report on how I was doing. So when Kluckholm indicated his mission to see Admiral Leahy about putting me on report, Captain Denfeld came to my rescue.

He said, "Did you ask a question that Lieutenant Austin wouldn't answer?" Kluckholm informed him that he had. Captain Denfeld said, "I don't understand that because I have been down there off and on a number of times this afternoon and I haven't heard him dodge a single question by any reporter all afternoon." Kluckholm said, "He refused to answer my question when I asked it." Captain Denfeld said, "Did you take your Turn?" He said, "No, I don't have to take my turn. When I have a question, I ask it."

Captain Denfeld said, "It's people like you that make these things hard for the people who are really trying to inform the American people through the medium of the press. You came in my door, so you know where it is. I'll give you a reasonable time, which is 30 seconds, to get the hell out of here."

Kluckholm never did go to see the Secretary of the Navy. I never heard anything about his efforts, until after it was all over, when the aide came down and told me about the exchange of punts between Kluckholm and Captain Denfeld.

Q: Leahy later became -- what was his title, Commander-in-Chief to the President?

Austin: No, he was the Chief of Staff.

He was very much against the use of the atomic bomb. He really did all that he could to prevent our proceeding along that path.

I was the first Navy member of the National Security Council staff. At one time, while Admiral Leahy was still in the White House as the advisor to the President, the Chief of Naval Operations sent for me and asked me to go and talk to Admiral Leahy about a certain National Security Council policy paper that was up for consideration. He knew that Admiral Leahy would advise the President to turn it down, because it had to do with our posture in the atomic weapons field.

I went to see Admiral Leahy. He was very kind and he gave me plenty of time to talk to him about it. I gave him the reasoning of the staff in producing the paper and the pros of the subject, as it were, on the issue. He said, "I really can't give you counter-arguments for all of those things. Just deep in the heart, I don't like to see weapons like that developed and used. I can't give you logical reasons why we shouldn't do it. Just my inner feeling tells me that we shouldn't. I just can't bring myself to support it."

Q: He felt very deeply.

Austin: He felt very deeply. This is the side of military men that few of our people in the country ever see.

Q: That's why it's so rewarding to me now to talk to you honestly, because as I told you about some of my experiences regarding officers in wartime who never seem to let down. After retirement, they never quite become real human beings. It's a shame.

Austin: It is.

Q: I think that the average citizen would feel much more kindly towards military people if they seemed less rigid in their outlook.

Austin: Unfortunately, a military man's training and his experience have to equip him for making quick decisions and acting vigorously on those decisions. Some people, as a result of that training and experience, develop the habit of not being as considerate of the others' side of the question, as of the one that they think is best. Because they do this quick mental computer process, they decide this is best for the country, this is best for the istuation, and full speed ahead. They disregard all the other arguments on the other side.

I have been fairly fortunate in being able to serve under people who weren't quite that simplistic and dogmatic.

Leahy was one of those people. There wasn't anything dogmatic about him. He could see the good and the bad, on either side of a delicate question that was delicately balanced -- As in the case of the newpaper headline, "Admiral Predicts War." He knew that was going to cause him an awful lot of unhappiness and pressure from many sources, but it didn't perturb him, because he could see the good.

So many military men in his position at that time, would have crawled down my throat and said, "You stupid young man, why did you do that?" And I, would have been his goat; or Woodward, or both.

But, Admiral Leahy was not of that type. He was not one who didn't have broad shoulders enough to carry whatever burden he had to carry, in order to do what he thought was best.

Q: That's why Roosevelt made him his Chief of Staff.

Austin: That's right.

Q: After serving as Press Relations Officer at the Navy Department, did you go to London with Admiral Ghormley?

Austin: Yes.

Q: Soon after that?

Austin: Immediately after.

Q: I think that's a most interesting period, and I'd like to have as full an account as you care to give of your experiences during that period.

Austin: Before we got to that it might be interesting to tell you a story about my successor.

As a young submarine officer, my first Commanding Officer was Robert Berry. When my time to leave the job — I was at the time that I left the Public Relations Officer acting — I had served in that job about five months between Commander Lovett and his successor, who came from the China Station (it took a long time in those days to get them back from the China Station) —

Q: Excuse me. Was Lovett the first Public Relations Officer to gain flag rank?

Austin: I don't really know. I couldn't answer that accurately enough.

Austin - 70

Q: I always identify him with his book.

Austin: Yes, CUSTOMS AND TRADITIONS.

He was a great man to work for, tremendous ability as a raconteur and he was an entrovert, of the first order; and would undertake anything, which got me into trouble.

He began writing speeches for the top people - the Secretary, the assistant Secretary, the CNO, the various Bureau Chiefs, and so on. As these speeches were well-done, he got more and more clients. As he got more and more clients, the fellow that he passed the job onto got more and more unhappy. Because he couldn't possibly do them all.

One week-end I recall, it was a week-end to remember, for me. I had three separate speeches to write for three very different occasions by three separate individuals. For one week-end, that's quite a task.

One day, Commander Lovett came into the office; it was shortly after this week-end to remember. I'd been going home and reading my evening paper and sitting down to write about ten o'clock at night. Then writing until two or three in the morning, and then getting up and being at the office at 7:30; which you don't do too long, even at a young age, without it beginning to get you down. That was the pace I had to keep up in order to do all of these speeches that he was throwing my way.

My wife, of course, couldn't see why I couldn't come home at six or seven o'clock and have my dinner, and get to writing speeches before ten o'clock. I don't think I ever explained it to her satisfaction.

I'm sure you know that you just have to unwind a little bit, in order to really produce anything worthwhile. Of course, there were the usual household noises. We had young children in those days. I found that I could do more per minute after ten o'clock, than I could before. I used that time to relax and read my paper. I had to read not only the local papers, but I had to read clippings from all over the country to keep abreast of my job at the office the next day.

Lovett came in and looked at me and said, "You look like death warmed over. I want you to get out of the office and I don't want to see you for ten days. Go some place and rest." I didn't argue with him at all.

I'd been told about a place called Capon Springs, not far from Washington. I went home and told my wife, I said, "Get the kids packed. We're going on a vacation." I got on the telephone and talked to the manager of Capon Springs, who happened to be named Austin also. I didn't know that until I called him. He said, "Yes, we'll take care of you. Come on down."

We went down and the first night I was there, the phone rang. It was one of these old country crank up types. I went to the phone and it was my office trying to get me. They had a problem. But I couldn't hear them, and they couldn't hear me. We were on the phone quite a while, and we got very little understood between the two ends of the line. So, they didn't bother me anymore and I had ten wonderful days of golf and relaxation and rest.

I went back feeling like a new man. I always had a soft spot in my heart for that place. The food there was wonderful.

I started out to tell you something and we sidetracked.

Q: You were going to tell me about your successor.

Austin: The choice of my successor.

When Commander Lovett left, Admiral Leahy allowed him to go before his relief arrived, provided I stayed on board until his relief arrived, and had an overlap with him.

In the menatime, I was told to suggest to BuPers the name of my relief. I was told to pick him from the class of '21. I was the class of '24.

Of the people in the class of '21, my old Commanding Officer of the R-10 was the one that I knew best. I knew that he had qualities that would make him a good Press Relations Officer. I felt that it wouldn't do him any harm to be in Washington, closely working under the Secretary of the Navy and the CNO, and going to the White House to all of the press conferences. And seeing the President, every few weeks, at least, when there

Austin - 73

was something from the Navy Department in the press that he needed background on.

Without feeling that I was doing him any disservice, I put his name on the list of those that I suggested be considered as my relief. When the list went through the usual process of being considered by various people from Admiral Leahy on down, his name came out as the number one choice.

When he arrived, I found that he was very unhappy about being ordered to the job. I think it was mainly because he didn't feel that it was proper and progressive, shall we say, for him to relieve an officer three classes junior to him who had once served on his ship as his most junior officer.

So, I took him down to meet Admiral Leahy and he acted all right. But when we got back to the office, he unburdened himself. He was quite unkind. He imputed to me motives which I had never thought of, in getting him to the job. He even said that I was trying to get back at him for a bawling out that he had given me once.

I went home that night and was very unhappy. Here, I hoped that I was getting a good man for the job, and here —

Q: Doing him a favor.

Austin: —and doing him a favor. Here, I couldn't escape the feeling that he shouldn't relieve me.

Austin - 74

The next morning I went to the office and I asked him if he would come in and talk to me. He did.

I said, "Bob, I realize that you were once my Captain. I was your junior officer. I realize full well that you went to the Naval Academy three years before I did. I could have been a plebe at the Academy, when you were a very upper-classman. I realize that there are other jobs that would require far less of your time on your shore cruise, than this job will require. You mentioned yesterday, how you'd been told what a slave-driving job this was - many hours, seven days a week, and all that. You just didn't want any part of it. I don't think that you should take the attitude that you are taking, because of the hard work. I don't reconcile that with your character, as I observed it for several years under your command. It must be the juniority of the man that you're relieveing, that bugs you. I was told to pick noone junior to your class as my relief. I did not make that decision. That was made by higher authority. I think it's a fine job. It is a hard-working job, there's no doubt about it. It gives you an in-sight into things that you've never been given an in-sight into as a naval officer at a shipyard, or some place like that, just doing plain every day navy work. It gives you an exposure to the media of the press and radio. It causes you, I think, to develop a broader way of looking at things.

It puts you in a position very often, of having to be the advocate, before very senior people, of giving to the public, information which they want to withhold. I have not slept well, since talking with you yesterday. You made me very unhappy, because I put your name among other names to be considered for this job, because I thought that you had the qualities that this job should have. I think it's an important job, not only to the Navy but to the American people. Frankly, I have been disappointed in you. I have been disappointed in you to the point that I am going now to Admiral Leahy to tell him that I was wrong to nominate you to this job."

Evidently, what I had said had gotten to him because he said, "I wish you wouldn't do that." Of course, there is the possibility that he didn't want the stigma on his record of having been ordered to the job, and then Admiral Leahy sending him out of it. I rather feel that it was a little bit more than that. I think that he did realize that I was sincere in disclaiming any of the very low motives that he had imputed to me, in his being ordered there. I do think that I did give him a feeling of the importance of the job, that he hadn't had before.

He said, "I will give you my word of honor that I will do a good job in this assignment - the best that I know how to do." I said, "All right, in that case, I'll sleep happier tonight because I know you have what it takes, if you'll just give it."

So, he became the Press Relations Officer. Later, he became Press Relations Officer under Forrestal, for the Secretary of Defense.

So, he was able to do a very able job. He's a very fine man. He's a man of considerable principle and statute. I am happy that my judgement in him was vindicated. It gave me a very unhappy interlude.

Q: What rank did he retire with?

Austin: He retired as a Rear Admiral. I haven't seen him much since. I've run into him a couple of times. I think he settled on the west coast.

Since I mentioned the time that he bawled me out, maybe I should say something about that --

In those days, the chief of the boat on a small submarine was quite an important figure. He is today, even with the bigger boats. The chief of the boat is the senior Petty Officer on board. He's really the sort of Exec's alter ego for actual minute supervision work and he's the interface between the officers and the men of the ship. He's a very important man.

The chief Petty Officer who was our chief of the boat on the R-10 was named Dorn. Dorn - I think I've alluded to Dorn before - had been in the R-boats since they were built many years before. He knew them from A to Z. He, as the chief of the boat, would check the boat before the diving officer checked it.

Actually the practice on the R-10 had gotten to be a little lax in the double check of the boat before diving. But the Captain had indicated to me when I became diving officer that he wanted me to check the boat after the chief of the boat. I knew that to be good practice. I didn't quibble with him. It was the Commanding Officer's wish. But I could tell that Dorn resented it. Up to that time he had checked the boat, reported to the diving officer in the control room that the boat was checked for dive, and was ready for dive. That was that.

Sensing that Dorn was a little touchy on this I would wait until Dorn had finished in the torpedo room before I would enter the torpedo room to check the various valves that should be checked, and the gauges that should be checked.

As was bound to happen, I guess, one day I found Dorn had pulled a booboo. He had put in x-thousands of pounds into the forward trim tank instead of taking that much out, to trim the boat for a dive. This was a little hard for Dorn to take. As diplomatically as I could put it, it was hard for him to take.

So a few days later I was in the control room, I had reported to the Captain on the bridge that the ship was rigged for diving. I heard the Kingston valves being opened. The Kingston valves are the valves on the main ballast tanks on the old R-boat and on an auxiliary tank - which was a very large variable flooding tank. The main ballast tanks are usually full, or they are empty. These Kingston valves are large openings. The practice was that the Kingston valves were never touched, except by orders of the diving officer.

When I heard the Kingstons being opened I looked over and sure enough Dorn was opening all the main ballast Kingstons. I said, "Dorn, close the Kingstons. I have not ordered them opened yet." The Captain heard that up on the bridge. The conning tower hatch in those little boats was not so long that you couldn't hear what was going on at the bottom of it, if you were in charge on the bridge.

I noticed that the Captain was, shall we say, very frigid towards me during the rest of the day. We got in and he sent for me. He bawled me out and he could do a pretty good job of it.

He said, "Don't you ever again question anything that Dorn does. If you do I'll bawl you out, not in private, but in front of the entire crew." I said, "No you won't, Captain. I'm requesting, as of now, a transfer to any other ship in the Navy. I will not serve under a Captain who gives me responsibilities that I cannot live up to. I cannot live up to the responsibilities of your diving officer without being able to ask questions and give instructions to those who are moving the Kingston valves of the ship, and other things that affect the safety of the ship."

He evidently didn't think that I was going to carry it through, but I did. I went straight to the Division Commander. He was a very human individual. He was one of the 'Red' Doyles, of whom we had several in the Navy at that time.

I went straight to Commander Doyle. I said, "Sir, may I request that I be transferred from the R-10 to any other ship?" He said, "Now Count, you don't want to do that. Let's go out here on the sea wall and sit under a palm tree and talk this thing over." He could feel that I was very emotionally upset, I guess, although I tried to be casual.

When we got out under the palm trees he said, "Now tell me what's the reason for your wanting to be transferred."

I said, "Commander, it's simply this – I think that my effectiveness as an officer of the R-10 has been terminated."

He said, "Now that's a very general statement. Just what is it that's bothering you?" I said, "Sir, I don't believe it would be ethical for me to elaborate any more than that."

He said, "Now I find this very difficult. I know Bob Berry thinks you're one of the finest young officers that he's ever seen. I can't understand why you'd feel this way." I said, "Well sir, I do. I want to be transferred to some other duty."

For a long period he tried to coax me and cajole me and to worm out of me just what had happened. I would not elaborate, because I didn't think it was quite fair to.

I felt so strongly that the Captain was so much in the wrong in this thing that although I may have been wrong in what I did certainly it did not justify the Captain to put me in the position - if I ever spoke in any way to this chief again about the rigging of the boat for diving I was going to be bawled out in front of the whole crew. I think he was wrong. I didn't want to tell this to his immediate superior.

Finally Commander Doyle said, "I'll tell you - it isn't long until the first of the year. If you will just bear with me until the first of January, I'm going to make a lot of changes in the personnel in the division anyhow at that time. I'll, at that time, give you your choice of any of the ten boats in my division that you want to go to, if you still want to leave the R-10 on the first of January."

I said, "That's fair enough, sir. I can stand on my head from now to the first of January if necessary."

I'm quite sure he had my Captain up for a little talk, because from then on the Captain was exceedingly nice to me. No more bawling me out in private or in public, and a lots of appreciation for my performances, and so on.

Q: It seems extrordinary to me Count, because I would just assume from my limited experiences in the service that almost invariably unless the Commanding Officer considered a junior officer completely in the wrong, he would back him in preference to a non-commissioned officer.

Austin: I'll tell you, Bob had been an enlisted man in the Marine Corps himself. He had such a feeling of dependence on this old chief. This old chief was a clever old fellow. He not only was very competent in his knowledge of that particular type of submarine, but he was a good public relations man too. Actually Dorn resented my being on the ship.

One night I had the duty and we had to put in the battery charge before I left the ship. I had the ship's duty, so I had to supervise the battery charge.

It was pretty late when we got our turn to get the battery hooked up, and we still hadn't gotten our turn to get air from the dock. After we finished the battery charge, I sent for Dorn.

I said, "Dorn, it's very late. You have to be here all night anyway. Would you see that the air charge is put in, when we can get our turn in?"

There were twenty boats there and the capacity of the little plant was not high, so you had to stand in line to get your air for your bank. It usually took much of thenight to get your turn.

Dorn very cheerfully said, "No, sir, you go on home. It isn't necessary for an officer to be here for an air charge." It was required that an officer be present during a battery charge, but not for an air charge.

So, I went home. As usual, I was the first on board the next morning. I was up on the bridge making the usual test of the main engines at the mooring, when the Captain came aboard. He called up to me rather cheerfully and said, "All set to go out?" I said, "Yes, sir, I'm quite sure we are. I charged the batteries last night, they're full. There's only one thing I haven't checked this morning, but I'm sure that's all right. That's the air banks. I left instructions for them to be charged before I left the ship last night. I'm sure that they're all right."

Dorn stepped up and said, "Mr. Austin, you didn't leave any instructions to charge the air banks."

Q: Was this the same Commanding Officer?

Austin: Yes, the same Commanding Officer.

Then, another little experience -- Dorn had been a chief machinist's mate, before he became the Chief of the boat. Actually, he served in a dual capacity. He was the chief machinists mate, number one engineer as it were, on the enlisted side; and chief of the boat.

When I found that the air starting gear on our engines was mostly missing instead of present and working, I inquired of Dorn about this. He had been with the ship since it had been brought out. He said, "Mr. Austin, I wouldn't worry about that. None of these boats have air starting gear that works."

I said, "Dorn, we have to affirmatively or negatively state on our engineering report every month that we have or have not made a successful air starting during the previous month." He said, "Well Sir, we always check that that we have." I said, "Dorn, we don't do things that way."

To make a long story short, I started getting together the list of things we had to have to get the air starting gear in shape. First I asked Dorn to get it together. He couldn't find the blueprints. So I found the blueprints and I got the list. I finally got the parts and we got them installed, much against Dorn's wishes and better judgement.

So the moment of truth arrived. We had the air starting gear in place, and we were to make our first air start.

Dorn came to me and said, "Sir, I think I should tell you if you try to start those engines by air, you're going to have cylinder heads popping all over that engine room."

I had had a very short course in diesel engineering at the Submarine School. I reckoned that I didn't know as much from experience as Dorn did, but I thought that was a little bit overstated, because you have relief valves just to prevent that sort of thing.

Austin - 84

I said, "Dorn, I know you've been against putting air starting gear on. I respect your experience, and your wanting to give me the best advice and all. But until the orders are changed about air starts, this is a military matter. If this ship in war time had to stay submerged until it's battery were too weak to start the engines, it would be a vital matter to be able to start them by air. That's why they were designed that way. Until somebody gives us some other way to start these engines, I'm going to make an air start."

So, we go all set. Everybody was at his station. I was in the engine room to supervise the first air start, Dorn had the throttle. He turned around to me and said, "Mr. Austin, I want to once more warn you that this is unsafe and that personnel are liable to be hurt. If you order me to start these engines, I will."

I said, "No, Dorn, I'm not ordering you to start the engines by air. I'll take the throttle. You may leave the engine room, if you feel that it's unsafe. Anybody else in the engine room who feels it's unsafe, can leave the room too. We're going to start these engines on air." Nobody left the engine room, including Dorn. But he did step back, because I told him to.

I said, "Give me the throttle." The throttle was a combination of two wheels. On an air start, you turn one to the right and the other one to the left. The trick of the trade was to turn the one that gave her the shot of air just enough to get her turning, and then give her the fuel with the other one.

I was very happy, when after a shot of air and I turned the one with the fuel; she took off smooth as a whistle. No cylinder heads popped.

It was just that Dorn had gotten the idea ---

Q: He'd gotten in a rut.

Austin: He'd gotten in a rut. He'd gotten away with not making air starts and just saying he had for all these years. So, he was reluctant to get out of that rut. He didn't, evidentally, think the probability of hostilities were very great; therefore why worry about something you're never going to need.

Q: There weren't too many chiefs in responsible positions during the war were there?

Austin: No, I would say there weren't. I would say, that in war time, Dorn probably would have had a different view of it. This was in 1927 to '31. Things were pretty calm in those days.

As a matter of fact, I remember we got a new division Commander out there, who was quite well-known in the Navy, being a pretty hard-boiled fellow. He found that all of the warheads for all of his ships, were stowed off the ships over on the ammunition island. So it would have been quite a job to have gotten his boats out in a war ready condition very quickly. He ordered them all to put the warhead back on board, which of course is standard practice ever since.

There was a lot of unhappiness about that, because it made for a more crowded area in the torpedo room. They were in the way.

Q: That really required some effort to get them aboard.

Austin: That's right. And to keep them from deteriorating, watching them, testing them for exudate of the charge, and all that sort of thing.

Q: Suppose we knock off at this time. Then when I come back again we can start with your assignment to London. I'd like to go into some details about that, if you would like to. That was a very very interesting assignment.

Austin - 87

Austin: I can give you excerpts from a diary I kept over there if you need it.

Q: I'd like to. I'd like to have your reactions to the politics of the country at that time. Had Churchill taken over?

Austin: Yes. As a matter of fact, Mr. Churchill welcomed Admiral Ghormley to London, and took him to the Admiralty, and personally conducted him through the Admiralty. He had taken over, because it was his conversations with Roosevelt that resulted in our being over there. He had recently been the First Lord of the Admiralty, so he personally conducted Admiral Ghormely through the Admiralty. On the conclusion of the tour, the welcoming aboard as it were, he said to Admiral Ghormley; "Admiral, if there is anything that you feel that you need that you have any difficulty in getting, you come to me personally and you will have it. That is the way I want you to feel. Anything you want, you get."

Q: He must have been a very very remarkable man. I've oftentimes thought that the TIMES cover of Churchill was most appropriate, stating that he was the outstanding man of this century.

Austin: He certainly was, for England at that time, the man of the hour. There's no doubt about that. Every place you went you heard the people singing his praises.

Admiral Ghormley and I were privileged to go on a few 'see what happened last night' expeditions, where you'd see him going around giving the victory signal, and people who were pushing their last belongings on a push-cart to some other place for the night, and him talking with them. He really had contact with the British people at that time, and he had their confidence. Whatever their policital inclination, they were going to stick by 'Winnie' until they won. Then they'd get back to politics. He was the man of the hour, there's no doubt in my mind.

Q: I understand that at the time he took over as First Lord of the Admiralty a message went out to the Fleet saying, "Winnie's aboard."

Austin: They had mixed feelings about him in the Admiralty, yes. While he was showing us through the Admiralty he took us through the war room. He pointed out the submarine loses.

The chap who later became a very close friend of mine, who had been told to sort of keep his eye on me I guess during this tour, Commander Goodenough, told me after the party got ahead a little bit, "Those figures are not the true figures. The picture's blacker than that. If you want the actual facts, I can get them for you. We don't dare put them up here where 'Winnie' sees them every day because we never know what he's going to give out to the public. We just couldn't have the true figures go out right now. It's too black, too discouraging."

So they loved him, but they knew his weaknesses, shall we say.

Q: He was very much inclined to be very frank in all his public utterances.

Austin: Yes.

He did not have a creditability gap. Frankly I don't think that a Prime Minister who allowed a creditability gap to develop between him and the British people would have been able to lead them through that. I don't think a creditability gap would have been acceptable in those circumstances.

Vice Admiral Bernard L. Austin
near Rockville, Maryland

by Paul L. Hopper
November 7, 1969

Mr. Hopper: Admiral Austin, as we concluded our third session as I recall, you had begun to discuss your assignment to London, during which time you were acting as naval aide to Admiral Ghormley. Would you like to continue along that line?

Admiral Austin: The estimate of Admiral Stark that this would be a rather short tour of duty did not turn out to be accurate, to say the least. He had used the term about six weeks, he thought.

At the end of six weeks it appeared that we were getting in deeper and deeper instead of completing our assignment. We were getting more and more requests and requirements from the Navy Department.

When we had first arrived there had been a little misunderstanding created quite innocently by a flag officer of the British Navy - slapping Captain Kirk on the shoulder at a party and whispering in his ear, "I heard that you're about to leave us, and that they're sending an Admiral over here to relieve you."

Our mission had been kept so secret that this was the first that Captain Kirk knew of Admiral Ghormley's coming. When he inquired by cable to either disabuse his mind or to confirm the report that he was about to leave; he was told that Admiral Ghormley was coming on a highly classified mission, and that he was not coming as his relief. He was given the gist of the mission that Admiral Ghormley was to perform.

Actually, Admiral Ghormley received his instructions orally from President Roosevelt. To the best of my knowledge, they were not reduced to writing.

The Navy Department, therefore, was a little reluctant to go into too much detail as to what the parameters of Admiral Ghormley's job were.

Captain Kirk had a limited staff for the increased work incident to the many inquires that were coming from the Navy Department regarding the war.

Q: Was he acting as Naval Attache then?

Austin: Yes, he was the Naval Attache.

His assistant Naval Attache for air was a Commander Hitchcock. Commander Hitchcock requested the Naval Attache to get the two aides to Admiral Ghormley assigned to his watch list, which was a quite normal attitude for him to take, in view of the fact that he was on the watch list himself. He represented to the Naval Attache that the watch list was so small that the people were quite hard-pressed to stand these watches. They had to stand them around the clock both day and night, because of incoding and decoding load.

Admiral Ghormley quite amiably agreed that his two aides would help out. Sure, he wanted to help out as much as he could. So, we were put on the watch list. I didn't object at the time. I thought that the more we ehlped, the better too. Being on the watch list, we'd probably be in a position to learn more quickly how to mesh our activities with those of the Naval Attache's office.

But, as sometimes happens, Commander Hitchcock decided that he should come off the watch list and the next senior officer, who was a Lieutnenat Commander Ammong, who was a little senior to me, would come off the watch list; when McDonald and I went on.

We didn't make any todo about that. We reckoned that the Commander was sufficiently embroiled in aviation intelligence and that sort of thing and that probably he shouldn't be on the watch list. Bill Ammong was sort of the communicator of the staff, so had some excuse too.

As things developed, we had excuse not to be on the watch list too; more than an excuse, a reason.

Commander Hitchcock required the watch stander for the night watch to also stand watch during the long British noon hour. You relieved the coding officer of the day in time for him to go to lunch and if he took one of these three hour lunches, you were still there three hours later. You were stuck, you had it.

This happened to me one day when I was late getting back to the Admiralty for a conference that Admiral Ghormley had with Admiral Bailey. Admiral Ghormley wanted to know why I was late, and I told him. He said, "Get yourself off that watch list."

I went to see Commander Hitchcock. I didn't ask to come off the watch list, but I did ask if he would try to find some arrangement so that I wouldn't have to be subject to the noon hour watches. He misunderstood my request or my attitude, and he said, "You're just trying to get out of your proper work." He started giving me a bad time.

During the time that he was upbraiding me for not having the proper attitude towards my watch standing, several other officers came in to his office. He continued to upbraid me in front of these other officers, which I didn't relish. When I could get a word in edgewise, I said, "Commander, if you think I'm trying to evade my proper duties; I think that you had better come along with me and we'll see Admiral Ghormley. You should tell him if I'm not doing my job, I think you ought to tell him so." He declined to do that.

A little later, he came into my office, and stuck out his hand and said, "Let's forget all those unpleasant things in my office and let's be friends." I'm not one to hold a grudge, so we shook hands, and that was that for the time being.

But, there had been planted in the Attache's office, this little bit of attitude of resenting the Ghormley mission. I think it was mainly due to the fact that they initially had felt that Admiral Ghormley was going to route their boss out. It was just loyalty on their part, to their boss.

Q: Admiral Kirk was a very splendid officer.

Austin: Yes.

Q: He was director of ONI, for a time, when I was there.

Austin: Yes. As a matter of fact, he came back from that job as director of ONI.

I had the pleasure of having him as my guest up at the Naval War College, while I was president there. He went over with me, he wanted to see the main building where my office was. We went over, and he reminisced about the time that he had lived in the War College building. His uncle was then the president. He had visited there as a little boy. In those days, they had apartments up there in the main building for the people who were on duty there.

Q: The classes were correspondingly small.

Austin: Yes.

I don't know just where to start here on this matter of my whole tour of duty over there in England. So many things happened during that time which are of interest. Do you have any suggestions on what you would like me to cover?

Q: Not particularly Count. I read over your diary which I thought was most interesting. However I think you purposely and very properly didn't improperly disclose any information.

Austin: Anything that would have been aid and comfort to the enemy, if they had found it.

Q: Yes. I was very much impressed by the extent to which you obviously made good use of your social contacts and the multiplicity of people which you came in contact with and apparently were friendly with, and obviously must have exchanged information with from time to time.

Austin: I said something about the three hour lunch period. Most of us over here are inclined to look down our noses at the British taking so long for lunch — these business lunches.

I quickly learned though, very often you could accomplish something at a three hour lunch; that you couldn't accomplish in much more time by letter and by phone calls. So, it isn't just a social proposition. It does have a practical function.

Q: Many business men, in this country, now do the same thing.

Austin: Yes.

I think the best thing to do is to sort of do a chronological approach to this.

The night that we arrived in London, we were shown to a suite of rooms that had been set up by the Naval Attache's office for Admiral Ghormley, at a very special rate, on the top floor of the Dorchester Hotel. It was interesting to note that we were the only people who lived on the top floor of the Dorchester Hotel.

Q: I was thinking you were *pretty vulnerable* as far as bombing went.

Austin: When someone raised this point with Admiral Ghormley, suggesting perhaps that it was a little dangerous to be on the top floor, with the bombs liable to fall; he shrugged it off and laughed and said, "I'd rather be on the top floor and come down with the building, than be on the bottom floor and have the building come down on top of me."

McDonald, Admiral Ghormley's aide, and I took the same attitude. We lived very happily there until a later date, which I will cover at the proper time.

The night we arrived, Admiral Ghormley was whisked out to the country by Captain Kirk. McDonald and I were shown to the hotel by a young reserve officer, who had been told off to see that we got to our diggings. While we were unpacking, this young officer was being very helpful to us. Telling us such things as - how to get to the Embassy the next morning; where our rooms were there, our offices; the details about identification cards; and all that we'd have to attend to the first thing in the morning.

The air raid alarm sounded. The young officer said, "We should go down to the air raid shelter right away."

McDonald and I said, "We're so close to the roof, couldn't we just go up on the roof and see what's happening?" He said, "Oh, no, that would be very dangerous to be up there."

I had about the same attitude that Admiral Ghormley had expressed about the danger thing. I'm not a Presbyterian, but I am a little bit of a fatalist, I'm afraid. I don't go looking for bombs to get under, but I, by the same token kind of felt that if one had my name on it; it would find me, and if it didn't, it probably wouldn't. There's no use to spend the intervening time worrying about it.

I told him, "If you don't mind, I would like to go up and see what an air raid looks like; where you can see the planes maybe, and see what the activity is going on throughtout the city, as it were." With great reluctance, he accompanied me to the roof of the Dorchester. We did get a good view of what was happening.

That was the first night that bombs fell on London proper.

The next day we got squared away at the Embassy with all these passes and whatnot. Among the other things that we got, were driver's licenses. I was somewhat amused when I read in my driver's license, that I was authorized to drive any kind of motor vehicle that traveled on the road or locomotive. I don't know whether someone vouched for my skill in driving locomotives, or not. I was amused that I had a permit to drive one.

Q: They must have felt that you American naval officers were truly versatile.

Austin: They were leaning over backwards to be kind to us, and they were. I have never belonged to so many clubs in my life, as I did during the time that I was in London. I was invited to join every club that I'd ever heard of, frankly.

Except White's - I don't believe White's ever extended an invitation. White's is a little bit snobbish that way, I guess. What I mainly referred to of course, was the various service clubs - The In and Out, the Senior, the Junior, the Bachelor's Club. There were more clubs than I could patronize, I can assure you.

Q: The British have always been famous for their numberous clubs.

Austin: Yes. It was one way to get a fair meal. The clubs seemed to be able to serve fair meals, not much meat, but pretty good meals. They had the very best of wines and cigars, and that sort of thing.

The pattern of our activity there developed after the initial sort of reception of Admiral Ghormley by the Admiralty and Mr. Churchill personally, and his going to Cabinet meetings and all that. It developed into a series of meetings with a British Admiral, Sir Sidney Bailey; who had been assigned as Admiral Ghormley's contact with everyone; both naval and political.

Admiral Sir Sidney Bailey was a charming gentleman. He had served under both Beatty and Jellico. As I got to know him better, I tried to pick his brains a little bit about the Jellico-Beatty controversy. But, he would always smile, and give me the polite brush-off.

Austin - 100

He was a very interesting man, and a very excellent contact for Admiral Ghormley to have.

I believe I covered the time that we received this long cable from Admiral Stark, asking for lots of information about the mandated islands.

Q: No, you didn't.

Austin: I didn't? I guess that was some one else I was talking to.

An illustration of Admiral Bailey's very great cooperations -- One day Admiral Ghormley received from Admiral Stark a very long list of questions, to which he indicated he needed urgent answers. They were all in the field of intelligence on the Japanese mandated islands After reading those questions, I wondered if we had any information about those islands at all.

Admiral Stark had indicated that he had been led to believe that the British intelligence did have information which would provide the answers to many of these questions, if not all Admiral Ghormley called me in and sent me down to the Admiralty to get the answers.

I saw the director on intelligence at the Admiralty, who was a very nice chap, but who evidentally took the attitude that Americans were just as much foreign as anybody else.

He was darned if he was going to open up his intelligence files to us. I quickly sensed that he was giving me a stall and a delaying response.

Admiral Stark wanted these answers by dispatch. I suggested that we needed them more quickly than it appeared that he was going to be able to get them; and that if I could be of any assistance in doing the digging, the sorting out, or looking for the specific answers; I'd be happy to do so.

He said, "We couldn't do that. We'd have to make our entire portfolio on that part of the world available to you." I said, "Maybe that wouldn't be a bad idea." He said, "You realize, it would take an affirmative act on the part of the Board of Admiralty to do that." I said, "Let's give it a try." He was still in shock, when we saw Admiral Bailey.

Admiral Bailey said, "I see no reason in the world why we shouldn't do that. I'm going to a meeting of the Board of Admiralty in a few minutes and I'll take it up."

I went back to my office and reported to Admiral Ghormley my lack of success thus far, and where we stood. I said, "If the board of Admiralty took the attitude that Admiral Bailey took, we'd quickly have all the answers we needed."

About three o'clock that afternoon, sirens sounded, and up to the Embassy drove a couple of motorcyles with sidecars and riders around them to guard them. And in came this officer messenger and plunked on my desk the entire portfolio of the Far East from the British Admiralty, and asked me to sign a receipt for it.

We immediately, of course, extracted the answers that Admiral Stark was urgently interested in; and sent those by several separate cables. Then we dispatched the entire portfolio by the next courier that went back.

Admiral Bailey was, throughout our dealing with him, one to inspire confidence and to promote real smooth cooperative effort.

He was assisted by a number of officers in the Admiralty. The one who was sort of his number one assistant was a Commander Goodenough, who was the nephew of old Admiral Goodenough. Goodenough and I became very close friends. It was a friendship, which I believe did promote the smoothness of our dealings with the British. I think I can illustrate that best by telling you about one evening.

This was after we had been there long enough for Goodenough to get a pretty good idea as to the metes and bounds of Admiral Ghormley's authority. And also, the metes and bounds of what we would or would not, agree to.

Admiral Ghormley always prefaced anything that he said, that might seem like a commitment, with the statement that he was not authorized to make any commitment. But, that he had been told to discuss these matters with the British and that he hoped the discussion would provide the basis for whatever commitments the two governments might wish to make.

Goodenough came up to my apartment, (this was long after we'd left the Dorchester), and he said, "Count, I need a drink." So, we had a couple.

Then he said, "You know, I don't know how to put this. I know what will get Admiral Ghormley's hackles up, I think. I have been unable to convince the people in the Admiralty who are about to put forward this paper tomorrow, to change it. They're set in their convictions. They say it's what we need, and therefore they're going to stick by their guns. I'm going to show you that paper because I feel that if Admiral Ghormley sees this paper for the first time tomorrow, that things won't be very pleasant across the table. He will feel that we have not listened to him all these meetings we've had. I think confidence will be destroyed to a degree that will not be in the best interest of either your country or mine."

When I looked at the paper, I said, "I think your analysis is absolutely correct. Admiral Ghormley would hit the ceiling if he saw this as a proposal of your side. If you let me keep this copy, I will propose to Admiral Ghormley reshaping of this in such a way that it will fit our instructions. I will tell him that you have visited me and that you have given us this preview of this."

At this point, Goodenough said, "For God's sake, don't let him inadvertently take that paper to the meeting, or in any way give away the fact that I've come to you with it. Because I would be fired forthwith if they knew that I was communicating this information to you. In my own conscience, I'm not doing anything wrong, and I think I'm doing right."

I gave him the assurances and I went over to Admiral Ghormley's apartment immediately after he left.

Admiral Ghormley and I worked over it. The reaction was just as Goodenough and I had predicted. The Admiral at first shrugged his shoulders and wondered if they had been listening to what he had been telling them for all these months. After I had calmed him down and explained to him how we could alter it a little bit and make it fit our position, he went in the next day and sure enough they tabled the identical paper that Goodenough had a copy of.

Instead of Admiral Ghormley hitting the ceiling, he said, "Now, if you recall, I've told you so and so and so and so. Therefore, I would have to strike out this and substitute that." And that's exactly what happened. They gave him exactly the changes that he asked for.

But had we not had this little behind the scenes liaison, I think the meetings would have foundered right then and there.

Goodenough was a very brilliant fellow. He later became a flag officer in the British navy.

Austin - 105

I might tell you an interesting little event that took place when I was the senior U. S. naval officer at Supreme Allied Headquarters under General Grunther.

I arrived and found a British Rear Admiral there who looked down his nose quite a bit at the newly arrived U. S. Rear Admiral, I could tell that.

Q: Was he senior to you?

Austin: No, he wasn't. I had flown my flag at sea before that. He had never flown a flag at sea, he had just been given the rank for this job. He only preceeded me there by a couple of months. He had gotten in the driver's seat and he was Mr. Navy at NATO Headquarters.

He worked for a French Admiral who was a charming fellow, former CNO of the French Navy, Admiral LeMonier. Admiral LeMonier let the British Deputy do all the work, and therefore run the office.

My job as the Deputy to the Deputy Chief of Staff to General Grunther for Plans, Policy, and Operations covered quite an area. It later was changed, after I left. It was changed to just Plans and Policy. Operations was split off.

I'd been there only a very short time when Admiral C. came into my office with a paper in his hand. He said, "I understand that you wouldn't initial this when it was brought to you by Colonel so and so."

I said, "That is correct, Admiral, I wouldn't. Furthermore, when the Colonel became quite impatient with my not initialling it and saying it was long overdue; I told him that I would go right with him to my boss, General Lohrio and explain to him why I didn't initial it. Then, if he wanted to initial it and let it go on, okay."

When I told the General why I wouldn't initial it, the General said, "I agree, write me a memorandum to General Grunther to that effect." The Colonel had told me that the paper had already been approved by Field Marshall Montgomery.

As a result of Admiral C's visit, I quickly detected that he had written the paper. The gist of it was that -- the Naval Deputy's office was going to have the veto on all matters having to do with navies in NATO. Despite the fact that the Plans, Policy, and Operations people were charged with overall Plans, Policy and Operations for NATO. That is, advising the Chief of Staff and the Supreme Commander on them. To split the Navy off wasn't quite in accordance with the way the Headquarters had been organized.

I heard the protest of Admiral C to the effect that after all I was a naval officer and he was a naval officer. It would have seemed to him that before I took the action which caused my boss to write that memorandum to General Grunther, and caused General Grunther to disapprove this; that I might have collaborated with him.

I said, "I think you have a point. We are both naval officers and we should cooperate on naval matters. You're the Deputy in the Naval Deputy's office and I'm the Deputy here in Plans, Policy and Operations. I think it is quite proper that we sort of touch base with each other and cooperate. But cooperation begins at the beginning. When you wrote this paper, it has as its purpose, the chipping away of the responsibilities of this office, of which I'm the Deputy. It seems that you might have come around and consulted me on it then. I'm perfectly willing to cooperate, but it's got to work both ways."

Several months later, Admiral Mountbatten arrived at NATO Headquarters with Goodenough as his brief-case man; Goodenough then being a Rear Admiral. Goodenough came to call on me, while his boss was having a conference with General Grunther.

Michael Goodenough said, "Count, how is "C" making out over here?" I said, "He seems to be working pretty hard, Michael. I don't have too much observation opportunities, but he seems to get around and do his social duties quite properly. The Naval Deputy office there seems to function all right." Michael smiled and said, "Count, you're not leveling with me. He's been getting out of his proper field over here." I said, "If you knew, why did you ask me?"

He said, "I'm going to tell you. Admiral Mountbatten has just come from his office. I'm going to tell you what Admiral Mountbatten told him, because we have received reports from this Headquarters from British officers that indicate to us that "C" is running around here as if he owned the place and stirring up trouble where he shouldn't be. Admiral Mountbatten told him, that he had put his stars on him to come to this job, and that if he doesn't improve in a very short time, he'll take them off of him and send him back to sea without them. Remember that Admiral Austin is not only senior to you, but I have utmost confidence and trust in how he does business. He has flown his flag at sea and you have never flown a flag at sea. From now on, stop trying to undercut him and usurp his job."

Q: That was a nice comment from Mountbatten because he was quite a person.

Austin: I had met Admiral Mountbatten before. Of course, I think his opinion of me had been shaped by Michael Goodenough. I think Michael had vouched for me.

I went to see them off at the airport. Mountbatten took me aside and personally told me just what Goodenough had told me. He didn't know whether Goodenough had presumed to tell me or not.

He said, "I don't want to put "C" in an impossible position. I know you well enough to know that if you know what I told him, that you'll help him instead of otherwise. That's why I'm telling you. I think he's got what it takes, he just got off on the wrong foot over here."

Sure enough, "C" came into my office a few days later, with the letter from Mountbatten. It said, "This is to confirm my conversation with you." He repeated it. "C", very much embarrassed, handed me the letter.

He said, "Admiral, I think you should see this. This has taken the wind out of my sails a great deal. It's caused me to do a lot of self-evaluation. I want you to know that I will do everything in my power to see that the relations in your office and my office, and between you and me, are what they should be in the future. Perhaps, I was wrong."

Q: The average British officer has real character.

Austin: Yes, they do.

I might say, "C" became a fast friend. He and I got along well. Our wives got along well. We found that we could work together very well.

As a matter of fact, I might tell you another little incident that happened while I was at the Supreme Allied Headquarters.

Austin - 110

Shortly after I arrived there, the requirement was put on General Grunther to send a study and recommendations regarding the future of naval forces in the NATO setup.

I was called in by the Chief of Staff and told that I would be the chairman of the committee, to work up this study and report for General Grunther. I went back to my office and outlined my approach to the problem.

We had many navies represented in NATO, but of course, there weren't very many that could contribute very greatly in the way of ships and men. But, as I had learned earlier in life, some times the smallest entity is the one with the biggest pride.

So, I got a representative of every navy in NATO on my committee. I gave them their say, just as much as I gave the U. S. representative. The result was a very hard working committee and a wonderful bit of digging and putting together of a report. The only trouble with it was, it was entirely too long.

Q: You mean the report?

Austin: Yes.

Q: I suppose the membership was really a bit unwieldly.

Austin: Yes, it was. But, we worked in sub-groups, which helped that a great deal. The report was a volumn that thick. When

I got through laboriously going through it, I realized that it would accomplish nothing. Because, the golden nuggets were buried under too much soil, as it were.

So, I had a meeting of the group and expressed my feelings on it. Strangely enough, Admiral "C" championed the full report. He said, "Perhaps it is long, but it's got everything in it. If you start cutting it, we're going to have to cut out something." I said, "This may be true. But, I feel very strongly that it must be a report that General Grunther can read. He isn't going to read this long report. I'm perfectly willing to leave intact the present report; but we've got to have a summary report that summarizes this, that is something a busy man can read and judge."

When we put it to a vote, I was supported by the majority. Then I made "C" the chairman of the sub-group to do the editing, and he did a marvelous job.

As a matter of fact, when the report was submitted, General Grunther happened to be out of town. I was sent for by General Schuyler, who was Chief of Staff. He told me that he was sorry to inform me that General Grunther probably would not send this report forward.

I said, "General, the standing group has required this of General Grunther. What's he going to send forward? I happen to know every line in that report. If there's anything wrong with it, I'm willing to defend it or change it if anyone can prove to me that it's wrong."

He said, "I'll tell you, I agree with you. General Grunther has got to answer the standing group's requirement. I'll show you a memo I just sent him yesterday before he left."

The memo informed General Grunther that this was a requirement on him by the standing group, that it was an excellent paper, and that he - General Schuyler - thought it should be forwarded. But he said, "I must inform you that the Air Deputy, General Norstad, takes grave exception to it's being sent."

I went home that night, this was late in the afternoon that he told me this, and I didn't sleep too well, because I knew that General Norstad had great influence with General Grunther.

The next morning I went down to see General Schuyler. I said, "General, I've thought over what you told me last night. I would like to discuss this with General Norstad, if you have no objection." He said, "No, not at all."

I said, "I feel so strongly about this General that I feel if this thing is swept under the rug, after it's been generated by the representatives of every navy of NATO, I think you're going to have unhappiness in all the adrmialties of NATO. I don't think General Grunther wants that. He is the Supreme Commander. He isn't just Commander of the Army forces, or the

Air forces, or the Navy forces, he's the Supreme Commander. He can't put himself in the position of being that partisan." Schuyler grinned and said, "Count, I agree with you."

I went back to my office, called General Norstad's office and made an appointment to see him. When I walked in there sat General Schuyler alongside of him.

Norstad's a very charming fellow personally. He and I had always been good friends personally and socially, and had always gotten along together officially. We didn't always agree, then sometimes we were on different sides of the problem.

General Norstad put on his most charming smile and said, "Count, I understand that you're very unhappy about my not letting General Grunther sign and send forward that paper that you and your committee produced." I said, "That's an understatement, but a correct one, sir."

He said, "I'll tell you, it's a good paper." I said, "Yes sir, I think it is. I think it's a correct paper. I stand ready to defend any part of it."

He said, "You don't have to do that. That's the trouble with the damm thing, it's too good. You know why I don't want this to go forward? I don't want to see every country in NATO stop spending money on airplanes, and start spending it all on the Navy. You make too good a case. That's the trouble with this paper, it's too damm good, it's too convincing. I have told General Grunther that I recommend that he not send it

Austin - 114

forward. I'll level with you, that's the reason. General Schuyler's told me how strongly you feel about it, so I'm withdrawing my objection." And, it was sent forward.

Q: Nordstadt later became Supreme Allied Commander.

Austin: Yes, he succeeded General Grunther. Then, Gen. Lemnitzer succeeded him.

Now, we've gotten off the track again, Paul.

Q: Very interestingly so, Count. Would you like to retrace back to London for a bit?

Austin: Let's jump back across the channel.

Q: Your entire story really, Count, is fascinating; and an interesting one; and I would like to have you say as much as you want to. I think it would be an interesting commentary for you to have, yourself, later on.

Austin: I find it difficult to know where to stop.

Q: Just kind of ramble on.

Austin: Let's go back to London.

These meeting with the so-called Bailey Committee, --

Q: Let me ask you this about your experiences in London. There was quite a lot of comment about the Cliveden Set in the early stages of the war. Did you sense that there were a certain number of highly placed people in London who would not have been unhappy if the British hadn't won the war, or they hadn't actually gotten into the war in the beginning?

Austin: Paul, this is a delicate question to answer. I wouldn't try to answer it in a few words.

Admiral Ghormley, and I, and his other aide, McDonald; were invited out to Cliveden several times. We were invited down to Plymouth, where the Astor's held forth. I had the feeling, from the people that I saw there and the little bit of conversation that you'd have with various people on various small topics, that there was a bond that tended to sort of keep this Cliveden Set together. I don't think it was anything approaching disloyalty to the country. I think they were simply in the same position that lots of our people in this country are today. There was a situation, they didn't see an easy solution to it. They were struggling for something less unacceptable than defeat by the German juggernaut.

Frankly, there were times over there, when it looked like that was what they were going to have to face. Still, I can't feel that people like Lord Halifax - he was one of them --

Q: He was close to Chamberlain.

Austin: He became Ambassador to this country later.

Q: He was Viceroy of India, when I first went out there.

Austin: People like Lady Astor - she was an interesting person, to say the least, if I may indulge in a very great understatement. I might just digress a moment to tell you about a little quip of hers.

When I arrived in England after the war, for my tour of duty at the Imperial Defense College as a student; there was a reception. One of these typical British receptions, where the majordomo announces the people as they come in.

My wife and my little daughters were more or less the guests of honor at this little reception. Lady Astor was one of the people who came. As soon as she got to the receiving line, she jumped on my middle daughter for dycing her hair. It embarrassed the little girl no end, because she didn't dye her hair.

As a matter of fact, she'd been accused of that at Holton Arms by the Assistant Head Mistress there. Although she'd gotten used to being accused of dyeing her hair (in those days it was not looked upon as the thing to do) to have someone as prominent as Lady Astor stop in a receiving line and say (she actually turned to me and asked), "Why do you let this beautiful young girl dye her hair?" was distressing to my young daughter.

Q: She had no inhibitions.

Austin: No, none whatever. She said what she thought and it could sound any way that it happened to come out.

They were giving a party for Admiral Ghormley when we first arrived there at the Admiralty. The only people invited were government officials, and not very many government officials were ladies. Lady Astor was the only lady that I saw at the party. They were all Cabinet officers, Whip, Parliament of all parties, so forth and so on; and sort of that type list of government officials at that time.

Q: Did she hold an honorary position of some kind in the British officialdom?

Austin: Oh, yes. She was at that time, a member of Parliament.

Austin - 118

She was, I think, on the committee of the Parliament that dealt with Admiralty affairs. She was invited. Not all the members of Parliament were obviously, it was not that big a party. But, she came, and she came late. She never stopped talking, as you know. She always had people to listen to her, because she was so unpredictable and so interesting.

She had this group of people around her and I was within earshot. She was explaining to them, why she was so late. She said, "It's a beautiful day out today. I just decided I'd walk down here. I was walking along Piccadilly and I saw this very attractive girl who was obviously a street walker. On the impulse of the moment, I just stopped, and started talking to her. I asked her why she didn't find a more honorable way of living. She looked me right in the eye and said, 'I like my present way of living'."

Lady Astor was very shocked, but was not shocked enough to avoid telling it in a group of men. So, she was quite an interesting person, quite a vivacious individual with tremendous energy. Her husband was 'just like an old shoe'.

Q: That's what I understood.

Austin: He didn't appear to have any energy. I guess he felt that one dynamo in the family was enough.

Let's get back to the Bailey committee, shall we? We went over a paper — it was actually a book, about that thick — which the British had prepared for the conversations with us. We used it as a sort of point of departure because Admiral Pound inadvertantly, or advertantly, I don't know; disclosed the existance of this paper. The British appeared to be very unhappy that he had disclosed the existance of this paper to Admiral Ghormley.

Admiral Bailey explained to Admiral Ghormley, when he asked if he could have a copy of it. He said, "Admiral, I frankly don't think there's a thing in it that you shouldn't see. But, it was prepared not for anyone other than the eyes of the British people. Some things may be expressed in there in a way that might make you unhappy. I'll have to check it out with the board of Admiralty, as to whether or not we can release it to you. As far as the disclosure of secrets is concerned, we have no secrets from you. We don't want to give you a paper that was written as an internal paper for us, without going through it pretty carefully and making sure that we aren't going to offend you in doing so." Actually, they did make it available.

We informed Washington of it's contents, naturally. We used that as a sort of departure for each phase of our talks with the British.

Austin - 120

The ABC conference, which took place later, was shorter and smoother and produced more agreement as a result of the conversations which we had had with the British on the chapters of this paper.

Q: What was the ABC conference?

Austin: That was held in Washington. We went over to London in '40. The ABC conference was in late '41, before Pearl Harbor, but after Admiral Ghormley had had his seris of preliminary talks with the British on the Bailey level.

Q: I was trying to tie in the granting of the destroyer deal for the bases in Trinidad and various other places. Was that decided at the ABC conference or brought up?

Austin: No. This was a government to government proposition. Of course Admiral Ghormley was asked for, shall we say, information on which to base a decision by our government. This was decided while we were over there. The main thing that our government was concerned about was whether or not giving the British fifty destroyers would result in their being turned over to the Germans. You can understand why. Because we were going to spend lots of money to get those ready for turning over to the British. They'd be, not new ships, but they'd be in pretty good condition. We didn't want to turn over fifty good destroyers to the British, and then have them cave in a few weeks later. So, Admiral Ghormely was very much queried about the prospects of the British being able to hold out. We had experts - Marines, for example - make a survey of all the beach defenses of Britain and all that sort of thing; to give us more than a top of the head type of response to the queries that Admiral Ghormley got from Washington. I'm sure many of those queries were instigated by either the President or the State Department, because they were not of a purely naval technical nature. They were more of a political nature. Yet they required naval expertees to give them some of the answers.

The bombing in London became progressively more discoboblating after we got there. While Admiral Ghormely was out of town, the Ambassador called me in one day.

Q: Kennedy was Ambassador then?

Austin: Kennedy was when we first got there. He was replaced by Ambassador Winant shortly after.

Q: As you say, this is a delicate subject for discussion. There has been, as you know, statements and rumors to the effect that Kennedy was very close to Chamberlain. The two of them were perhaps not as aggressive in making preparations, in view of what was obviously the state of affairs at that time. I wondered if you had any comments on that?

Austin: I'm afraid that the basis for any comment would have to come from someone who was privy to a little higher level meetings, than I was privy to. I only saw Mr. Kennedy a couple of times, the whole time I was over there.

Mr. Winant, I saw much more frequently. Because Mr. Winant, not only came to the office every day, but he lived right in the building that the Embassy was in. He lived in an apartment in the building right next door to it.

It was Mr. Winant that sent for me, and he told me that he felt that the probability of Admiral Ghormley being damaged by German bombing was too great and that I should get accomadations for us outside of London proper.

It was at that time, that we did succeed in finding accomadations at the home of a dowager Lady Smiley. We lived there, the Admiral and both of his aides, for quite a long time.

Q: She must have been a very fine person from your accounts in your diary.

Austin: She's a charming person, a very forthright individual, with some of the same qualities of Lady Astor. She was a much larger person. She was a direct decendant of William the Conqueror, and stood very high in Burke's perage. As as result of that, she 'drew a fair amount of water', as it were, in certain areas.

For example, one night, she said, "Would you like to go to the Easter service in WindsorCastle tomorrow morning?" I said, "I'd love it." She went to the phone and called the Lord of the Castle and said she'd be there with a guest.

Q: As simple as that?

Austin: Yes. We arrived, and it was a most impressive occasion for me, as I'd never been to Windsor Castle before. The little chapel there is quite long and narrow, with the pennants of all the knights of the garter hanging from both sides. All the pews are hand-carved. When we arrived, of course, it was still dark. Because of the blackout regulations, they didn't start putting the candles on until it began to get light outdoors. So, you had this very interesting combination of lighting effect from the dawn outside through the stained glass windows and the gradual lighting of a few more candles as the dawn came up. It was extremely impressive, being in war time, and not knowing really how long the nation might be able to hold out, at that time. I was very grateful to Lady Smiley for being an ancestor of William the Conqueror.

Q: That was a wonderful experience.

Austin: After the service, the Lord of the Castle took us over to his private quarters, and we had sherry and chit chat. Then, we drove on home.

It was quite a thrill for one to ride with Lady Smiley at night. As you know, during the war, they had theee little slits of light that they were allowed on their cars but no more. Lady Smiley usually drove herself. She had a big Damiler car. Some of those little roads in England are not expressways, by any means. They are winding and narrow.

Q: It must have been a thrill.

Austin: It really was a thrill to ride with her at night with the blackout regulations being such that you couldn't see where the heck you were going. She knew those roads though pretty well. We always managed to get there and back. But, it was a thrill.

Q: How did you end up your mission in London? You were re-assigned, or you had asked for change of duty before Admiral

Austin - 125

Ghormely came back, as I recall.

Austin: Yes. I had objected to going to London because of the shore duty aspect of it. Admiral Stark, at the time, assured me that he would personally see that I did not suffer from accepting this job. He said, that the President wanted Admiral Ghormley to have whomever he wished to go with him, and that I should forget all about it being shore duty.

While over there, Admiral Ghormley, at the end of a year; wrote a letter to Admiral Stark and said that I had been to all the conferences in London with him and that lots of the information that I had in my head was nowhere else to be found. Therefore, he thought that it was illadvised to have me relieved, by anyone. He suggested, in fairness to me, that the Secretary of the Navy designate my duty there as sea duty for rotation purposes.

Mr. Knox, was then Secretary of the Navy. Evidentally, Admiral Stark agreed with Admiral Ghormley. Mr. Knox signed such a statement to BuPers. At that time, the Chief of BuPers was Admiral Nimitz. I still have in my files some place, all of the correspondence - Admiral Ghormley's letter to Admiral Stark, Admiral Stark's memo to Mr. Knox, Mr. Knox's endorsement to the Bureau of Personnel. Admiral Nimitz had the entire correspondence returned to me, with a note on it --"At such time that I came up for selection, a determination would then be made as to whether or not my duty in London had been sea duty for rotational purposes." Which really put it right back in my lap and didn't give me any assurance that I would not fail of selection *for lack of sea duty*.

When I'd been there a little over a year, I began to get worried about being away from sea duty so long. Because I had stayed extra time in the Navy Department to temporarily relieve my boss, until his relief arrived - as I told you before. In those days, if you didn't get your sea duty in, you just simply had had it.

When the selection list for the class of 1923 for Commander came out, there was a Captain Wentworth on the staff at the time. This was after the staff had begun to build up, from two aides to a proper staff. Captain Wentworth was the senior member of the staff, other than the Naval Attache who was the Chief of Staff designate, in the event that we started functioning as an operational staff.

Every night Captain Wentworth would come into my office and look over the day's dispatches and ask me to highlight for him any that he should be interested in.

One night, he was looking over the dispatches and came across the selection list for the class of '23. He said, "Count, which class is yours?" I said "I'm '24, sir." He said, "Gettin pretty close, isn't it?" I said, "Yes sir, it is. Captain, could I ask you a theoretical question?" He said, "Sure."

I said, "If you were on the selection board to select Lieutenant Commanders to Commanders; and you came across a record of one Lieutenant Commander who had never been to sea as a Lieutenant Commander, but who had had command of a ship for three years as a Lieutenant, and no matter how good his record happened to be; would you select him for Commander? If he'd never been to sea as a Lieutenant Commander?" He said, "Why, no." I said, "That's the position I'm going to be in, a year from now, if I can't get Admiral Ghormley to let me go in the meantime."

Captain Wentworth thought that was serious. He was a very nice person. He came in to see Admiral Ghormley every morning. So, the next morning when he came in to see Admiral Ghormley, I took in the mail while he was still seeing Admiral Ghormley. I put the selection list, that he had noted the night before, on top. When Admiral Ghormley glanced at it, he said, "Oh, selection list." He was always interested in that sort of thing.

He looked up at me and said, "Count, where does this put you?" I said, "Admiral, it puts me right under the guns. My class will come up next year and that's why I've been pestering you about getting to sea, sir."

Captain Wentworth took the cue and said, "Admiral, you can't keep Count any longer. You've got to give him a chance to get to sea and have some sea-going report in his files before he comes up for selection."

Austin - 128

Admiral Ghormley listened to him for a little bit and said, "All right, send in my writer, Martin."

So, he dictated a letter to Admiral Stark and told him, he would appreciate if if he would personally select someone to relieve me. That he felt in fairness to me, he had to let me go.

Admiral Stark sent over Commander McManus, class of '22. He was my relief. I left just before Pearl Harbor. I was in Estoril, Portugal when I learned about Pearl Harbor.

We got to Estoril and the airways were a little clogged with passengers. Gunther, the author, and I got to running around together while we were waiting for our place on the priority list to be reached. We were staying out at the Hotel Estoril. We'd go into town each morning.

The American newspaper men, while we were there, came to me one day and said, "Do you know that you're being shadowed by the head of the Gestapo here in Lisbon?" I said, "I wondered who that big fellow is, who looks like a German, that seems to be everywhere I go. I didn't know that he was shadowing me, but I do notice this one fellow. If I go up to the cabaret, he'll appear. If I go into town, he'll appear. I hadn't any proof that he's shadowing me, but it's a great coincidence. I've been/tempted to invite him to have a drink with me a couple of times." They said, "He is the number one Gestapo man here, and he is shadowing you. We have noticed this. We thought you ought to know."

I did have a very important letter from Admiral Ghormley to Admiral Stark to be carried by me and given to him in person. I don't know what was in the letter, but it was impressed upon me to take proper care of it. And, if I stopped along the way, I should put it in the Embassy's safe. Which I did, as soon as I got to Lisbon.

That was rather amusing too, because I had the letter on my person, not in my baggage of course. While we were waiting for customs, I could see the Portugese take the German by the door that I was looking out of, into the next door room where they had taken my baggage. I could hear from the conversation that the German had inspected my baggage and said, okay. I guess it was the way that the police in Portugal were able to walk the tight rope of neutrality. They let everybody see everybody's else's baggage.

Q: But the Portugese had long had a treaty of friendship with England.

Austin: With England, oh, yes. But, you saw British planes and German planes landing right alongside of each other there in Portugal. They were neutral, but they were giving the Germans quite a bit of access there.

Q: I suppose, next to Switzerland, that Portugal was probably the top spy center in Europe.

Austin: Yes, I think it must have been. Because, it was a place where they could all meet.

Anyway, they didn't find my letter because it was in the Embassy safe.

When Pearl Harbor happened, I was out reading the Portugese newspaper. Which of course, I couldn't read very well. But I could get enough out of it to know what was going on in the world a little bit.

There was a young Coast Guard officer who had come down on the same plane with me, who came up to me and he was very much upset. He said, "Commander, it's happened, it's happened." I looked at him and said, "What's happened? You seem to be very upset. You mean that the Japanese have struck us some place?"

He looked at me and said, "You're not surprised." I said, Sit down, and tell me about it. I'll see whether I'm surprised or not." When he told me that they had struck Pearl Harbor, he'd heard it on the radio, I said, "Frankly, I am surprised that they struck Pearl Harbor. I'm not too surprised that they've taken an aggressive act. Things have been getting pretty tense here of late. I'm not surprised that they decided to cut the Gordion knot."

He really thought I had the inside dope, and knew it all the time.

Q: Are you getting kind of tired?

Austin: I'll finish this little episode because it's rather amusing.

The next morning, Gunther and I went in to town to check Pan Am again. He was ahead of me in the line and when he went to the man at the desk, the man said, "No, not a chance Mr. Gunther. I'm sorry." When I asked him, he said, "Stand by your hotel."

Gunther and I walked out together. He said, "I can see the handwriting on the wall. With you military chaps getting top priority now, I'll be here 'til hell freezes over. I'm going to go out to the nearest bar and get tight."

I went back to my hotel. On the train back, there were only three people in the coach that I was in. Going in, the train was crowded. But going back, which was in the middle of the day, there were only three people in that coach.

One was a little old lady who'd been to market and had her market basket. The other, the number two, was me. The third man was my German gestapo friend. He hadn't lost track of me the whole time. Gunther and I had done a little shopping and everything; and he hadn't lost track of me. He was a good tail.

Austin - 132

Q: He must have been a rather obvious one though.

Austin: Yes, he was such a large man to begin with. He was not an inconspicious individual and he was rather large. Always appeared to be not watching you, he was very clever that way. But he was always there within sight.

That night, when I got back to the hotel, I received a phone call in the afternoon - telling me to be at the airport about two o'clock in the morning. So, when we got to the airport, I naturally had all my luggage with me. As soon as we started to weigh in, they said, "You'll have to limit your luggage to seven kilograms."

There was a General McNarney who was coming back. He saw them make me throw out my officers overcoat and various other things. He stepped up. There was a lady going back on this plane, who was the wife of the Pan Am manager in Lisbon. She was pregnant, and I think that was the reason for her being put on this plane. She had a pretty full kit going with her, including a set of golf clubs.

This was a little too much for General McNarney. He stepped up to the man who was throwing away most of my kit, saying it couldn't go. He said, "You mean to tell me that you're going to let one person take golf clubs back; and you're not going to let this young naval officer, who's going to sea in a destroyer probably, take his overcoat with him?"

That didn't phase the guy. He'd been told seven kilos, not an ounce more. So, I left behind most of my kit right there; and it never caught up to me until a year and a half later. I'd had to replace every bit of it in the meantime.

The amusing little finale of this was that they began to look for Gunther. Some one said, that I ought to be able to tell them where he was. So, they asked me. I said, "All I can tell you is to look around the bars nearest your Pan Am office. The last word I had from him was, that he was going to the nearest bar and get crocked."

At the last minute, there'd been a 'no show'. And they were going to put him in, because his office had evidentally been using a little 'suasion on Pan Am. If he'd been available, he could have gotten in that plane. But, he missed it.

Do you think that's a good place to stop?

Q: Why don't we stop, Count, there for the day? That will just about finish out this reel.

Then, we will start next time, when you took over command of the destroyer.

Interview #5

Vice Admiral Bernard L. Austin
near Rockville, Maryland

by Paul L. Hopper
November 21, 1969

Mr. Hopper: Admiral Austin, I believe when we completed our last interview, you were about ready to assume command of the WOOLSEY. Would you like to begin there?

Admiral Austin: Yes, Paul, I was ordered to the USS WOOLSEY; which was then on the so-called neutrality patrol. On reaching the United States I proceeded to Washington, delivered a letter from Admiral Ghormley to Admiral Stark, and then proceeded to Norfolk, Virginia where the ship was then expected to return and when I had a brief visit with my family.

Actually I joined the ship in Boston, because the information that had been given to me as to her coming to Norfolk, had been in error.

When I reported aboard to assume command of the WOOLSEY; I recalled that on termination of my first shore duty, I had thought that, to broaden my naval experience, it would be a good idea to get in a little destroyer duty. So, I had requested, on my fitness report, destroyer duty.

When the time came for orders to be issued for people in my status at the Naval Academy, everybody got his orders but me. And as usual, my little wife began to get anxious and wanted to know 'where next.'

So, I ran up to Washington and went in to see the detail officer. He informed me that I was going to a submarine tender. I said, "But I asked for destroyer duty to broaden my experience. Now, you send me right back to submarines, except on a tender." He said, "That's just too bad. If you go to general duty, if you don't go back to a submarine, you will have to take a tour of duty on an auxiliary. That's the policy of the Bureau for your class and those classes close to you. If you haven't had an auxiliary cruise, you've got to have one." I said, "You mean, a whole sea cruise?" He said, "Yes." I said, "Let me go back and see the submarine desk man."

I went back and Swede Hazlett was the submarine detail officer at that time, Commander Hazlett. He was a very fine gentleman. I said, "Sir, I wondered if there's any chance of getting duty in submarines. I find that the general detail desk is going to send me to a tender for my next duty." He said, "You didn't ask to come back to submarines, so that automatically took you off of our list. Would you like command of a submarine?" I said, "Yes, sir. I'd like any duty just to avoid getting a tour in an auxiliary, for which, I don't think I'm trained particularly. I don't really see, from my viewpoint, how it's going to broaden my experience a great deal." He said, "If you want command of a ship, we had you lined up for one until we got your fitness report, requesting destroyer duty."

To make a long story short, I was ordered to command a submarine and commanded it for three years.

When I reported aboard the USS WOOLSEY, I could not help feeling that perhaps the judgement of the Bureau of Personnel was not perfect, in denying a young officer the opportunity to work his way up in destroyers the hard way when he wanted to at a younger age; instead of sending him aboard one as a Commanding Officer with the United States then being in a state of war. When I boarded that ship to assume command, it was my first day of duty in a destroyer.

I inspected the ship of course, with the Commanding Officer, who was a very fine officer, an officer who had been primarily trained in engineering. I'd rather not indicate his name here, because I don't think it's too pertinent. He did suffer from seasickness, to the extent that he had a hammock swung on the bridge for use at sea. Undoubtedly as soon as the ship docked, he got ashore to get a little rest as soon as he could.

As we inspected the ship, I found conditions that were rather shocking to me. I realized that the ship had been in the North Atlantic on neutrality patrol, and had not been given very little time in port for upkeep and maintenance. But, it was practically a new ship. It had only been out of the builder's yard about eight months. And yet, it was unable to make more than 16 knots because of rusted reduction gears.

When we got to the paint locker, it was about two inches deep in varied colored paints. I looked at the fire extinguisher bank and saw that it had never been connected up to the hand toggle that actuated it. I reached up and pulled the toggle, which unfortunately caused the Commanding Officer to have a little moment of concern because he thought it was connected and that I would waste all of his CO_2 ~~sealed tube~~. When he told me that, I said, "No, Captain, I don't think this has ever been connected."

When we got to the provisions store room, which was of course practically the double bottom you know, you couldn't enter without putting a handkerchief over your nose. Because of the stinch that exuded from cans that had been punctured in rough seas and never removed. I was given the mess accounts as, I believe it was, $1,300 in the black. Actually when the first correct ration report was submitted, after I relieved of command, we were some $900 in the red.

I, of course, had to survey all of this decayed food; which was partly the responsibility for the ships going ~~being~~ from $1400 plus to $900 minus. But, my young supply officer found out that every single ration record since the ship had been commissioned, had been sloppily and incorrectly submitted. And that the actual stores that were alleged to be on board, actually weren't there. If they had been there, I could have surveyed them and got credit for them. It wouldn't have been out of the mess pocket, as it were. But they just weren't there.

I went back to my hotel in Boston and I did lots of thinking. Then, I sat down with my notes and I wrote a letter refusing command of this ship. Not simply because the Executive Officer was in his room under arrest for having had improper relations with 31 known members of the crew, but because the condition of the ship I thought was such as to be unsafe to take out in a war zone.

But, as I sometimes do, I slept on it. The next morning I read the letter over again, tore it up, and threw it away.

I went down in my best suit of blues, saluted and said, "I relieve you, sir." Then, I started holding mast. There were 13 mast cases pending when I took over. I was a little strict in my punishments, I meted out some bread and water.

So, the word got around pretty quick that the new Captain was a tough guy. That wasn't my purpose in being firm. My purpose was to restore discipline in the ship, where it had disappeared.

I had the misfortune to run the ship aground the first time out of harbor. This was preceeded, of course, by a change in Executive Officer. Because the one who was in his room under arrest, was brought to trial by court martial and was convicted.

Therefore, I fleeted up the gunnery officer, a young red-headed Irishman of great enthusiam, but not much experience at that time; named Henry Wier. I fleeted him up to be Exec.

The senior destroyer officer in Boston called me up and told me that he had given lots of thought to my situation. He'd been very helpful in getting transferred off the ship the known rotten apples.

He said, "I want to help you as much as I can. I think the best help I can give you is to find you a real good Exec." I said, "Well, sir, I have a good officer who has been on the ship. He's never had experience as Exec, he's too young. But he knows the ship and it's problems. If I get an Exec who's just as new to the ship as I am, I think that we may go off in the wrong direction. This young officer has been very helpful to me in advising me as to those that can be trusted. I'd like to keep him." He said, "It's your funeral. It's up to you."

I kept Henry Wier. Although, he may have contributed to my grounding on exiting from the port our first trip at sea; because I was pretty much engaged in watching my propellers go through the net gap. The gate was not too wide and it was a little straggly. As soon as I got through the net, I turned to the navigator, who was the Exec also. I said, "Mr. Wier, what is my course now?" He gave me a course and I looked in my binoculars, after we steaded on that course.

I said, "Mr. Wier, better check that course. Things don't look quite right with the buoy system up ahead." The buoys were completely iced, it was winter time. So, you couldn't be absolutely sure what color a buoy was. You could say it was ice-colored, but that's about all.

Shortly after my telling him to check the course, he very honestly and not too comfortingly said, "Captain, I don't know just where I am." I said, "All back, emergency." But, before the head way of the ship had been removed, we touched bottom.

We went back in and we inspected the hull and propellers. There was no damage done whatever. But, I had grounded. I got a letter of hate out of it, just because I'd touched ground.

The ship was fundamentally a good ship. It was built at Bath, Maine and they build good ships. But the reduction gears, for example, were rusted because of just plain negligence - poor administration. I think this was attributable to two factors - that the Captain was a chronic seasickness fellow, and he trusted his Executive officer. He was really distraught about the Executive officer, he trusted him implicitely. The Exec was one of those smart fellows, who was able to pull the wool over the Captain's eyes.

Q: Were they both regular Navy?

Austin: Yes, they were both regular Navy. The Exec had, I found later, been suspected of homosexuality earlier in his career. But it had never been proved, and a man is not guilty unless he is proven guilty. Here he was Exec on a ship where the Captain was a seasick man, and he ran the ship.

After I'd been on board for about three months, I had quite a few experiences that were difficult for a young Commanding Officer on his first destroyer in war time or in peace time.

For example — When I got to sea and called for my dispatch board, they said, "What dispatch board?" I said, "Don't you keep a dispatch board of dispatches that the Captain, the Executive Officer and the heads of departments should see?"

They said, "No, if a message is addressed to the ship, we just get somebody to decode it, if it's in code; and if it looks like the Captain ought to see it, take it up to him. We don't have any dispatch board."

When I gave my first drill at sea, I designated an imaginary target after we had gotten manned for general quarters; which took quite a long time, I might add. It took two minutes and forty seconds to get on this first imaginary target with the gun director.

Let's say, we started trying to correct these things. We had to take some drastic measures to restore discipline.

For example — The first mail I opened, after becoming Commanding Officer was a letter from Sears Roebuck. This letter asked for the fifth time, if the government intended to pay the bill owed to Sears Roebuck. It was an open purchase by the USS WOOLSEY. So, I asked to see the previous correspondence. There was no previous correspondence according to the first class supply chap, who was acting as the Supply Officer.

In those days, destroyers didn't always have an officer as Supply Officer. The senior storekeeper was usually designated as the Supply Officer.

I had noted that among my young reserve Ensigns, I had one that had been to business school. So, I sent for him. His name was Stevenson, from South Carolina.

I said, "You are hereby designated as the Supply Officer of this ship. Before you report to me that you have assumed your duties, I order you to make thorough inspection of the supply department - it's records, it's files, and it's correspondence. When you report to me that you are ready to assume the responsibility of Supply Officer, everything that's gone before will not be your responsibility; but everything that goes after will be your responsibility."

He was a young reserve Ensign and this was a pretty tough assignment for him, but he did a good job. He came back to me with a written report of the conditions that he found in the supply department. He found the previous letters from Sears Roebuck. They'd never been opened. They'd been thrown in a bottom drawer by the first class storekeeper, who'd received them. He'd never opened them, as he had not opened many letters that were found in this same place.

The things found wrong in the supply department, by this young reserve Ensign, went through the alphabet once and half way through it again - all major items.

I sent for the first class storekeeper, and I asked for his side of this. It didn't sound too good. He started evading and lying. So, I told the Executive Officer that we'd hold preliminary mast on this case.

At the preliminary mast, the storekeeper lied so much he just completely exhausted my patience, I suspended the preliminary mast and went to the telephone. We happened to then be in port and I called the Bureau of Personnel. I asked to speak to the Chief of the Bureau.

At that time, Admiral Denfeld was the assistant Chief of the Bureau. He answered, he said, "The Chief wasn't in, could he take the call?" I said, "Yes, sir. I have a situation on the WOOLSEY, with which you may or may not be familiar." He said, "Oh, yes, I know about the situation you found on that ship, Count. Everybody down here does. I sympathize with you."

It was then Captain Denfield, I'm pretty sure. I said, "Captain, I have a situation that I don't believe was envisaged by those who wrote the BuPers Manual. I want your authority to reduce a first class storekeeper at mast, to a seaman." He said, "Oh, Count, what do you want to do that for?"

I said, "I'm going to start reading sir. When you've heard enough, you stop me." Then I read this report. I summarized the lead-off, and then I started with the particulars, that had been found. I got about to J, and he said, "My God, go ahead. Reduce him to an apprentice seaman if you want. If we tried him by court martial, we'd have to send him to jail. Reducing him to seaman, is not unfair. The Bureau will back you up, and disregard BuPers Manual."

So, I held formal mast on this case; and I reduced the first class Petty Officer to seaman. The first class Petty Officer was quite a sea lawyer. He spread the word around, "The old man has really flipped his lid now. He can't make this stick. I know BuPers Manual. He can't reduce me at mast." But, when he drew his next pay check, he began to change his mind. So, we got the supply department cleaned out.

We got the reduction gears hand-cleaned. Every tooth of those reductions gears had to be scraped. I came back one night in Boston and at my request, the yard had undertaken to clean these gears. They had this crew aboard for this purpose.

I came back to the ship about one o'clock that night. I went down into the engine room and asked the man in charge, how they were getting along. He said, "Captain, I hate to say this because I invented this system of cleaning reduction gears. I've used it successfully on many ships laid up in the back channels for years, and I've never had to admit failure before. But, I can't clean your reduction gears. Nobody is going to be able to get these gears to where you can make full power, without hand-cleaning every single tooth. My process is not that.

Q: With a wire brush?

Austin: Yes, a scrapper and a wire brush. So, that's what we had to do. The ship's force did most of it, because we were in a hurry. We put as many men on it as we could work with, and we got it clean, and we made full power afterwards.

About three months after I'd assumed command of the WOOLSEY, the young doctor came to me and said, "Captain, could I just talk to you sort of informally?" I said, "Why, sure, doc, sit down. What's on your mind?" He said, "Sir, I'm not a regular naval officer at all. I just was caught, they put a suit on me, and they sent me to sea as your doctor. I'll admit, I was getting scared. I don't think I'm yellow, but I was really scared on this ship. But, when I see you up there now designate an imaginary target and the guns are on the target in a matter of a few seconds; I'd kind of like one of those doggone German submarines to tackle us. I think we could take him on."

Shortly after the doctor's visit, the senior Chief Petty Officer on board came and knocked on my door one night in port.

He said, "Captain, could you spare me a few minutes? I'd like to come in and talk to you." I said, "Why, sure Chief come on in. Sit down." He said, "Sir, you may know, I'm your senior Chief on this ship. I was on here under the old regime. I feel that I ought to come to you and assure you that you don't have any rotten apples on this ship anymore. And that discipline is restored. We tried hard, Captain. Those of us that were trying to maintain discipline on the ship, trying to keep her a fighting ship; but it was an uphill struggle. We'd put some young fellow on report for sassing us, or refusing to do what we told him to do. Then we'd find that he was one of the Exec's fair-haired boys, and we'd get called up and put on the pan by the Exec. You can be sure now, sir, that discipline is restored. And that all those Petty Officers that you kept on board from the old regime are loyal to you 100 percent. They'd go to hell for you, sir."

My young red-headed Exec came next, about a week later. He said, "Captain you you worried me a lot - (he was a pretty serious young fellow) - when you first came on this ship. I was afraid somebody might drop a moneky wrench on you." I said, "Henry, I was not unaware of the fact that I was requiring things that hadn't been required before."

For example - The officers at the first meal I had on board, after assuming command, came in in bathrobes and all

Austin - 147

sorts of disheveled costumes. In a calm tone of voice, I turned to the Exec and said, "Mr. Wier, officers will never sit at this table to eat a meal, without being in the uniform of the day."

The Exec went on to assure me that things were all right on the ship now. He thought I could walk under ladders without fear of monkey wrenches dropping.

He turned out to be a fine Exec. About a year later, when I was relieved of command on return from the North African invasion; it was to him that I turned over the ship.

We got credit for sinking a German submarine on the North African invasion. I might say, we didn't get credit then; we got credit many years later when the German records were available. But, we were pretty sure that we'd sunk it.

He got credit for sinking two submarines after I had left the ship. The USS WOOLSEY received very high praise and commendation for being the best destroyer in the Atlantic during the Atlantic war period, the battle of the Atlantic period, in both engineering and gunnery. So, I was kind of proud of her.

I might pause here a little bit to give a little story about a reserve officer on board.

This was a senior reserve officer for a destroyer, he was a senior Lieutenant. In fact, he was next senior to the Exec; when I fleeted Lieutenant Wier up to be Exec. His name was Wallace. He was a jovial fellow, he was a very likable individual. But, he had not had to work very hard in his early life

life evidentally. He came from a fairly well to do family, I think. He worked in the family business as the public relations chap. If he told good stories to the clients that he had on the golf course, I guess everything was fine.

The Exec came to me one night and said, "Captain, I'm at my wits ends with Mr. Wallace. I can't find a job to put him at that will get him to really roll up his sleeves and go to work." I said, "I've noticed that you've been having difficulties there, Henry. I too have noticed Mr. Wallace is fine at telling stories and fine at getting along with people; but he doesn't seem to address himself to any job very seriously. We can't afford, on a destroyer in war time here in the Atlantic we're so thin - to have just super cargo. We've go to have everybody produce. It's almost fitness report time. You give Mr. Wallace as fine a report as you think he rates, and then, I'll look it over."

Wier brought me Wallace's fitness report and he had laid it on the line pretty well. So, I sent for Mr. Wallace and said, "Mr. Wallace, I've just looked over the fitness report that the Executive Officer suggests that I sign on you. I think he has been very generous. I want you to read it. And, then I have a few words to say."

Wallace looked at it and returned it to me, with sort of a silly grin. I said, "Mr. Wallace, that's about twice as much praise as you deserve. You have ability, but you're not applying it to the job assigned on this ship. Anybody on this ship will help you acquire the necessary technical ~~confidence~~ Competence that you need, in any job that you're assigned. I'll help you, the other officers will help you, the Petty Officers will help you. You've been assistant navigator now for quite awhile and I have never even seen you try to take a star sight, or a sight of any kind. I'm telling you, I'm not going to reduce this report from it's present level. But if you don't roll up your sleeves and start to work, I'm going to ask that you be sent to some other duty."

Wallace looked at me and smiled and said, "Sir, you've given me something to shoot at." So, you've heard of the turning over of a new leaf - Wallace turned over a new leaf.

The next day, I saw him up with the quartermaster getting instruction on how to take a sight, among other things.

When I received my first letter from Wier after I got to the South Pacific with my new assignment, he said, "Captain, you'd be surprised to know that my new Exec is Mr. Wallace. He is one of the best Execs in the Atlantic fleet. He has certainly turned over a new leaf, and has worked like a trojan ever since you gave him the talk in your cabin that night."

It goes to show, that very often, you've got a lots of potential; but if you don't know how to connect it up, it doesn't mean very much.

I might say a little bit about personnel here that will help you to understand the sad situation that the whole Navy faced at that time. It wasn't just my ship.

I had, when I took over the ship, the previous engineer officer, who was a senior Lieutenant and was a post-graduate in engineering. But, he had orders to be detached. He was to go as the assistant to the Commanding Officer that I was relieving, who was going as the engineer officer of the USS MASSACHUSETTS - a battleship.

I got on the phone to BuPers and I pointed out that my ship was not able to make full power, due to rusted reduction gears, and that I therefore requested that the orders of this officer be held in abeyance until such time as the ship made full power. The Bureau granted this request. So, I was able to keep him for a matter of weeks; until we got this situation corrected.

His assistant engineer officer was a young Ensign reserve. A very smart young man named Connally. He had been a chemical engineer. He'd been trained for that at college and had therefore gotten the word engineer on his card in BuPers. So, he'd been sent as the assistant engineer to this ship.

What young Connally didn't know about steam engineering and mechanical engineering would fill quite a few tapes. We won't go into that. But, he was a smart young officer. He was able to pick up in a hurry and he did have the advantage of being given instructions by a real post-graduate engineer officer of a destroyer. I didn't kick about that.

I said, "We're at war. As Admiral King had said, and we'd had repeated to us many times - you've got to do the best you can with what you've got." So I didn't complain about it.

But after my first trip at sea, we got back into port and we had orders for Connally to be transferred to be the engineer officer of a new destroyer fitting out.

His relief, of course, was to be the young officer that had been fleet up to be his assistant engineer and understudy, who was a reserve Ensign, who had never had engineering experience in his life. So I bit my tongue and said, "Do the best you can with what you've got." I realized that they had to try to fill the billets on the new construction ships.

So we went to sea again. We got back again and I had orders to transfer that young officer to be an engineer officer of a ship going in commission. That left a very young junior officer, reserve Ensign, who had just come abaord and had only a few days instruction under this former Ensign that had been the engineer officer, who had been instructed for a short time by a reserve Ensign, who had been instructed by a real engineer.

We were entering New York harbor at night. The area down near the narrows there was just filled with merchant ships that had anchored all over the place. It was inside the net. They were safe from submarines there so they just dropped their anchors in a not too orderly fashion sometimes.

I was twisting and winding my way through this mass of ships, when we lost suction - all power gone.

I called down to the engine room and said, "When can we get some power?" Of course I had way on and I could still steer. The poor Ensign, who was engineer officer said, "Sir, I don't know but we're doing all we can. All the Petty Officers are working like mad down here. We'll give it to you as soon as we can." I said, "If you can give me just one engine even, give me one, and we'll worry about two later on."

To make a long story short - I was about to drop my anchor because my way on the ship was getting to where it was not very noticable. I was having to watch that I didn't drift into another ship. When cheerfully the poor young engineer called up and said, "Captain, we can give you power on the starboard engine now." So we went ahead on starboard engine.

We rounded the Battery and headed into Walabout Basin, where we were going to go in for a sort of voyage repair job. Instead of a tug meeting me off the entrance to the Basin as requested, I had to get in and dock with one engine at a very unfavorable state of the current off Walabout Basin. It's not an easy place to enter, even at normal times. I finally got tied up without banging anything.

The tug captain came down the dock to explain to me why he didn't meet me. I was still so disappointed in his not meeting me that I told him - save his explanations, I no longer needed him, good-bye.

But he insisted on coming aboard and I did listen to his story. It wasn't his fault. It was simply that an emergency had arisen, and they had to have his tug to handle a gate in the drydock in a hurry. I gave him a cup of coffee and we parted friends.

Shortly after that I entered Casco Bay, where the Commander Destroyers Atlantic was in his flag ship. Commander Destroyers Atlantic at that time was Admiral Oscar Badger.

When we got in and we got our mail, lo and behold, I had orders to transfer my engineer officer again.

Q: You were sort of conducting a training for engineer officers.

Austin: That's right.

I told the Exec, "I want my gig. I'm going over to see the Commander Destroyers. This is too much."

I got over and his Chief of Staff was a very nice gentlemanly fellow who smoked a long smelly pipe, always had a curved stem on it as I recall, Captain Porter. I went in to see Captain Porter and told him that I was anxious to see the Admiral and told him why. He said, "Now listen. You know Admiral Badger well enough to know that if you go in there with this request of yours, he's going to throw you out on your ear. He's just come from being right under Admiral King. He's so much a mirror of Admiral King's — you've got to do the best you can with what you've got — he isn't even going to listen to you."

Admiral Badger was a pretty forceful type of individual. I don't know whether you ever knew him or not.

Q: I knew his wife better. She worked at Garfinckel's for a time. My wife was quite well acquainted with her.

Austin: He was a very meticulous type of Admiral who had been given the Congressional Medal of Honor. He was, shall we say, not easy to convince on things.

I insisted that I be able to see the Admiral. Captain Porter said, "All right. It's your rear extremity that you're going to land on and not mine." So I got my appointment with the Admiral and went in to see him.

Admiral Badger was quite talkative. I started to tell him my story and he started talking. I was watching the clock and I listened patiently. And I listened, and I listened, and I listened. Finally I did a very indiscrete thing under ordinary circumstantces, at least. I said, "Admiral, I came in here with an important matter to take up with you. You haven't given me a chance to talk. If you do all the talking I'll have to leave here probably when somebody else comes in, and you still won't know what I came here to tell you." That stopped him.

Austin - 155

He glared and me and said, "Young man, tell your story and it better by a damned sight be a good one." I knew this before I stuck my neck quite that far out. So, I told him.

I said, "Admiral, when I relieved as Commanding Officer of this ship six months ago about, I had an engineer officer on board who had been trained as an engineer officer. He'd been given a post-graduate course in engineering. His understudy was a young reserve officer, who'd been trained in chemical engineering but had never had any mechanical engineering experience. He was under instructions for a matter of weeks, under this good well-trained officer, when the well-trained officer was ordered away. Five weeks later, Admiral, this young reserve officer was relieved because of BuPers orders - for him to go to a new ship as engineer officer. He was relieved by a reserve Ensign, who'd been under instructions for only five weeks by a reserve Ensign, who'd been unders instruction only a matter of weeks by a competent engineer. About seven weeks later, we got into port and we had the same experience. We lost our engineer, and so to relieve him; I now have on board a young reserve Ensign who was trained by a reserve Ensign, who was trained for a few weeks by a reserve Ensign, who was trained for a few weeks by a competent engineer. Admiral, I've just gone through a rather agonizing experience entering New York harbor."

Then, I told him of the failure of power. I said, "I don't think you want your destroyers in the Atlantic fleet to be so inexpertly manned, as this sort of a system is going to result in,

Austin - 156

their being manned." "Why, hell, no," he said, "I certainly don't. Is this going on all over the Atlantic fleet?" I said, "Sir, I don't know. I can only tell you about my experience because I've been at sea. Captain Kephart, your engineer officer on your staff, can probably tell you."

He sent for Kephart. Kephart said, "Yes, Admiral, this is happening to every destroyer. Maybe not quite as bad, but the same general thing is happening. There's no other alternative. We've got to provide engineer officers for these ships going into commission. It's better to send a reserve Ensign that's had a few weeks instruction, than it is to send one right out of an induction center with no instruction."

Admiral Badger turned to me and said, "Have you got a better answer?" I said, "Why certainly sir. You've got a destroyer that was torpedoed. It's engine room is still in good condition. Why don't you take a ship like that and set up a destoyer engineering school on board? Use a good engineer to do the instructing and train 50 or 100 - whatever number you need at the same time. And let us fellows that are trying to run the ships at sea alone for a few months."

He said, "You know, I think it's not a bad idea." He turned to Kephart and said, "Do it." I think that's the way that the destroyer training program for young officers got started.

I didn't get tossed out on my ear. In fact, Admiral Badger was very kind to me when I departed. He said, "I appreciate your coming over and telling me this. I didn't realize it.

Austin - 157

I think it's something that does need correction. What do you need to help you out now?"

I said, "Just to be let alone Admiral. He said, "You don't need more Petty Officers or soemthing to bolster up this young officer that's trying to be engineer officer?" I said, "No, sir. If you just let me alone and let me keep him until I can get him trained."

I think that gives one insight into the personnel situation in the Navy on the officers side. I might at this time, give you a story about another ship, but it's on the same subject of personnel.

When I came back from the North African invasion, I received orders by a dispatch late in the afternoon of the day of my entering Norfolk; to turn over my command to my Executive Officer and to proceed to Bath, Maine to put in commission a new ship, the USS FOOTE.

I sat up most of the night turning over to my Executive Officer, because we had no forewarning of this. I went through Washington on my way to Bath.

In the Bureau they said, "Count, you were over in London for a long time. You've been at sea, without getting to see your family, in the Atlantic. We decided it was time to give you a little blow. We're sending you to put this new ship in commission, about four months before it goes in commission. So, it will give you a chance to see your family."

Austin - 158

On the strength of that, I stopped through New York, where my family was living out on Long Island. I told them to get their things in storage the next day, and get in the car and go with me to Bath, Maine; which we did.

I arrived in Bath on Sunday, the last day of my proceed orders. I went to the office, and there I found the prospective Executive Officer, who had reported in twelve hours ahead of me. I asked him what the personnel situation looked like. He said, "I think it will be all right in about four months. Right now, you and I are about it. Incidentally, sir, the president of the boat building company here has aked me to extend to you his warm invitation to this party that they're giving for this ship that's about to go down to Boston to be commissioned tomorrow. He'd like very much to meet you and would like you and your wife to come." I said, "All right."

So, I went to this party. The president of this boat building outfit, said, "We'll have you out in two weeks." I said, "Two weeks, sir? I'm the prospective Commanding Officer of the FOOTE. They told me in Washington, that it wouldn't be finished for about four months." He said, "We have a hard time getting it through to those people down there. We're ahead of schedule here. We'll have your ship out in two weeks."

They did. In two weeks, we cracked the ice, backed out, went to Boston, and commissioned it. But, we didn't have much of a crew on board.

My Exec was a very fine officer, with some destroyer experience. So, I went into a huddle with him, I said, "We've got a problem. You can't man guns and engine room and all with pieces of paper. I notice that the senior fire room man that we have is a water tender second class, who's never been to sea in a ship. He's gotten his rate on a donkey boiler on a shore station. He isn't going to be too much help. He may have studied enough out of the books to pass his exams, but he's not going to be too much help. We've got to have an intensive training program. I want you to assume that we have a low level of experience on board. Get all of the people that have experience and make them instructors. Find out what they know. Don't assume, like in the case of the water tender, that he can instruct people in how to fire up a destroyer oil burning boiler. Find out what he does know and let him teach that, but nothing more. All the way through the rates do the same thing. Then we're going to arrange the non-rated people into groups according to the alphabet. This seems like a shotgun system of doing it, but we're going to have to start somewhere."

I said, "I want all of the engineer personnel to be instructed in all the engineering subjects in which we can find expertise on in the ship. I want all the deck side people to be instructed in all the deck side things - like handling lines, how to talk on the telephone, nomenclature of the ship, and that sort of thing. Don't try to make a jack of all trades of all of them, but use your time efficiently and the talent you have on board efficiently. It isn't much, but use it the best you can."

We did pretty well in many ways. We were only in the yard for a very short fitting out period. Then we were to go to Guantanamo, Cuba and be checked out underway down there, to see if we were ready for the battle front.

I knew we were going to the South Pacific. I had secret information to that effect. So I wanted to be sure that we were properly trained before we got there.

When we started to back out I told the pilot, Captain Pierce, I said, "Captain, I've never handled one of these 2100 ton destroyers. If you don't mind I'd like to take her out. You just sit there in the Captain's bridge chair and have a cup of coffee. If I need you your tugs can come in and help me. I'd like to see how she handles in taking her out." He said, "Fine, that's the way I like to earn my living."

I got up forward of the binnacle and gave the order, "Single up all lines." I turned around to say something to Captain Pierce and I kind of sensed that the ship was loose. I turned around and looked and instead of singling up the lines, they'd thrown them all off.

I backed clear and then we got going ahead. I turned to the quartermaster and gave him an order to the wheel. I said, "Rudder amidships." Then I saw that we needed to meet her a little bit. I turned and said, "Meet her." I noticed that the ship's head wasn acting just right. I turned around and looked at the rudder indicator. Here stood this little second class quartermaster, grinning from ear to ear. He said, "Captain, I never heard that one before." So, I gave him orders to the rudder - right so many degrees, left so many degrees - until I got him on course.

After we got about half way through our check-out down at Guantanamo, one night this quartermaster and the other second class quartermaster came to me. They said, "Could we come in and talk to you Captain?" I said, "Sure, come in."

The little fellow that acted as a spokesman for the two of them looked like one of the seven dwarfs. He was short and broad. When he smiled, he smiled all over his face - a lovable character really. He said, "Captain, we know that you know that we don't know nothing about being quartermasters. We appreciate your patience with us. We'd kind of like to explain to you how we got to be quartermasters second class without knowing anything about being quartermasters."

I smiled at that point and said, "Yes, I would like to know." He said, "Sir, we went off to war together in World War I. We were very young fellows and both under age, but we got in. We got as far as Sound Listeners School in New London, Connecticut before the war was over. When the war started this time, we got together one night and decided we weren't too old to be some help. So, we decided we'd go sign up again. We went to the recruiting office. The recruiting officer said, 'Have you ever been in the Navy before?' We said, 'Yes sir.' He said, 'What did you do?' I said, 'We went to Sound Listeners School in New London'. He said, 'That's enough. You're both quartermasters second class'. Captain, honest we tried to tell him, we didn't know anything about being quartermasters. But he piped us down. He said, 'I need quartermasters so bad, that anybody that's been to Sound Listeners School is going to be a quartermaster. At least you know something about bearings!"

Those two fellows really applied themselves, and they got to be pretty good quartermasters. I did appreciate their honesty and forthrightness in coming to me and explaining to me how it was that they didn't know anything about their rate.

Q: You must have practically conducted a training school at Guantanamo.

Austin: We did.

The Commodore down there, after he checked us out, I had him stay aboard for lunch; he was very commendatory. He said, "I think you've got a fine ship here. You're ready for anything." I said, "Commodore, don't kid me." This was in my cabin, where nobody could hear it. I said, "Don't kid me. This ship is not ready for anything. I just hope to hell, we'll have her ready before we get where we're going. We passed your little test, but that's ABCs. The real fighting ability we don't have in this ship yet, but we'll get it."

I think we did have it by the time we got to the South Pacific.

I want to go back a little bit. When the Executive Officer and I decided on our training program, we worked up a legal size sheet. I told him I wanted it all on one sheet, didn't want pages and pages. We asked every man on board questions. All he had to do was check - yes, no, or four months, or a year, or whatever the answer was. We so-worded all the questions that they could be answered simply with a check mark or a brief statement like four months or a year. When we compiled the data from this set of questionaires, or this questionaire;- it was the same one that went to everyone - it was rather shocking.

Very few of all the crew had ever been instructed in handling a line. Very few had ever been instructed in how to use a sound powered telephone. Very few had ever had any instruction in the most used terminology that you have to know on board ship, to know your right from your left. 250 of our crew were marched down in the snow the morning we commissioned, straight out of boot camp - 250.

So, when I got through looking over the summarization of this data, I called my wife who was in a hotel ashore. I told her to get me a reservation for the train that night. I wanted to go to Washington to talk to the Bureau of Personnel. She called me back a little later and said, "I can't get you a reservation, unless you're under orders. They won't give you a reservation." So, I called BuPers.

I got Admiral Denfeld on the phone and told him what I wanted to do. He said, "All right, you have oral orders by telephone. Go down and get yourself on the train and get on down here."

I went to see him the next day and took him this set of data. I fully expected to get tossed out, to be perfectly frank with you. Because I was critizing BuPers policies, which resulted in a situation such as I had. But, he didn't throw me out. He had known me in the job when I was in the Department in Public Relations. He said, "Count, this is the first time, we've had definitive information in this field. We've had lots of complaints about people not being adequately trained when they got to ships, but you're the first fellow that's given us something that we can put our teeth into."

He gave me the names of three Captains that he wanted me to see that were heads of the pertinent parts of BuPers - training recruiting and so forth. I went to them and again I thought they might throw me out - maybe not out of the front office, but when I got down to these boys where they were going to get the boom lowered on them, I might get thrown out. But, they were extremely cooperative and appreciative. They asked to be able to keep my summary and mimeograph it and use it in the work to correct it.

Captain Denfeld told me, "We have been thinking very seriously of starting a program to give preliminary training to a crew of a ship, before it's sent to the ship instead of just sending people from hither and yon and have all the training done there. This pre-commission training idea, we've been toying with it, but since we've got your data I think we'll have the necessary leverage now to go ahead with it." And they did.

A year later it was an entirely different story. I talked with Captains that put ships in commission later. They got pretty nicely trained crews to start with.

Q: It was a group of men who could work together.

Austin: That's right, and who knew right from left, and didn't throw the lines off when you said, "Single up," and that sort of thing.

The general situation at that time was tough, I know best about the Atlantic, because that's where I was. It was just as bad in the Pacific, if not worse, because they'd suffered the loses at Pearl Harbor and had to spread themselves pretty thin over a vast area. In the Atlantic, for the year that I was in it, I would be sent out to cover a coastline say from the northernmost tip of Maine to the Delaware Capes. While I was out there to cover that vast strip of coastline, I would be ordered hither and thither and yon to submarine contacts.

I'll give you one experience we had that I think will typify it. I went out from New York full of depth charges and I was going to a reported contact with a submarine. I was proceeding at top speed. I got about half way between Ambrose Light and the point that I was to go to, when I got an urgent message diverting me to a more urgent situation. And before I got to that point at top speed, I got diverted a second time; which meant my third assignment.

As you know, you don't do much sound work at 31 knots. All I was doing was churning the ocean up and advertising the whereabouts of the only destroyer on that whole northeast coast at that time.

I got into port from that assignment and the Chief of Staff called me in and asked me how things went. So, I told him.

So, the next time I went out, they had a blimp assigned to work with me. I tried to call the blimp on the assigned frequency and got no answer. Finally he flew over me. I told him by flashing light that we were not able to raise him on the assigned radio frequency. So, therefore, we would communicate with him by light until such time as we could establish radio communication.

When I got back in from that trip, the Chief of Staff asked how everything went this time. I said, "The only way I could get the blimp was to say 'hey blimp' by blinker. The communication instructions that we were given in our op order, just simply didn't work." I told him about our experiences and he said, "Like you say, it's kind of harsh, but I'd like the whole staff to hear it first hand. Do you mind if I have a staff meeting and have them all in here?" I said, "No sir. I'll say to them, what I say to you. I'm not talking behind anybody's back."

When he had the staff meeting, I told my story. The communication officer, who was a heck of a nice guy - I later lived with him in the same house at Admiral Nimitz's headquarters - said "What communication annex did you have with your op order?" I told him. He said, "No wonder you couldn't communicate. That wasn't the right one. You should have had annex A3b." So, we got that ironed out.

The next time we went out to work with the blimp, we could communicate; and it helped. The blimp was a good viewing platform.

The whole situation though on the east coast was so thin, that you literally were never able to get the repairs that you needed. You weren't able to take the time to go in to get more depth charges when you needed them, lots of times.

I was assigned to escort a single fast ship to Puerto Rico once. I received my orders and went back to my ship. Receiving the orders was rather amusing.

I went to 90 Church Street to get my orders. They said, "You go down and get your orders from the convoy and escort outfit at Battery place." So, I got a cab and went down there. They said, "No, we think the Chief of Staff ought to issue the orders up there. This is not a convoy, it's a single fast ship. You're operating directly under CNO, so we better not issue your orders. You go back and get him to issue you orders." So, I went back and told them what had been said. He said, "Oh, I'm not going to get into the convoy and escort business. You go back and tell them --."

I said, "Captain, you tell them." He said, "No, I'm not going to tell them. I told you to go back and tell them."

I said, "Can I use your telephone?" He said, "What do you want to use my telephone for?" I said, "I want to call CNO. I'm operating under CNO. If I can't get orders, I'm not going to wear out the street between here and that convoy and escort place. I've been both places now twice. I want somebody to decide who the hell is going to issue my orders. Or I'll ask CNO from whom I should take the orders."

He got off his high horse, and called the other place. The other place finally issued our orders. I had to go back there once more.

That was early in the war and things hadn't gotten ironed out.

That afternoon late, when I got back to my ship with my orders, the merchant ship skipper came to see me. He said,

"Will you authorize me to get underway and shift anchorage away from the pier?" I said, "I don't think I'm the right one to shift you from a pier to a berth out in the anchorage. I'm not the port authority and I'm not the owner." He said, "I know, and I shouldn't be asking you. I'm not going to have a crew if I stay at that dock any longer. I've got to shift before night fall, or I'm not going to have a crew to go on this trip." I said, "All right. As far as I'm concerned, you can shift out to the anchorage. I'll give you the following signal, when I pass." He said, "I can anchor right near where I am at the pier now." And he showed me where he was.

I said, "All right. When I pass there tonight -(we were to get underway at two o'clock in the morning) - I'll give you the following signal." And it was arranged. Sure enough, I got underway, gave him the signal, and he fell right in behind me. He was ready to go and he had his crew on board.

When we got to Puerto Rico, we were told to stand off. The channel was not clear. They had had German submarines working down there. A ship had just been torpedoed and they were trying to get it inside before it sank.

Finally they let us come in. I got tied up just about one o'clock. I went up to the headquarters - naval headquarters - and I was shown to a Captain. My young doctor went along with me just for the ride. He'd never been to Puerto Rico, and he wanted to see what he could see on the way up.

The Captain said, "We need you to take a ship on down to Trinidad." I said, "Captain, I'd like to lay alongside the dock until morning if possible to get refueled and re-provisioned. And to get ready for my next assignment, which I think you know is such that I can only tarry a very short time here." He said, "Young man, do you realize there's a war on?"

Having been through the battle of Britain and having been in the Atlantic about six months in a destroyer, I think I was justified in the answer that I gave him. I said, "Captain I'm not where I can read the daily newspapers, delivered to my office like you have them delivered here each day. Judging by the number of assignments that I've had for my ship, which have resulted in my crew not being able to get ashore to put their feet on land for about three months, I would judge there's something near a war going on, if not a war. I'm prepared to believe that, sir."

This was not a reserve officer, this was a regular officer who'd been called back to active duty. He just didn't have quite an overall view. He saw things from his viewpoint. He needed a ship to escort this ship down to Trinidad and he was nabbing what he could.

The operations officer for the headquarters was out to lunch at that time. And I hadn't had any lunch. In fact, I didn't get any lunch that day. But, before I was let go by this Captain - who really hazed me after that, he really did - this regular Captain officer who was really responsible for my operations, came in.

He said when he saw me, "Come on in, we're awfully sorry about not relieving you before you came in to port. I realize your next job is an urgent one. You've got to be up off Ambrose Chanel Light at a specific minute. We're awfully sorry we couldn't relieve you, but we've been/so short-handed down here with all these ships being sunk, that we just couldn't relieve you. What can we do to help you while you're in here?" I said, "Captain, just let me stay where I am until daybreak and I'll be gone out of your hair." He said, "Don't you need a tug to pull you out in the morning?" I said, "No, sir. It's easy to get out of there without a tug. Just let me get some oil, some water and some provisions. I would like, if possible, to let my crew just go ashore and stretch their legs a little bit." He said, "You give them whatever liberty you want. They rate it." This was quite different from the other fellow.

The other fellow was just taking advantage of having a young destroyer skipper that he could push about a little bit. The doctor, when we left there, said, "You know, Captain, I know that you aren't supposed to strike your senior in the

Navy, but I wondered why you didn't slap that first fellow in the face. He certainly gave you plenty of provocation."

Q: I expect you're getting kind of tired, Count. You've been wonderful this morning, as you always are. Suppose we stop for the present time, and then we'll take up again.

Interview #6

Vice Admiral Bernard L. Austin　　　　By Paul L. Hopper
near Rockville, Maryland　　　　　　　November 28, 1969

Mr. Hopper: As I recall Count, as we ended our fifth session, you were leaving Puerto Rico. You were bound for the southwest Pacific. Would you like to take it up there?

Admiral Austin: There are a couple of experiences while still in the WOOLSEY that may be worth a little time.

After the North African landing, a task force was detached and was proceeding back to continental U. S., with oilers to refuel on route. The afternoon before our scheduled refueling the next day, the weather reports began to look a bit ominous to me. I was the senior destroyer Captain in the escort group, so I felt it appropriate that I convey my concern to the Task Force Commander.

He did not appreciate my suggesting a change in his schedule. I thought that if we refueled that afternoon, we'd be sure of getting our fuel; whereas if we waited until the scheduled time the next day, we may not. I was given a rather curt reply to my message, which could be summed up in about these words - "I'm the Task Force Commander. I have as much information as you do. I will make the schedule and you adhere to it."

The next morning the weather deteriorated really more than I had anticipated. It was really rough. I was ordered to go alongside one of the tankers first. The USS BROOKLYN, a cruiser along with us, was ordered to go alongside the other tanker.

The BROOKLYN was commanded by a very able Captain, who later became my boss in the Pacific at one time.

So, we proceeded to line up astern of these two tankers, to go alongside for alongside fueling. The tanker that I was approaching was pitching and yawing to such an extent that I could not only see the rudder, but I could see the bottom of the rudder when he pitched. His yaw was not a degree or two, it was in the magnitude of ten degrees a side.

It was not the kind of weather to try to fuel alongside. I conveyed this opinion to the Task Force Commander and was told to carry out my orders.

Whereupon, I gritted my teeth and did the best I could. I got alongside and I got connected up. I got about 30 minutes oil before the inevitable happened. Luckily, I disengaged without injury to a single person on board the oiler or my ship. But the ship suffered some superstructure damage - needless to say.

When I got clear, I informed the Task Force Commander of the collision with the tanker. It wasn't exactly a collision. We rolled together and my upperworks hit his. We were rolling 30 or 40 degrees.

I said, "Unless otherwise ordered, I will proceed back alongside." I got 'otherwise' ordered very quickly.

Then, a little later after I resumed my position in the formation, I received one of the nicest compliments that I had ever received from a senior. He commended me for my superb seamanship and complimented me highly on no loss of life and no injuries to personnel and all that sort of thing. I think that's the only time I ever got commended for bashing up a ship.

The BROOKLYN never got connected up to it's tanker. Of course after my experience, the task force Commander decided that it was no go and called the fueling off.

He had to detach the destroyers and the BROOKLYN because we didn't have enough oil to get to the other side. At least, the destroyers didn't. There was some question as to whether or not we had enough to get back to the side that we'd just left. I think the BROOKLYN was probably included in our group going back as an emergency souce of fuel in case one of the destroyers, or more, gave out. So, we proceeded back to North Africa.

While waiting outside of Casablanca for my turn to go in for fuel, my sound man got a contact. I personally went in to the console and listened to it and it sounded good. My plotting officer was plotting this contact and had it moving in a very logical way for a submarine that was trying to run slow and be undetected, but maintain it's depth. I reported over the voice circuit to the task force Commander that I had a submarine contact and was proceeding to attack.

I was told by the task force Commander to proceed to the inside harbor for fuel, never mind my contact. He said, "I don't think you've got a contact anyway. You just picked up one of those sunken ships out here. We've had lots of destroyers getting contact on them. Go on in and get your fuel."

By that time, I had made my first attack. The plot showed that just about the time we dropped our ashcans, the submarine went into a tight circular turn; and we missed it. I was so convinced that I had a good contact that I went back on the voice circuit to the task force Commander. I said, "Indications of firm contact so possitive, request permission to remain with same, until it is sunk."

Evidentally it took a little time for this to be communicated to the boss from the fellow who took the message, so I had a little time. During this time, we were making our second approach on the target.

This time I figured that he would do the same sort of trick that he did before, but I wasn't sure he would turn in the same direction. So, I gave instructions to the man who was doing the plotting. I said, "As soon as you get an indication of any turn, you assume that he is going to make a tight turn in that direction, and we will lay our course accordingly." That time, I think we got him. Because, that's exactly what he did. He turned again, but in the opposite direction.

About that time, I got the task force Commander's reply. He was a bit irate. He came on the TBS himself. He said, "You're holding up the whole parade over there. Get on in and get your fuel." I said, "Sir, I am absolutely certain now that we have an enemy submarine. I request that you relieve me by another destroyer, before I leave this contact." He relieved me with two destroyers.

Some ten years later, when I finally got a Bronze Star for having sunk this submarine, the other two destroyers I think got the same credit that I got.

The task force Commander was so engrossed in trying to get this fueling off on schedule. This was fueling from inside the harbor. It's not a big harbor, as you probably know. You can only get so many ships in there at a time. He had this sort of line of ships out there waiting for fuel. We had a couple of aircraft carriers in the line.

Two nights before, a German U-boat down at Fedala, almost in sight of Casablanca; had played quite a bit of havock with the shipping down there, including one destroyer. I'm quite sure that fellow was waiting to try to get a big ship. He didn't want me, I was too small.

Q: Probably the aircraft carrier.

Austin: That's right. The German records did show that we actually had a bona fide contact and it was sunk in that spot at that time.

Q: It must have been an immense sort of satisfaction, when you found that out.

Austin: Yes, it was, because it isn't easy to buck the task force Commander. It's much easier, shall we say, in the military organization to always say, "Aye, aye, sir." But, one doesn't always do one's duty; when one just says, "Aye, aye, sir;" when he has information which is not available to the person issuing the order that he's saying, "Aye, aye, sir" to.

Q: To phrase an old saying - "That's what separates the men from the boys."

Austin: I think our training should help people to speak up. And I think it did, in the days when I went to the Naval Academy as a young officer. On many occasions, I had the courage to speak up on something. And I never recall having been punished for having done so. You should be right, but if you're right, your superior officer appreciates your speaking up, rather than holding it against you.

I had several experiences as a young Ensign on a battleship, which at the moment I thought would result in my career being rather foreshortened. But, they turned out, I think, rather to enhance my fitness report, rather than otherwise.

I'm afraid that today, one can't say this with the same degree of conviction. I'm afraid that today, the officer who speaks out when he's not in tune with the moment and with the thinking of the moment, may have it held against him; more than in the days when I was coming along. I feel that this is one of the regretable developments of the so-called civilian control of the military. I don't think that any properly motivated military man in our country would ever wish to have other than civilian control of the military, if by civilian control one means that the political decisions that fall in the political military area shall be reserved to those politically responsible. But then, we've gone beyond that. We have reached the point, and this had been reached before I left the Pentagon, where the energies of officers were devoted so much to answering innumerable queries from civilian sources not conversant with the situation, that they had very little time to do the things they should have been doing to make the plans they should have been making. They were always defending what had already been submitted.

Q: Political decisions?

Austin: Yes. I'm afraid in our war in Vietnam, we have suffered from this tendency. I've known a number of the officers who have been in high places in this war. I know them to be very fine men, but I'm afraid that little by little their ability to contribute to the military success of that war was eroded by the overweaning political dictates, as to just how and where and when military operations should be or should not be carried on, in persuance of our national policy in that area.

Q: I deeply agree. I think we would have had the war in Vietnam over long ago, if the military had not been hamstrung.

What you say intrigues me, in a way too Count, because it would seem on the basis of the extreme latitude and independence with which youth operates; that there would be more tendency for a chap to speak out and state his mind - whether he's going to civilian school, or possibly even the Naval Academy or West Point.

Austin: I think you do have a sort of a paradox. Paul, that is a good question. It's difficult for me to give you a good answer to it. I am sure in the days when I was a young boy growing up, our society was far more disciplined that it is now. Therefore, it was not as easy for a young man to buck the establishment, or constituted authority, or his senior officer, even to the extent of suggesting a change in his orders.

Today, with a more permissive type of concept, we would expect young men in the military to be more willing to express their slant on something, and to suggest changes and orders of seniors. Perhaps this is an index of the degree to which we have civilianized the military. We have extended civilian control to a degree far beyond that which was envisioned by our founding fathers. I think that they did not envision civilianization of military matters, but civilian control over military undertakings - overall control, policy control as it were.

I might cite an experience while I was the Director of the International Affairs Division in the Navy Department.

I received a call from an assistant Secretary of Defense. He said, "I understand the Navy is putting a carrier into Buenos Aires in the near future." I said, "That is correct, sir." He said, "I would like that visit cancelled." I said, "Sir, that visit was not initiated by the Navy Department and therefore I don't believe the Navy Department could initiate the cancellation of it. Mr. Dulles personally requested that visit of our Chief of Naval Operations. I was given the task of setting up the visit."

There was a bit of humming and hawing, and he wanted to know why Mr. Dulles had asked for the visit. I suggested that

Austin - 182

I could give him what I thought Mr. Dulles might have had in mind, but it would probably be better for me not to attempt to determine what the motive was, and for him to ask the State Department.

He commented during our discussion on the phone, that the reason he wanted the visit cancelled was because the Air Force had scheduled a visit by the THUNDERBIRDS to Buenos Aires, which would overlap with that of the carrier. And that the air staff was very unhappy that the carrier would be there at the same time. They thought it would erode the normal effectiveness of the publicity obtained with the beautiful flying of the THUNDERBIRDS.

I suggested that perhaps if the State Department were motivated by desire to show military prowess in the United States in that area at this particular time, perhaps the two visits might be more effective than one. The Secretary reiterated that the Air Force was very unhappy about this and that they had requested him to have it cancelled and that he wanted it cancelled. He would contact the State Department and he would call me later.

He said, "Why don't you put that carrier through the Panama Canal? Buenos Aires is a long way down, and from there, you're probably going to put it on down around the Cape."

I said, "Yes sir, we have to put it around the Cape, because it won't go through the Canal." At this, there was a short silence and then he said, "You don't mean to tell me the Navy's been stupid enough to build carriers that won't go through the Panama Canal?"

I said, "Yes sir, we have several carriers that won't go through the Canal. It's not entirely due to stupidity, Mr. Secretary. The advance of the state of the art of the airplane has been such that the carriers that we now have that will go through the Canal, are a bit out date; just as would be the planes that you could fly from them, if we continued to insist on having that as the guiding criteria in the building of our carriers."

This is not too much to be unexpected. An assistant Secretary is an appointive office and you can't expect him to know all about all of the services. But, by the same token, he should not assume that because he's appointed to this job; that he knows more about all the services than the people who have been working at it as a life time profession.

I'll give you another little illustration that I think will indicate how the civilianization of the military has eroded the expertise available in the military establishment for the production of good results.

While I was the Director of the Joint Chiefs of Staff, the Secretary of Defense decreed that all chiefs of military advisory groups had to be personally approved by the Secretary of Defense.

Now, of course, let us be fair. I always try to be, I don't like to get subjective in my veiws at anytime.

This, undoubtedly came about because at one time or another one of the services as a detail inconvenience probably sent some officer as the chief of a military advisory group to some country who wasn't ideally suited for the job. That can happen in any detailing of personnel.

But, as a result of this one situation that was brought into the spot light, the Secretary of Defense was convinced by his civilian assistants in his staff, that he should personally approve every chief of a military advisory group, so that this wouldn't happen again.

The chief of the military advisory group in Japan at this time was an Army officer. This Army officer was due for a promotion, but he had to go to the unit in which he was going to get this promotion, in order to get it. As you know, the Army works that way. He could not get the promotion while still the chief of the military advisory group in Japan.

So, the Chief of Staff of the Army asked General White, who was then the Chief of Staff of the Air Force, if he would hurry up and get that Air Force officer out there that was scheduled to relieve the Army officer. General White said, "No. This puts me in a heck of a spot. The reason we haven't gotten our officer out there is that we just don't have one right now, who's a Brigidier General rank, who is suited for that job, that we can spare." He turned to Arleigh Burke and said, "Arleigh, could you by any chance furnish a Naval officer for that job? If you will, I'll take your turn in furnishing the chief of the MAG out there when it comes up next. I'll have my man relieve yours. In the meantime, that will get me out of this bind that I'm in. And I'll have time to plan for it - get him sent to Language School to learn a little Japanese and that sort of thing."

Admiral Burke, of course, was always willing to take on anything. So, he said, "Why sure. I've got an officer that I have here in Washington now at Language School. I'll just shift him from studing Portugese to studying Japanese. I'll send him out there. There's no rush to get him to Portugal right now. I'll pick somebody else, and swap with somebody else."

The Joint Chiefs, when they met, were told of the discussion that had gone on between the Army, the Air Force, and the Navy Chiefs. They were asked if they agreed that this would be the best thing to do - to let the Navy take the Air Force's turn, and the Air Force to take the Navy's turn when it came up next. The Chiefs all agreed to this. Now, of course, that means that five four-star officers had given the thing fairly good consideration. They had determined that the overall best interest of the government would be served if this was done.

Admiral Radford though, when the Chiefs finished their meeting that day, turned to me and said, "You'd better go up and clear the way for this. Otherwise that General may be sitting out there a long time waiting to be relieved. You go up to SecDef's place and clear the way for it."

At that time there was a Lieutenant General Fox, who was the head of the part of the Defense staff which handled these matters. I knew Pat very well. I went up to him and said, "Pat, the Joint Chiefs have just decided that this change in turns will be in the overall best interest. The chairman asked that I come up and pave the way for the SecDef's approving the Navy's nomination for the job, so that this Army fellow can get out and get his second star." Pat said, "Well Count, the Secretary of Defense has undertaken to do so many things like this in person that he can't possibly do them all. Many of them have been delegated to me. There're only so many hours in the day and I can't do them all. So I've had to delegate them. We've taken away so many of the prerogatives and the final decisions from the Chiefs, and from the individual Chiefs of service that we've got everything focused up here now. I've had to delegate this to a Colonel. I'll call him and ask him if he can see his way clear to give approval for the Secretary on this. He handles it with the Secretary."

So, he called this Colonel. The Colonel said, "Oh, no. I can't approve that. We were asked by the Ambassador in Japan who would fill the billet next time, who would relieve this Army General. By the Joint Chiefs own schedule, it is to be an Air Force officer. The Secretary of Defense is on record as having replied to the Ambassador in Japan, that it will be an Air Force officer. I cannot reverse the Secretary of Defense."

I got the gist of this conversation by the one-sided reply of General Fox. I said, "Pat, it happened that I saw that exchange of messages about this job; and brought the messages to the attention of the Joint Chiefs at the time that they considered this change in the schedule, or in the rotation procedure. They figured that this was not anything that would interfere with the change. That the first message was undoubtedly generated by the young Brigadier General out there, who was anxious to get out and thought that if the Ambassador asked the Secretary of Defense who was going to relieve him, it might sort of spur things on. So, they saw no harm in the Secretary of Defense now saying that it was going to be a Naval officer."

Austin - 188

Pat communicated this to the young Colonel. The young Colonel hesitated quite a bit. It took quite a little argument on the part of Lieutenant General Fox to get the Colonel to agree to approve what five four-star military men had already considered, in greater depth than he was considering it in fact, and had decided it was the appropriate thing to do. But, he finally gave in.

I think these two little incidents are only feathers that indicate the way the wind is blowing, but I could go on and on and on if we had the time, to give you many more.

I saw this process, or this gradual overweaning influence of the civilians in the military; and I tried to do something about it.

Q: You probably did, when you were President of the War College.

Austin: By that time, I saw it from many angles.

As the Director of the Joint Staff, I was in a pretty good position to see how the wind was blowing. To be perfectly honest with you, it was not entirely the Secretary of Defense's fault, it was not entirely the civilian staff's fault; Because most of the people that the Secretary of Defense brought in as appointive people, were pretty well chosen, pretty highly motivated people who wanted our military establishment to be efficient and work in a way that if we went to war, we could win it. But, the trend of the times got to be such that the military, in many ways, helped produce this overwhelming civilian influence. I will cite you one case, that will illustrate what I am trying to get across.

The Joint Chiefs of course are a committee, it's true, you might say. It's a group of men with a corporate responsibility, much like the directors of a corporation.

The Joint Chiefs must, in my opinion, be willing to give their best advice without splitting it every time; if they're to be useful to the Secretary of Defense as military advisors and useful to the Commander in Chief, the President, as military advisors.

There developed a great tendency for the Chiefs to take too long to give answers. There developed a tendency for them to give answers that were not as definitive as was desired by those in the civilian staff of the Secretary of Defense who had to go up on the Hill and take a position.

For example -- one day an Assistant Secretary of Defense came down to me. I had known him personally before he became Assistant Secretary of Defense. He said, "Count, I need the following answer and I've got to have it today. I don't want to go off half cocked on it. I know if I write the Chiefs a memorandum and ask them for the answer, I won't get it until next week or maybe next month. Can you help me?"

Austin - 190

I said, "I can give you staff assistance on it. We have people in our logistic division who are quite knowledgable in this field. I'll give you all the help I can." He was most grateful.

The Joint Chiefs were not quoted in this. They were not represented as agreeing to the information or advice that we gave to the Assistant Secretary of Defense. In fact, they might have rung my neck if they had been aware of the fact, that I was giving it to him. But, I did tell a couple of them about this. I pointed this out as an illustration of why they must become more responsible and more timely in their giving of advice.

This was only one of many approaches I had from various people in the Secretary of Defense's staff. I tried to always be helpful and I think they found me so. I still have good relations with several of them to this day.

Q: Don't you think Count that this relief of military responsibility by the civilianization of the services that you refer to, has been brought about to some degree by officers assigned to the civilian side of the military establishment? Like this young Colonel that you mentioned who was reporting to General Fox.

Austin: Yes.

Q: Who feel that the way to get ahead is to play up to the civilian side, even though it costs them the esteme of their brothers in arms?

Austin: That is correct. Many of those young fellows who went up to the Secretary of Defense's establishment - that is to his staff - got promoted very quickly.

There is though another very important factor in this equation, that is the introduction of atomic weapons into the stockpile of nations.

When the Cuban crisis arose I was President of the Naval War College. I kept my finger pretty closely on the pulse of what students were thinking up there in many ways. And so, I got a little concerned about their reaction to the degree of control of the ships on the quarantine duty by people in the White House. I'd heard these stories too, things like that get around.

I felt that it was important enough that I called an assembly of the students in the auditorium. I undertood to try to explain the situation to them. I said, "Now gentlemen, I understand that many of you are quite perturbed at the danger inherent in civilians in an air-conditioned room in Washington dictating details of speed and course and positions on a line of a ship that has a pretty delicate task to perform in this quarantine situation. In the first place, I want you to realize, as I'm sure you do, but you may not have had it in the forefront of your mind when you formed your opinions about this; that we are in a situation today where it is in the best interest of our nation that military forces sometimes be used as political pawns in a rather complex chess game. This Cuban situation is such a one. It is, at the same time, not in the best interest of the country for some one who is not responsible politically; but who only works for some one who is responsible politically, to assume military tactical control over situations that have been given to the military people to handle. Let us be very careful that we do not be too broad in our opposition to the proper use of political control of military forces, which are actually being used as a political tool at the time."

I found that my discussing this with them, I let them ask questions and I answered them forthrightly and as best I could, took a lot of the unhappy element out of their reaction to what they had heard about the ships being moved around on the line by amateurs across the river.

I think one must realize that every time there's a misunderstanding, if you could get people face to face and see the other fellows view; very often the misunderstanding would, if not disappear, at least be lessened.

Q: If we could just all communicate more effectively.

Austin: Yes, that's right.

I'd like to go back just a little bit to this matter of the Joint Chiefs' responsibility and the manner in which they discharged it.

Q: That's very interesting Count, because I'm sure you've heard the story, I've heard it numerous times, it's possibly without foundation — that the line of separation between North and South Korea was discussed at the Joint Chiefs of Staff, and they were unable to reach a consensus on it. And it was finally suggested that they just simply flip a coin, and let go one way or the other.

Austin: I was not there at that time. I'd rather not comment Paul on something that I don't have first hand knowledge of. But I was there when this happened —

The second year that I was the Director of the staff of the Joint Chiefs of Staff, I kept a curve of the split decisions of the Joint Chiefs prior to my taking over as Director of the Joint Staff and after I took over. I was very proud of the lessened number of splits during the time that I'd been there. The curve was most encouraging frankly, because the split decisions were becoming less and less. I think that the operations deputies had a great deal to do with this. They were all very able people at the time. I presided at their meetings, as the Director of the Staff. I tried to be a catalyst for understanding, rather than just a chairman of the meeting. I think we were beginning to have some success in bringing the Chiefs more together on issues that the service Staffs had been poles apart on.

When it came time for the Joint Strategic Objective plan to be considered by the Chiefs, we had many meetings at the operations deputies level before the Chiefs got this plan. We had resolved many difficulties. We started out with splits numbering between 50 and 100. We'd reduced this number of splits to just really one, one from each service. I saw that I was not going to be able to get the operations deputies to resolve this last difference of opinion between the services, because it involved an aircraft carrier with the Navy, and another division for the Army, and another Strat Wing for the Air Force, and something (I forget exactly what it was that they considered very important too) for the Marines.

We had the Chiefs meet on the matter. The Chiefs listened very attentively while the joint staff gave them pretty good presentations on the issue. The Chiefs really had informed themselves better than you could expect on such a long plan and such a detailed plan as this. I was very hopeful that they were going to resolve their differences. I therefore was quite disappointed when at the end of the meeting, instead of resolving the differences, they hadn't even reduced their differences. They were all going to submit a separate opinion. The poor Secretary of Defense was going to be left with no consensus on this.

I asked the chairman if I might address the Chiefs. He hesitated, but allowed me the priviledge. I got up and said, "Gentlemen, you have done a commendable job on informing yourselves of the issues here. The Secretary of Defense isn't going to have the time that you have taken to go into this matter. He's going to need definitive guidance in this. If you do what you're proposing to do gentlemen, and send him four different views on this, you are abdicating. It is your responsibility to give the advice which you are refusing to do." Those were a little strong words, I'll admit for a Director of a Staff to give to his bosses. But I felt it so strongly Paul, I'd seen this thing coming so much. I knew exactly what was going to happen, if they sent this up split four ways; who was going to give the Secretary the advice he needed. Some fellow who didn't know a heck of a lot about it, and who may not be as objective as the Chiefs.

Q: Otherwise, the only thing he could do would be to just shut his eyes and read each one of the decisions and --

Austin: That's correct. So, at the end of my dissertation, there was a silence. No one spoke up. So, the chairman banged the gavel and said, "We're adjourned." So the paper went up split.

The Chief of Staff of the Air Force walked alongside of me as we went out. He said, "Count you were one hundred percent right. I want you to know that I felt that what you said was appropriate."

Admiral Burke didn't speak to me for about two months. Max Taylor, who was the Chief of Staff of the Army at that time, later became the chairman of the Joint Chiefs of Staff in the Kennedy administration.

One day, while I was President of the Naval War College, I got a letter from Max. He said, "Count, every time I go into that room which is irreverently called the 'tank' I think of what you told the Chiefs that day when we split on the JSOP. You were so right and I don't know whether we will ever again be able to exercise our proper function, because once you have abdicated it's hard to regain the power."

Q: It means your civilian control is going to tighten up.

Austin: That's right. Really this civilian control has gotten beyond what I think it was intended to ever get, and certainly it has gotten beyond what is in the best interest of our country.

I doubt that you or I either will live to see the pendulum swing back to dead center. It could swing too far the other way again. Although we say it can't happen here, there are situations which could conceivably cause that pendulum to swing too far in the other direction.

Q: I've often times pondered that. Our society is moving in such a way that if it's going to hold together at all we may have to face up to a dictatorship — either extreme right or extreme left.

Austin: I'm sure that some of the poles that we have both read cause one to be concerned along those lines.

Q: Count, I think it is the feeling of many of us that while in no sense would we like to see all four of the services in one common uniform, that if there was more cooperation among the services in striving for a common objective, be it a political situation or actually in time of war, and less jealousy among the services in maintaining their own separate identity, that we would have a better overall military effort.

Austin: I've given a great deal of thought to this, Paul. While I was Director of the Joint Staff I proposed a solution.

Austin - 198

It's difficult for a Chief of a service to spend ten hours a day on the detailed problems of his service, and then spend two hours being briefed on the problems of the Joint Chiefs. He's tired by the time he's spent ten hours on the other problems. He is too much inclined, I think, to take the recommendations of his staff. This, I think, is not always the best thing to do. Particularly is it dangerous when a staff is prone to tell the Chief what they think the Chief wants to hear.

I might give you an illustration of this. I think I can do it without getting into highly classified things.

While I was the Operations Deputy for Admiral Burke, - that's the title of the job as Deputy CNO for Plans and Policy - it was my task to have him briefed on all JCS matters. It was also part of my job to represent him at the Operations Deputies meetings, when we were trying to solve things for the Chiefs, without having them have to go into them in detail.

One day the briefing sheet came up for a problem and I send for the team that had prepared the brief, who were in my shop. I said, "Gentlemen, I find it difficult to agree with you on this position that you recommend that Admiral Burke take."

They said, practically in one voice, "That's the right position sir, because that's what Admiral Burke said four years ago. Admiral Burke said, 'It's not in the best interest of the country to have more and more and more big bombs. We need some of that material for our use and for the Army's use. We shouldn't put it all in big bombs!"

I said, "I don't disagree with that overall premise. Here we aren't faced with that simple problem. The Air Force is asking that they be given a more modern version of an older type weapon, which will enable them to put X times as many on the B-52s as they can put of the others; and each one of them will have just as much effect. It isn't going to take any more material. Material that's in the old ones can be used for Navy or Army equipment or weapons. I just can't see that I can advise Admiral Burke to do something which lessens this country's ability to strike an enemy, by an order of X to one."

They didn't see it that way. "Oh, no, you agree to this, and they'll have all the stockpile."

I told them, "Gentlemen, you are the experts in this field and this is a specialized field. I'm going to allow you to make your presentation to Admiral Burke just as you think it should be when we go to brief him. I forewarn you, I'm going to disagree with you."

So, we went down and they briefed Admiral Burke just the way they started out briefing me. When they had finished, I told Admiral Burke that I regretted that I had to disagree with my team and I gave him the reasons.

I said, "At the Op Deputies meetings; I have been able to get the Air Force Deputy to reduce the number they were asking for, of the newer versions, by an order of about four to one. Now, we have arrived at the one figure, on the basis of being able to completely arm their inventory of B-52s, with one strike of this type of weapon. They wanted enough for repeated strikes. I've gotten them down to this figure and I suggest to you that if you and the other Chiefs insist on bucking this figure, that the Air Force will go back to their original request and will take it all the way to the White House. They've got a wonderful case to win."

Admiral Burke went to the meeting. General Lemnitzer was the Chief of Staff of the Army at that time. He came in and he and Admiral Burke sat next to each other at the table. I was on Admiral Burke's left. So Lemnitzer turned to Admiral Burke and said, "My staff has briefed me to oppose this number one item on the agenda here. They tell me that you're opposed to it too. Your staff is opposed to it." Arleigh said, "Yes, I am." Lemnitzer said, "Arleigh, I don't see how we can oppose this. After all, it increases our national capabilities so much and at no cost really in number of pounds of material."

Arleigh turned to me and said, "What do I do?" I said, "Admiral, I tried to suggest to you what you should do and I still am of that opinion, sir."

General White came in. As soon as the meeting was called to order and item number one on the agenda was brought up for discussion, he said, "Gentlemen, I'd like to say a word before any one else says anything on this. My Operations Deputy has agreed at the OpDeps level, to reduce our required numbers of these from what we asked for to this low figure that you now have before you. I do consider it a low figure. If there is any voice raised in the Joint Chiefs against that figure, if anything is sent to the Secretary of Defense tending to cast doubt on our need for this number; I'm going back to my original figure and I'm going all the way to the White House." The paper was approved without dissent.

I'd only gotten home that evening and had my first martini in my hand about to take my first sip and the phone rang. It was about eight o'clock, because the Chiefs meeting had lasted until about six and I got back to the office and found a stack of stuff that had to be acted on before I went home - as usual. It was Admiral Burke.

He said, "Count, why did you advise me to sell the Navy short today?" I said, "Arleigh, I didn't advise you to sell the Navy short today. I advised you not to sell your country short." He said, "The boys that are experts in this field have been up to see me since the meeting. They're very unhappy that I agreed to this. They've convinced me that I've sold the Navy down the river on it."

Austin - 202

I said, "Do you want me to come back to the Pentagon now and explain it to you in greater detail?" He said, "No, I'm tired, I'm going home. I'll see you tomorrow."

I think he still holds that against me. We're good friends. But I don't think he ever saw the fallacy in the play back to him of his own words. In other words, he had said, that once, and he couldn't be wrong.

I found, when I went to the Pentagon as Deputy for Plans and Policy, a terrific tendency for the staff there to play back to him what he had said four years before, three years before, two years before, or last year. I had one heck of a time in my own outfit, getting them out of the file cabinet process of arriving at proper advice to the Chief on JCS matters.

If this went on in the Navy staff, I'm sure it went on in the other staffs. Now, we get back to my suggestion for getting away from this.

I suggested that the Chefs do what the National Security Act of 1947 says they should do. That is - to consider their duty as a member of the Joint Chiefs of Staff as primary -

Q: And the responsibility to the respective services as --

Austin: As secondary. Each has a four-star officer as a Vice Chief, and they should leave to him the minutiae of running that service; while they address themselves to the bigger problem of giving sound, well rounded - from every viewpoint - advice to Commander in Chief and to the Secretary of Defense.

I realized that as long as they sat up in their own part of the Pentagon, they would never do this. Sure, you could have the briefings for the JCS come the first thing in the morning instead of late in the afternoon. You'd be putting it first, in a way; but not in reality. The only way I figured that they'd ever really address themselves to their JCS duties primarily and to their service duties secondarily; was to be given offices alongside of each other, down in the area where the Chairman of the Joint Chiefs of Staff had his office, and adjacent to and convenient to the Joint Chiefs of Staff staff. And that they would agree that they would always be briefed on every agenda item by the Joint Staff before they got a single service staff's view. Then, they could call on all of the single service staffs for their views, if they wanted to. The same briefing to all, instead of the Air staff briefing the Air Chief with a slant that wouldn't be made available to the other Chiefs; and the same for the other services.

Q: As a matter of fact, it might be even better to have the Chiefs briefed individually by the staffs of each one of the separate Chiefs first; and then have your joint staffs briefing of all the Chiefs.

Austin: That would certainly be a possibility.

I went to Admiral Burke with this suggestion and he said, "I don't think the Chiefs will buy this. I'll discuss it with Lemnitzer and see what he thinks about it." He discussed it with General Lemnitzer. I think General Lemnitzer was pretty much inclined toward it. But it never got to first base.

When I saw that Admiral Burke was not going to do anything about it, I heckled him a few times about it. I said, "If you won't bring it up as a proposal of yours to the Joint Chiefs of Staff, would you discuss it with the Secretary of Defense as something that has been suggested to you and which you are turning over in your mind?" He said, "No, I won't. You have my permission to talk to Tom Gates about it if you want to."

So, I made an appointment with Mr. Gates and I made my proposal to him. He said, "Count, I agree with you 100 per cent; except I would go one step further. I'd take the Chiefs out of the services entirely." I said, "Mr. Secretary, that I think would be a mistake. Then you get an ivory tower organization. They have no responsibility for the execution of the plans that result from their advice to higher authority. I think they should remain in their services, but be physically separated therefrom; and let them know that their primary duty is what it says in the law. And they are to get the benefit of

Joint Staff briefings, as well as single staff briefings."

I still think that would have saved a lot of our sad sad failures of the military advice getting where it should get, on time and with the proper degree of agreement.

Q: What you say about Admiral Burke is interesting, because as you well know, he is now the head of the strategic studies group at Georgetown University.

Austin: Yes, I know.

Q: Which certainly takes one of deep objectivity, I think, to perform the duties properly.

Austin: I know Admiral Burke pretty well. We were together in the South Pacific. I was his Division Commander. I've been shot at by him, I've been decorated by him, and I have served him in several capacities since then. So, I know him pretty well. He has lots of highly commendable qualities, but like all of us, he is just another man. And no man is perfect.

Q: Count, before you left the WOOLSEY; do you recall any special instances or experiences that stand out in your mind as involving rather unusual stress and anxiety which you prefer not to relive?

Austin - 206

I might briefly describe one of our experiences in the North African invasion. As destroyers, we were assigned to screen the larger ships from possible torpedo attack because they did have indications that the Germans knew that we had some nice juicy targets there and had dispatched some submarines in that direction.

There was one shore battery over at Fêdala that continued to harass our landing. So the order was given for the squadron of destroyers, of which I was a part - Squadron 13, to silence this battery. It was a job that destroyers had to do because to get at it, you had to go well inshore. The cruisers just couldn't get in there. The airplanes had not been able to silence it thus far. They decided that a squadron of destroyers at point blank range might do the job.

So we were ordered into this spot, given a geographical position to which to proceed before opening fire, that having been determined by the angle that they had from their intelligence on the fort that was still firing. We were practically in the breakers before the point for opening fire was reached.

It was not something to make a Commanding Officer of a destroyer happy, even if the enemy weren't firing at you, which he was, of course.

Q: He was firing with bigger guns than you had.

Austin: Oh yes. It was rather difficult not to be able to open fire until we arrived at this designated point.

Q: Until you could see thw whites of their eyes.

Austin: Yes. Lo and behold, just as we arrived at the designated point; we got orders not to fire on Fédala. And Fédala was still firing like heck at us. And there we were, looking right down their gun muzzles. Fortunately, their aim was not too good. None of our ships were sunk or hurt badly. So, we got out of that all right.

Another time I recall was, I had been in an escort of ships to Londonerry, Northern Ireland. I had been released from my escort duty and given my orders to return to the States. I was up at the club having a fairly deserved drink.

The chief of staff to the U. S. officer who was the senior destroyer officer for the U. S. in Londonderry came to my table and said, "I've got orders for you. The Commodore wants you to take a deck load of depth charges up to Greenock. They're desperately in need of the depth charges and they are available here in Londonerry. He wants you to load with depth charges right away and take them up to Greenock and deliver them to the following ships."

I said, "Have you read the weather reports?"

He said, "Yes and the Commodore has too. He realizes that it's going to be nip and tuck for you to get there before the storm that's coming up the Irish sea makes it impossible for you to get there and unload. He asked me to tell you that he realized full well it's a dangerous assignment, but has no choice but to try to do it."

I wasted no time, I can assure you, because I knew that every minute I wasted was going to increase the probability of getting caught by that storm. We got our depth charges as we headed out the channel from Londonerry. The depot that we had to pick them up from was on the side of the channel, as it were. We got them on board as quickly as we could, and we lashed them as well as we could, so as to not have them charging around like wild bulls on the deck. We had a full deck load of depth charges.

I started out at best speed. We were fortunate enough to get to Greenoch and to get every depth charge unloaded to the ships designated. We had to peddle them around, like a milkman delivering milk.

Unfortunately though for me, between the time I left the last ship and the time I approached the buoy that was assigned to us for mooring the storm hit. And it hit with a wallop. I had one heck of a time getting tied up to that buoy, because the buoy was so located that to steam into the wind, my stern was pointing right towards the shallow water which was not very far away.

It was the last line of buoys toward the shore. I've never seen a better bit of seamanship on the part of the men that I had to put on that buoy in that rough weather. That's one time that I order the doctor to break out medicinal alcohol, when they got back aboard, because it was cold weather and they deserved it. I was afraid they would come down with pneumonia, if they didn't have it, frankly.

Most of my assignments during my time in command of the WOOLSEY had to do with escorts. They were difficult but not too thrilling, as a rule; except for the North African show and the individual jobs that I had on the east coast.

We were very thin on destroyers at that time. I remember one time Chiot Wood and I, our two destroyers, were all that we had on the east coast north of Hatteras. That is, for anti-submarine work.

Q: Were you involved in actually escorting convoys back and forth?

Austin: Yes, indeed. As a matter of fact, I might describe one escort that my people contributed to the safety of.

We were under the command of an escort commander whom I had relieved in command of a submarine at New London, Connecticut. I had a message brought to me which indicated that there was a

German wolfpack consentrating right on our line of approach. This was a pretty valuable convoy that we were escorting.

I asked the Squadron Commander if he had received the message. He came back and said - no, he didn't have it. So I gave him the gist of it. In fact I quoted the message to him. It was an intelligence message. I quoted it to him by blinker gun.

After about thirty minutes the convoy course was changed about thirty degrees to avoid this wolfpack. We got safely around it and no harm came to us. In fact I'm quite happy to say that no ship that I helped to escort was ever sunk. I don't claim credit for it, I think it was a coincidence, and I was lucky that I didn't have to spend more time picking up survivors.

Q: That must have been a horrible sort of experience for a destroyer commander - picking up survivors.

Austin: I've seen ships blow up, but they weren't ships under escort.

There was a destroyer that was commanded by an officer in the class of '23, named Max Haynsworth. We were escorting a group of ships to the Western approaches where they were to be taken over by local escorts.

The task force Commander was in a cruiser. The visibility was zero. He ordered the destroyer that Haynsworth commanded to contact by voice one of the tankers and give him a message.

While Haynsworth was feeling his way in toward this tanker in the convoy the task force Commander unfortunately urged him to hurry up. It wasn't very long after that he contacted the tanker. Unfortunately the contact resulted in his ship and the tanker exploding.

I believe only three people survived from his ship, and they were people on duty in the five inch gun director. The ship went down so fast. I don't know how many from the tanker survived, but I did get the information on Haynsworth's ship.

It was a sad thing. The visibility was zero, but the flash was such that I could see it from where I was in the escort. I was on the bridge at the time.

Q: What actually happened Count? Was the ship torpedoed or was it a collision?

Austin: I think probably the collision caused sparks or a detonation of a depth charge in the rack, or something that initiated the explosion. You had a tanker there, and the ammunition and depth charges on the destroyer. Once you initiate that, it's hard to tell just what happened. You don't run ships together like that, without great danger of having them explode.

Shall we call it a day? I think our tape has just about run out.

Interview #7

Vice Admiral Bernard L. Austin, USN (Ret.) by Paul Hopper
Rockville, Maryland   December 5, 1969

Mr. Hopper: As I recall Admiral Austin, when we concluded our last get together you were getting ready to go out to the southwest Pacific. Would you like to take it from there on?

Admiral Austin: Paul, on the way out we had a few experiences which may have some interest.

We were escorting carriers from the east coast to the west coast. When we got to San Diego, one of the carriers had developed difficulty with one of her elevators and so we stopped there for a look see at her elevator trouble.

When we had docked the captain of one of the destroyers, under my administrative jurisdiction as senior destroyer officer of the group, came to me and said he was sorry to bother me about such a matter, but he had a burned out boiler. He had gone up to the destroyer base to see if they could replace the burned out tubes for him, while we were there waiting for the carrier.

He said that he had had very little luck. They didn't seem to be inclined to help him out. He felt, in view of our destination, it was necessary to report it to me.

I thanked him for so doing and asked him to accompany me up to the repair officer of the base.

I think the reason for the reluctance to complain to me was the fact that this Captain was a classmate of mine. He felt that he should be able to get his destroyer repaired without bothering his classmate, who was just a little senior to him.

He accompanied me to the office of the repair superintendent of the base, who was the repair officer of the base. I did the talking and asked the Captain, who was sitting in the seat of responsibility there, to please indicate to me why they couldn't repair this boiler.

He said, "Very simple, we don't have the tubes here to put in." I said, "Couldn't we get them from Mare Island?" "No," he said, "they haven't got them either."

I said, "May I use your telephone?" He said, "What do you want to use my phone for?" I said, "I want to call the Bureau of Ships. I think that they should know that there are no boiler tubes for a standard destroyer boiler on the west coast. I think they should start to get them out here."

He was very reluctant to let me do this, but he gave in. I called the Bureau and I was assured that there were plenty of boiler tubes in Mare Island. I told them that an inquiry by the destroyer base repair office had been given the answer that they did not have them in Mare Island. Therefore, I requested BuShips tell Mare Island where they had them and to put the heat on getting them down for us. This the officer in the Bureau agreed to do, and did.

At that point, as we started to walk out, I asked the repair officer, "Now, Captain, that the boiler tubes are on their way, or at least BuShips assures us that they will be, will you go ahead and put your men down and get the old ones cut out so that we can reduce the time of the repair job?"

He said, "No, I won't, unless you take full responsibility." I said, "Responsibility for what, Captain?" He said, "If I cut your boiler tubes out and the others don't get here before you have to sail, I'll be on the mat for disabling your boiler." I said, "Captain if that's all that's bothering you, I will take full responsibility. After all, the boiler's no good with the burned out tubes in it."

So he sent his men down and started to work. The next morning the new tubes were there and the boiler was repaired. We were on our way happily and with greater battle readiness than we would have had if we had just taken the word of the local people that they couldn't do the job because they didn't have the material.

When we left San Diego, our next stop was San Francisco. When we got inside, after a very foggy approach to the entrance, my little flag ship was given a blinker signal which said, "Proceed to Mare Island."

Then we were about to come to a course to the left of our then course, and we got another signla. It said, "Go to Hunter's Point."

The Captain came to me and said, "Commodore, what do I do?" I said, "Captain, obey your last order first, very simple. We'll have to assume between the time you got the first one and the time you got this one something came up that changed the will of the authority of the port here."

So we went to Hunter's Point, and that turned out to be where we should have gone. When we tied up, we hardly had the lines doubled up when this swarm of workmen came aboard with blueprints under their arms and cutting torches in their hands.

So I asked one of the leading men. "What is this all about? This is a brand new ship."

He said, "We got orders to put combat information centers in your four ships. We've got just exactly 30 days in which to do it." I said, "Do you mean to say we're going to be here for 30 days?" He said, "Yes sir, you'll be here 30 days according to our present orders. If I've got any judgement, I don't think you'll get away from here in 30 days. We've got pretty high-powered orders that say we've got to get you out in 30 days, but I don't see how we can do what we've got to do in 30 days. Because we've never done it before."

So I gulped. We cooperated with the yard as much as we could.

Incidentally this turned out to be a very nice thing personally for me, because as soon as I got back to the St. Francis Hotel I called my wife. We were not together very much for the period of 1940 to '46. This was the longest period that we had together, during this time in San Francisco, in all that span.

I called her and caught her in a state of economic unreadiness. I couldn't tell her anything over the phone that would be very definitive, as to how long I'd be there or anything. I just said, "I suggest strongly that you consider a trip to San Francisco. Let me know when you start and where to meet you."

She went to her best friends and they happened to have enough in the cookie jars so that she could get away. It was on the week-end and she couldn't get to the bank.

She arrived in San Francisco and we had a very pleasant month together, exploring all the good eating places in San Francisco, which I'm sure you know about.

During this period of installing the CICs, I noted that there was not a uniform degree of enthusiasm about getting the work done. The leadingmen and most of the artisans were really striving fiercely to get us out.

But I noticed a welder who was working in my cabin, sort of taking it easy, taking it easy to the point of sitting on the bunk springs and doing nothing for a couple of hours each day. After observing him for several days, I was in and out of course and I didn't know how much time he was sitting down, and of course it wasn't my direct responsibility to keep him working. Finally I had observed him well enough to know that he was soldiering on the job.

So one day I said to him, "Are you waiting for someone to bring you some material or something? Or why is it that you have to sit down and waste this time that's so valuable?" He said, "No, I'm not waiting on anything, except the time for my relief to come to take over. After all, I've done my share for this turn. Let him do his share now."

I said, "You and the members of the other shifts have been working on that bracket for two days. I'm not a welder myself, but I would think you could weld it up there in a few hours." He said, "I've done my share, let the other shift do his share. I said, "You don't work on the basis then that you work as much as you can during the time that you are being paid to work?" He said, "No, I just do my bit."

I told the man, "Frankly, I'm not your boss. I'm just the Commodore of this division of ships, and this happens to be my cabin, but I'm going to find out why the work doesn't progress as it should on the ship. I'd like your name and your number." He, of course, reluctantly was to give me his name and number, but he did.

I went up to see the manager of the yard. I gave him the man's name, which I had obtained from him, and his number.

When I gave the manager the story and the data he said, "You know, we've been having a little difficulty here. We've had to expand very rapidly. Most of the workmen that we've taken on are really commendable in the way that they pitched in and learned and do. But we've had a little element here that has been saying, 'we'll lay so many bricks a day and that's all we'll lay, war or no war.' I'm glad to get this case, it sounds like a good one, a solid one. We will have this taken up by our labor relations people and have them get their own data."

So they did. They found that this bracket had been worked on for about 20 times as long as it needed to be worked on. And that the installation of this bracket was holding up the installation of the equipment that the bracket had to be installed for.

So they actually fired this man, which is rather unusual in war time. It's unusual any time.

The manager came aboard and informed me as a result of my report, this workman had been fired by the yard.

Q: You don't suupose that was sort of an intentional slow down by more than just one man.

Austin: I got the feeling that he was not alone in this, and that he was obeying instructions from some other source than his own conscience and his own mind.

I thought that might be an interesting little side light because we all know that during the war full and by, we had remarkable performance by the civilian segment of our economy in factories as well as in shipyards. This was an illustration.

A few days later, I was in a cab and I recognized one of the leading shipfitters as a man that was standing waiting for a cab. So I asked him if he wanted to ride with me. "Yes, he'd be glad to have a ride with me." While proceeding into town, we were talking. I said, (I told him about this little incident.) "Do you have any difficulties like this with your shipfitters?" He said, "Frankly, sir, in some cases we do. Habit is a hard thing to get over. The rules of what size pipe one union can handle, and what size pipe another union can handle, on a ship this can get to be a very sticky thing. Lots of our workmen are very very patriotic. They take a chance of being scolded by their own unions, and go ahead and help out whenever they can. But there are a few that will sit on their hands for hours, because they won't touch something that they are perfectly competent to handle but it's not technically their unions area of expertise." I said, "What do you do about it?"

He said, "We have tried to get the unions to call a moratorium on these agreements and some have. It's not an easy thing to deal with. The only saving grace is that most of our people are good conscientious patriotic Americans who want to do the best they can to get the war won as soon as they can."

Q; I think what actually happened was that they were most fortunate that there were enough patriotic loyal Americans, among our working force, who did enough more than they would normally do to make up for these people who sat on their hands.

Austin: That's correct.

In Australia for example, it was almost impossible to get shipyard work done there during the war. You would have thought that, that was a place that was right on the front line at one time for the Japanese advance, this would have caused their workmen to be willing to forego some of the pleasures of protection of rules and agreements among the labor people. But it was not so. They seemed to have difficulty in getting work done at a rapid pace in a shipyard in Australia during the war.

Q: Australia, as I recall, has been stronger in the sense of unionization than almost any other westernized country.

Austin: I have that impression. Of course, I'm not an expert in those fields so I really couldn't say.

I do know that when I arrived in Sydney with my ships, for ten days leave and recreation just before Christmas, we were planning, when we left, to give the usual party to repay social obligations. We had planned to have a party that would require a band. When we inquired about the hiring of the band, we found that we couldn't hire one band. We'd have to hire two bands, and that we'd have to pay time and a half for both of them. This got up into quite a bit of money. So I said, "We'll do without a band. We'll make up a plan so we can have a nice party, but we won't have a band."

It seems that we were there at the wrong time. During that period, the bands had a rule that you had to have a standby band and you had to pay them this extra amount or you didn't get them. In other words, there were lots of requirements for the few bands that were available.

Let's leave San Francisco if we may, and proceed out to Pearl, which was the next stop.

When we got to Pearl, my outfit was given the job of screening a task force which had been placed under the command of then Rear Admiral Radford. They were working up down off Kahoolawe, in that area. So when I reported, I was given the job of screen commander.

We got along fine for about a day and a half. Then a Captain Thompson (I was a Commander at that time), class of about '21, came in with parts of his squadron. I immediately assumed he would be taking over the screen commander's job. So I began to transfer the information to him by a signal, at which point I received rather peremptory orders to retain command of the screen.

So we finished the day up and I got my fuel reports in and looked the situation over. The fuel situation wasn't too good. We were getting kind of low, because we had been chasing around at top speed all day long.

So during the night, I promulgated an order to the screen to limit speed in reorientating the next day to 30 knots. That's still pretty fuel eating speed, but I figured that if I could keep them from just throwing the throttles open we might be able to have enough fuel to get back to Pearl. We had no provision for refueling.

The next morning after the first reorientation, I received just as peremptory orders as I had the previous day to turn over the screen to Captain Thompson. I didn't question the order, I immediately proceeded to carry it out, but it smarted a little bit.

I was still thinking about this when I got in. So I called Admiral Radford's flag Lieutenant and asked for an appointment with him. I was given the appointment.

When I was shown in I said, "Admiral I know you're very busy but after telling me to retain the command of the screen the other day, very shortly thereafter the next morning you ordered me to turn over the screen with a sort of a connotation that I wasn't doing very well. I'd just like to know what I wasn't doing right, because it's not obvious to me, sir." He said, "Yes, I'm glad you came over to ask. Your ships weren't fast enough reorientating the next morning."

I said, "That was my fault, if there be any fault about it. I had ordered them to limit their speed the next morning to 30 knots, which was slower than we had been responding to your reorientation program the previous day. I kind of suspected that this might be at the root of things. I brought along a little card here on which I have indicated the fuel capacity of these ships and their endurance at various speeds. The order that I gave I think was justified in view of the fact that the state of fuel oil in the ships was getting down to the worry point."

The Admiral looked at the paper and said, "You mean to tell me that these ships can't go any further than this at top speed?" I said, "That is correct, sir. That is the best data that we've been able to get on these ships. Frankly I think it's a little on the optimistic side."

So I started to make my getaway and the Admiral said, "Wait a minute. If you aren't pressed with another engagement, I'd like to talk with you a little bit." I said, "No sir, I just thought I shouldn't take any more of your time."

He said, "You seem to know more about these new destroyers than anyone I've run into. I don't know a thing about them. If I'm going to be working with them, I should know about them. If you don't mind, sit down, and I'd like to ask you some questions."

At the end of about an hour of his questions and my trying to answer them for him, I thought I'd better make another move to go. At which time he said, if I didn't mind he'd like to ask some more. So it was about two hours before I got away.

It was very pleasant conversation. At the end of it, the Admiral said, "I've asked you lots of questions about destroyers. Tell me, is there anything the carriers can do to make the destroyers job a little more bearable? Is there anything that we do that could be improved on?"

I smiled and said, "Well Admiral, it does perplex us sometimes when we see 'turn 1 8' go up on your starboard yard and ' 1 8 turn' go up on your port yard. It causes us to hesitate a little bit, to see which signal is the one that you really want executed. We do different things for the two, you know."

He really laughed a little at that. He said, "I know of the instance that you refer to. I had just gotten a new signal officer, he'd just come aboard, and I didn't realize that he wasn't quite up to the caliber of the old one. I know just exactly what you're talking about, it happened. I was very much embarrassed, because one of my fellow flag officers had just come aboard to observe operations with us and he called my attention to my flag bridges confusion."

Admiral Radford was a very good task force commander to work for, he was one that you could talk to. I was very happy that he asked me to go with him on his next operation, which was a very small operation, the Baker Island job.

During that operation, I recall, one of his carriers came so close to doing what the Australian carrier did to our destroyer that it wasn't at all pleasant or reassuring.

Admiral Radford, quite correctly, called the carrier commander, in this case, to task. Because the destroyer had done exactly what he was supposed to do under the circumstances and the carrier had not. So the near collision which was avoided, I might say, by the destroyer taking action and the carrier plowed right on as if nothing was going to happen. Admiral Radford really roasted that carrier Captain.

The aftermath of that first little operation with Admiral Radford was interesting. I was going up to CincPac headquarters for dinner that night with a friend of mine, who was on Admiral Nimitz's staff. At dinner, this friend of mine asked me how everything went on my operation with the task force off Kahoolawe. I told him, I said, "There was a little bit of misunderstanding on the task force commander's part about the fuel endurance in our destroyers, and therefore how long they could run at top speed. But I went over and saw Admiral Radford when I got in and we've got that all squared away now."

But the next day I got summoned through the Type Commander, Commander Destroyers Pacific, to report to Admiral Ofstie, who was the senior aviator on Admiral Nimitz's staff. Evidentally Admiral Ofstie's office had indicated that they wanted me to explain why I had been running around saying scurrilous things about aviation Admirals.

There was a contemporary of mine who was in DesPac headquarters at the time that this order was given to me to report to Admiral Ofstie. He said, "I've been operating with these carriers. They don't show enough knowledge of seamanship to suit me. They certainly don't know a darn thing about destroyers. I'll be glad to go along with you, Count." I said, "Fine, I may need some help. I know Ralph Ofstie, but Ralph can get pretty tough. I have nothing to hide. I've not gone around talking through my hat at all or making unkind statements about Admiral Radford or anybody else, but evidently he thinks I have. So I may not get a very good reception."

So this fellow went with me. We went down into the basement where Ofstie's office was. We went along the corridor, and as we approached the entrance to Ofstie's office this very large famous football hero officer who was going to go help me tell them off said, "By the way Count, I see old so-and-so's name down here. I've got something I've got to see him about." And he left me cold.

Q: Your support evaporated.

Austin: My support evaporated.

I went in and the first thing that Ofstie said was rather bellicose, rather firm and unkind. He said, "I want to know why you've been running around here saying what you've been saying about Admiral Radford, in particular, and flag officers who are aviators, in general." I said, "Well Ralph, in the first place I think we'd better find out what I've said and what I haven't said as opposed to what you allege that I have said." I told him exactly what took place at the dinner table the night before.

I think that what had happened was that the destroyer officer that I had been talking to at the table that night had been having a sort of a debate with his aviation friends on Admiral Nimitz's staff. And he used this little bit of information from me to reopen the debate. Or as it were, to pull the wedge out from under the rock that had been poised ready to roll down the hill anyhow.

Because when I got through talking with Ralph Ofstie, we were just as good friends as we'd ever been. He knew me well enough to know I had never been a carrier-hating or an aviator-hating type of officer. So I got the thing all squared away and everybody was happy.

But my friend really found he had an urgent bit of business to take up with somebody else as soon as we got opposite Ralph Ofstie's office.

Ralph was a very able fellow. He remained a bachelor for a long long time and finally married Joy Hancock, the head of the WAVES. He's deceased now.

He was a very able officer in many ways. I had known him on other jobs where we had been not necessarily under the same immediate command, but we had had enough contact with each other to know each other's characteristics.

Q: Coming up as a young officer Count, there must have been other officers with whom you served from time to time who were not always too easily gotten on with-who were perhaps harsh and bellicose at times in their contact with you.

Austin: In the days when I was coming up as a young officer, the relationship between senior and junior I think was quite different to what it is today. I think this resulted in some highly dedicated officers becoming what some people termed as 'sundowners'. Others had less complimentary names for them.

While I was an Ensign on the NEW YORK, the executive officer was changed. Commander Shoemaker, who was being relieved, had been a very fine officer, a very understanding and easy-going type of exec to be brought up under.

I was, at the time, at Range Finder School here in Washington preparing for the job of Range Finder Officer on the ship. Admiral Dutch Will, then Ensign Will, was the Range Finder Officer and I was to relieve him.

I had become well acquainted with a certain bachelor Lieutenant while in Washington on this assignment. We were at the country club one night and he asked me if I'd seen the orders for the new exec to the NEW YORK. I said, "Yes, I saw it in the ARMY-NAVY JOURNAL this morning." He said, "Do you know him?" I said, "No, I've heard of him, but I don't know him." He said, "Well, I do. I want to give you some advice Count. Don't go back to that ship. Go get yourself ordered to any ship or station other than that. He has the reputation of giving more young officers court martials than any other officer of his time." I said, "Thank you, George. I've got to learn how to work under tough guys as well as good guys, so I think I'll take my chances."

There were times when I regretted that decision. One of them was one night when I and the other young officers in the gunnery department of the ship had been up to Camanera, after a fairly successful gunnery performance during the season. We'd done a little celebrating, which involved a little drinking. On the way home in the boat, it was quite obvious that some of us had probably had a drink or two that we might have done without.

I convinced my roommate that I should check us in. So I was trying to find his name, it started with P. The light over the check-in board was a small light and not too bright. Frankly my focusing powers were not normal. So I was trying to find Patterson when the executive officer came out of his door, which was right alongside the check-in board, and engaged me in conversation. He said, "How were things up at Kamenera tonight?" "Oh," I said, "They were fine sir. We had a good time."

About that time down the hatch, which he was facing and which was behind me, two Ensigns were taking a third Ensign. One had his feet and one had his hands, and he had his voice, which he was using in a most unbecoming manner. The Commander was quite aghast at this performance and allowed it to go on until it was down below. He then told me, in a very firm tone of voice, to go below and find out the name of that young officer who had been uttering such unseemly language and come back and report it to him.

I had seen the group in the boat coming home and I knew pretty well the characteristics of my fellow members of the J.O. mess, and I'd heard the voice that he objected to. So I had a pretty good idea as to who it was.

I went below and told the first junior officer that I saw that I'd received these orders from the Commander and I therefore would have to make a thorough search of J. O. country.

I would start aft and go in every room until I got forward. If I found out who it was, I'd have to report him.

I found the one that I thought was most likely to be it (from the voice), snoring peacefully when I got to him. The usual J. O. comradery had resulted in his getting clipped on the chin, and he was not indicating that he had a few minutes before been uttering unseemingly language.

I went back up and reported to the Commander that I had attempted to carry out his order. And that he would recall that I was facing away from the hatch and he was facing the hatch, when we were talking, and the incident occurred. I reminded him that he saw the individual and that I only heard him. I said that as a result of my inspection in every room in the J. O. country, I had not been able to increase my knowledge of whom he had seen and heard, and whom I had only heard going down the hatch at the time of the incident.

The Commander was not pleased with my report. His facial expression left no doubt of this. He gave me orders to go below and return with the correct report in ten minutes.

I went below and I returned in ten minutes and reiterated my former report. At this point, he was even less pleased than he had been before. He informed me that I had evaded his order and that I was going to be given a court martial if it were in his power to give it. I was ordered to go to my room and consider myself under arrest until further orders.

The next morning about seven o'clock, one of the junior officers came to my room and said, "Count, I think you're in for it. The exec's been up with the Captain now since six-thirty. I'm afraid he's recommending you for a court martial. We've been trying to listen and get as much information as we can, but it doesn't look good."

About quarter of eight the Marine orderly came down and told me the Commander wanted to see me in his working cabin. I went up promptly and I walked in. His working cabin was fairly long and narrow. His desk was at the far end from the door. He sat gazing at the entrance, strumming his desk.

I said, "Good morning, Commander." He did not reply. For what seemed to me an interminably long time, I guess it maybe was a minute or a minute and a half, all this time he just strummed and looked intently at me. He finally said, "Good morning." "I believe you have the eight to twelve watch," he said immediately after. I said, "Commander I was scheduled to stand the eight to twelve watch. But if you will recall sir you placed me under arrest last evening. And I, therefore, have no watch sir." "You will stand the eight to twelve watch," he said.

This was good news to me, because you don't stand the watch under arrest pending court martial. So I said, "Is that all sir?" "No," he said, "that is not all. You weren't so sober yourself last night, were you?" I said, "No sir."

At which point, he became very confused. He obviously had expected me to argue the point of my sobriety, which I didn't. Because there was nothing to argue, I hadn't been too sober. Let's face it.

So he hummed and hawed a bit and finally said, "Well you carrying your liquor like a gentleman, we'll forget that." So I said, "Is that all sir?" He said, "No, that is not all. Until last night, I thought you were the finest young officer I had ever seen in the United States Navy. I haven't changed my opinion."

At this point, his voice broke and the control of his body broke down. He jumped up and down and banged on his desk and said, "I have reversed it." I said, "Commander is that all sir?" He said, "Yes, stand your watch." And I did. It was a very taut watch, I can assure you.

One shouldn't tell stories of that nature about that type of officer, I think, without telling another story that might put the officer in better perspective.

One morning I was due to relieve my classmate, Abdil, on the eight to twelve watch. I went up at the usual time, about twenty minutes of eight. I read the morning orders carefully and saw that they were very involved, very fast-moving, and that the most important mission which had not been reached yet was the sending away of a second motor boat on a errand.

Abdil was a very efficient and able officer. I wouldn't like to have anything implied that he hadn't done a good job on the four to eight watch.

But sometimes engines and boats don't start, sometimes boat crews are not as prompt in coming alongside as they should be. This boat should have been sent about ten minutes before I said, "I relieve you sir."

I turned to the bugler and said, "Bugler, call away second motor boat double time." Before the second motor boat came alongside, Commander Haines was alongside of me. He started bawling me out.

I had heard him bawl many people out. In fact, he'd bawled me out before. But I'd never heard him quite as mean in a bawling out as he was on this occasion.

I was standing where I could see the clock in the officer of the deck's booth. I tried to break in a couple of times, but was not allowed to. When I finally was able to break in, he had just finished saying, "If you can't carry out my orders any better than that, I'll carry them out myself."

At this point I said, "Commander, I've had the deck now for seven minutes. Six minutes of that time you have been preventing me from carrying out your morning orders. I hope, sir, that you can do better than I."

I handed him the spyglass, which he was so surprised he took. I asked his permission to leave and started to do so. Whereupon he called me back, thrust the spyglass into my hand and told me to resume my duties as officer of the deck.

About two hours later after things had gotten calmed down a bit and we'd gotten through most of the hectic part of the morning orders, he came up and caught me by the elbow. He said, "Look let's go back by number five turret."

When we got back there, out of earshot of anyone else, he said. "I want to apologize to you. I had no right to say the things to you that I said this morning. I want you to accept my apology and forget it."

This is the side of Gordon W. Haines that very few people knew. Because it isn't easy for someone who is normally harsh in the performance of his duties to admit that he's wrong. I'm sure that it was even more difficult for someone like Gordon W. Haines to admit that he had been wrong. But he did do so.

Years later when I was on a submarine going out of commission in Philadelphia, I was down in the engine room. I'd been inspecting machinery that had been coated with rust etc. So I wasn't exactly a fashion plate model. My clothes were a little wrinkled and my hands were covered with grease. A messenger arrived and informed me that a

Captain wanted to speak to me on topside. I got some rags and got off as much grease as I could and went up topside.

There stood Captain Gordon W. Haines, immaculate, beautiful gold braid, well-brushed blue uniform. He was always immaculate, as I recall him.

He was a bachelor, I believe, and seemed to have the wherewithall to dress very very well. He had a good tailor and he was always a good example to young officers as to how to look as a naval officer.

He told me that he had just learned that I was in the yard on this submarine, and that he was the senior destroyer officer at the yard. He just wanted me to know that if there were anything that he could do to assist me while I was there that he'd be most happy to do so.

This also is a side of the Gordon W. Haines type that isn't always seen, because only I and he were there. Whereas the times that he bawled out the first Lieutenant on the NEW YORK, many people were there very often.

I think that when one hears stories about these old timers who were such difficult individuals, one should realize that many of them wanted to be good guys. But their sense of duty was translated, under the circumstances then obtaining, into a harshness that sometimes was not very easy for a young officer to understand.

Q: Did Haines attain flag rank?

Austin: No, he did not.

He commanded a cruiser. He was very well liked by his seniors, I believe. He was highly regarded by his seniors. But unfortunately, many of his juniors did not like him.

During World War II, I went into New York harbor as Commanding Officer Destroyers one evening. A former messmate, Bob McFarlane, was commanding another ship and got in touch with me and suggested we go ashore for dinner together. Which we did.

During dinner Bob asked me, "Count do you realize that every J.O. on our ship under Gordon Haines is commanding a ship in this war today?" I said, "No Bob, I didn't." He said, "I just sort of went down our J.O. list the other day. That's a fact. Every one of them that's still alive is commanding a ship today."

So some of that training, that seemed harsh, might have been in the long run conducive to a competence in time of stress and strain, such as war, that it was worth the experience.

Q: You mentioned that he was very well thought of by his superiors.

Austin: Yes, he was very highly regarded by his superiors I'm sure because I've heard them speak highly of him. We had a flag officer on board, and I know he had a very high regard for the Commander of the ship.

Q: Why do you suppose he was not promoted to flag rank? Did the fact that many of his juniors felt as they did militate against his attaining flag rank?

Austin: I think it must have, because he certainly went up the ladder as an executive officer of a battleship. He went to command one of our fine new cruisers, the MINNEAPOLIS. I think it was a surprise to him that he wasn't selected.

He had always been the type of officer who was always on board, always on the job, always highly competent in all of the things, such as seamanship and that sort of thing.

I think frankly that he must have been surprised not to be selected. Although I've always said, and I still think, that any officer who assumes that he is going to be selected for flag rank is being unwise. Because the number of fine Captains that come up to be considered each year is so great, and the number who can be selected for flag rank is so small, that I don't think anyone should ever assume that his previous performance is a shoo-in for flag rank.

Q: What you say about Captain Haines is interesting to me, because I have had contact with some men in the Army who attained the rank of Major General who seemingly, practically all during their career, were almost *cordially* hated by men who worked under them. And yet, they seem to have gotten by and were selected for General officer rank.

Austin: I don't like to say anthing that could be interpreted as being unkind to a sister service, but I think that the situation in the Army and in the Navy is quite different.

In the Army, the separation between the officer and enlisted men I think is greater than it is in the Navy. I think the separation between senior officer and less senior officer is greater.

On board ship, it has to be pretty much of a family situation. It's true, the Captain is the patriarch and he's the boss and everybody knows. The exec is his appointed alter ego, and everybody knows. But, there is a *camaraderie* and an understanding on board ship which is certainly greater than you could ever have on an Army post, for example.

Then there's another element here. That is that the ladies are not mixed up with professional reputations in the Navy nearly so much as they are in a service that is more on land, where the ladies can be present.

I think I can cite my experience in submarines and destroyers to sort of collaborate this general statement.

I had command of a single submarine for three years. During that time it was commended on several occasions for being a very smart ship. Yet I never had to raise my voice on that ship in three years.

I would stop and look at something that needed correction. It was corrected and probably a couple of things that I hadn't seen. It was just a joy to command a ship like that.

I don't think that ship was too different from many others of the same type. The thing is in a submarine particularly this element of necessity to trust each other and to depend upon each other is heightened more than it is even in other types of naval vessels.

I later commanded a destroyer. I tried very hard to get the same degree of camaraderie, the same degree of pride in the ship, the same degree of pride in our battle readiness. I practically broke my heart trying to get the same degree of all these things in the destroyer that I had had in the submarine with far less effort, but it was not possible. It was a bigger ship, and we didn't live quite as close together. We didn't understand each other's problems quite as well. We didn't have the same degree of mutual trust and interdependence.

For example on the submarine, the steward's mate was on an important valve at diving time. If he didn't do his job, you'd be just as likely to be in trouble as if a quartermaster first class, second class, or third class might not be alert and on the job.

So there was a feeling of interdependence. A feeling of — I've got to do my job, because all my shipmates are depending on me to do it. So this breeds a respect, a mutual respect, that is difficult to find in any other military organization.

Q: I suppose the Marines actually come closer to that concept perhaps than the Army.

Austin: I think the Marines have a very high esprit. I think that is partly due to the fact that they have a smaller organization than the Army. So, in a way, the same principal is applicable there, yes.

Interview # 8

Vice Admiral Bernard L. Austin, USN, Ret.

Rockville, Maryland

by Paul L. Hopper

March 6, 1970

Mr. Hopper: As I recall Admiral Austin, at the time we broke off the last time you had gotten out to the western Pacific and were beginning to be quite actively engaged in combat. Would you like to continue?

Admiral Austin: Paul, I don't know whether I covered the small operation called Baker Island operation, or not.

Shortly after the experience that I had as screen commander for Admiral Radford's task force during it's working up period, Admiral Radford was sent in command of a task force to neutralize Baker Island. I was sent as his screen commander.

During the operation we had rather vigorous reorientation from time to time, incident to Japanese planes being seen on our radar scopes. During one of these reorientations a carrier did not follow doctrine. As a result, it almost ran down one of the destroyers. Luckily the destroyer maneuvered in time to save his hull.

Admiral Radford saw the incident from his flag ship. He immediately came on the TBS and gave the carrier commanding officer a dressing down such as I never heard before or since, because he had violated doctrine and taken the truck driver's attitude that he was bigger than the other guy and had hogged the right of way. Which might have resulted, of course, in a sad situation such as the Australian carrier running through our own destroyer out in the Pacific when they were conducting exercises recently.

Admiral Radford was very keen in seeing that the destroyers were treated right on that operation. I think that my little talk with him had probably given him a better feel for some of our problems. He is, fundamentally, a fair minded individual.

After that operation my ships and I were sent on to the south Pacific, which was our destination.

Q: Is there anything that you could say particularly about the Baker Island operation that would be of interest?

Austin: I don't believe that it was enough of an operation to warrant it. We were able to shoot down all the Japanese snoopers who came out to see what the hell we were doing out there. As a result, we had a very successful operation with no losses to our side and several to the other side. We accomplished our mission with mimimun cost.

It was not a strongly opposed situation. The opposition was in the air. That was, frankly, well within the competence of our carrier planes to cope with. So it was just a small operation.

When we got to the south Pacific, I was reminded of an experience which I don't recall having told you about.

When I was fitting out my destroyer in Boston, I was mindful of the fact that electronic spares were very scarce in the south Pacific. I'd had correspondence with some of my contemporaries down there and I knew that this was a very vital thing in the south Pacific.

So I called my young supply officer up and instructed him to make absolutely certain that we had our full set of spares on board. He had difficulty doing this, and I had to help him out. We got our spares on board.

Then I called my electronics chap up and I said, "I want to know the list of those electronic spares which have the highest usage rate in our equipments." So he brought me the list. Then I said, "Now I want to get individual parts of these very high usage rate spares." We also had difficulty when we started to do that, because the supply officer thought we were being a little on the hoggish side and he didn't want to honor our request. But with a little personal attention we finally got them.

So when we got down there, the first thing that happened was what I had anticipated. We had visitors from the tender, from other ships begging to know if we had such and such electronic spares to get their equipment back in operation. Luckily we did have, so we were a welcome group of ships.

The situation at that time in the south Pacific was rather nip and tuck. We had just had the sad loss of several of our cruisers.

Q: Would you point out the time, Count?

Austin: I believe it was November of '43.

I remember the morning after we arrived, the SELFRIDGE came limping into port without it's bow. The front end of the ship had just been lost, just forward of the bridge.

The tempo of operations was quite high. There was not time really to get a reasonable amount of rest between operations up the Slot, as they called it.

Our task force commander, Admiral Tip Merrill, who was in his cruiser flag ship, quite wisely I think used his destroyers for these night prowls rather than mixing cruisers up among them. This was not only wise from the viewpoint of saving the few cruisers we had left down there, but it also made the operation a little simpler from the destroyers viewpoint. Because at night, even with the help of radar, things can get confused.

Q: Big ships are better targets too.

Austin: The big ships are better targets. So frankly I think he was quite correct in using his destroyers on these night prowls.

The operations were usually that we'd leave Tulagi somewhere around five o'clock in the afternoon, depending on how far up the Slot we were going, and we would have our rendezvous with anyone that we were rendezvousing with well after dark.

One night we were sent up to go through a little strait between Kolombangara and a little island to the west of it. I think the name of it was Choiseul. This Gizo Strait was very narrow and Japanese were on both sides. It's understandable that one would have some reluctance going through it under unfavorable conditions.

The operation for the night called for us to rendezvous with another group of destroyers that had gone around the northern end of Kolombangara. We were to come in from the south, through Gizo, and do a pincer movement on a Japanese replenishment operation that was coming from the north and west.

So just as we were starting through Gizo Strait, we saw lots of gunfire up to the north of us. The squadron commander came up on the TBS to me, I was the second in command, the division commander under the squadron commander, and said, "I think we'd better turn around. It looks like we're going into something pretty heavy up there." I said, "But Commodore, we can't turn around. That's Duke Chandler up there. The enemy wouldn't be firing at themselves and so it must be

Duke that they're firing at. He may need our help."
So the Commodore did go on through, we did go to Duke's aid, and it was Duke.

Duke Chandler later became President of William and Mary down in Williamsburg.

He was a very good destroyer officer. I couldn't very well see Duke left up there at a disadvantage, when here we had all that squadron of fire power down there, just because it was a little risky to go through there.

In the interest of historical accuracy I think I should say that this was the last operation for this particular squadron commander. After this he was relieved by Arleigh Burke.

We had mixed emotions in this squadron, at losing this squadron commander. He was a very fine man, he was a jolly fellow, he was a likable fellow, and yet he was not quite tempermentally suited for the kind of warfare that we were up against at the time. He, I think, was a little too humanitarian. He probably hated to take his ships in to situations where he knew he was going to get some mauling. You just had to do that in those days down there, it was that kind of a war.

So I had a very kindly feeling for him, but I was pleased to have a more aggressive commander to replace him. That's why that's a little delicate, and I haven't used his name.

Our operations down there were pretty much stereotyped, except for very few. There were a few that stood out. Most of them were simply going up the Slot, trying to be as inconspicuous as possible, and be where the Japanese were trying to land reinforcements for the places that we were trying to eventually take. We were working our way up to the north.

We had one experience one night. Our motor toperdo boats were working in that area too. I could hear the motor torpedo boats talking to each other on their voice circuit. The leader of the group said, "I've got them in view. You go in from the starboard bow, I'll go in from the port bow, and we'll blow them out of the water." I came up on the TBS on his frequency that I was listening on, I said, "You'd better not try to blow us out of the water, because we're U. S. just like you are. If you come within range of my five inch guns, we're going to blow you out of the water, because we've got you on our screen." We didn't have any more trouble with those boys that night.

As I say, most of these operations were pretty much of a stereotype nature, except for the Bougainville operation and for the Buka bombardment. And the action off Buka, where we intercepted an attempted evacuation of aviation personnel from Buka. I'll cover those, if you want, one by one.

The largest of these engagements was one in which the cruisers participated, because we were sent as a task force to interpose ourselves between Japanese task forces, which were coming down to intercept our landings on Bougainville.

We had to send the destroyers in for refueling on the day before this night battle. Arleigh Burke took his division in first. We had a little fuel stashed away down there near Kolombangara. So he took his division in first and got his fuel. I was due to go in after he got back, and give my boys a drink. But, unfortunately by the time Arleigh got back we had Japanese task forces showing up on our screen. So I wasn't allowed to go in for fuel.

The combatant ships of this task force were in a column with Arleigh's division of destroyers in the lead, then the cruisers, and then my division in the rear. So when we made contact that night, the ships were coming in from our port bow formation from the north and west. Due to the displacement, Burke could get them on his radar before I could get them on mine, because they were coming from his direction.

So Admiral Merrill released Burke's division to go in for torpedo attack on this task force, but he wouldn't release me.

So finally when I reported to him that I had the task force on my screen, and could I be released, he said, "All right, if you have them on your screen, go ahead."

So I gave a signal to break away from the column by simultaneous movements. One of the ships of my division executed it wrong, so he got kind of left behind for the time being. He finally caught up.

This is an interesting point about this engagement - this is the first time that I had ever had all four ships of my division together under my command. And it was in a night battle.

That's the kind of situation we were up against in World War II, not just as an exception, but many times. People were short on opportunites to train together for the real thing that they were going to have to face, because of the lack of ships in certain categories. The destroyers, of course, were always in short supply, always at a premium. So instead of giving us a chance to train as a division, they had to nip them off as soon as they were ready and send them to some job.

That was the first time that we had been able to operate together, and it was a night battle. I can tell you, even when you're well trained, a night battle can be very confusing

So we took off. As a result of this misinterpretation of the signal by one of the ships there was a slight collision between two of the ships of the division. But luckily it didn harm either one, it was just sort of a sideswipe. They were both going at pretty good speed, so if it hadn't been a sideswipe it could have been very bad news.

We were proceeding toward a part of the enemy formation which was a group of cruisers. I was up on the bridge during the early part of this. We began to get gunfire which was uncomfortably close to us from a ship up to the north of this group that we were attacking. They were proceeding in our direction silently and saying nothing to nobody.

So between the time that I went down from the bridge and the time that I got in the CIC, where I was going to conduct the torpedo attack, the CIC officer had confused the situation a little bit. Because when I asked him for the course and speed of this group of ships that I was making my approach on from the bridge, he thought I was making an approach on something else. He said, "Oh Commodore those are our ships." I said, "I think you're wrong." He said, "No sir. I've been tracking those ever since we've been in this formation. Those are our cruisers."

I couldn't believe it, but you don't shoot torpedoes at your own cruisers - it was the same number and all - and I had to take in to account that he had been down there without anything to bother him except to do his tracking and had been tracking them all the time. He was so emphatic in his opinion that I said, "All right. Give me then the course and speed of this fellow to the north. I know he's not one of ours, because he's been shooting at us."

So we missed one of our most golden opportunities to fire a salvo of torpedoes into a cruiser division of the Japanese navy, on that occasion, because of the confusion of the battle and the unwillingness of the division commander to shoot at three cuirsers that his CIC officer assured him emphatically were his own.

Q: But it could have been otherwise.

Austin: It could have been otherwise, he could have been right. And I could have been wrong.

So we did fire on the fellow that had been firing at us, and we were able to check him off as one of the casualities on the Japanese side. Somebody else had already hit him, so I don't think that our damage to him was needed, but it was delivered.

We then took off after a group that had been the target for Arleigh's division. After Arleigh's division had fired, they had turned away and had separated themselves quite a distance from this group, because one had turned this way and one had turned another way. So I took out after this group of ships.

During the time that we were being fired on by the ship that we did attack, we got one hit through our hull. As we persued the group to the northwest, I got a report that we were getting salt water in the fuel oil. So finally, we lost power. I had to have my Captain turn out of the formation and turn it over to the second in command of the division. Luckily we were able to regain suction on an uncontaminated tank of fuel oil and got moving again.

Shortly after we got moving again, we picked up a ship that was sort of lying dog-o. It was a destroyer type.

This time again I had conflict as to whether this was friend or enemy. It was the Captain this time that questioned whether or not it was friend or enemy. I told him to open fire on this ship. He said, "Oh Commodore, that ship is the THATCHER, one of our ships." I said, "No, it isn't, Captain." He said, "It certainly is, sir." I said, "I will give one TBS transmission to make you feel better. And then you open up, if we don't get any answer from THATCHER."

I said, "I have a ship bearing such and such distance approximately such and such from me. I'm about to open fire. If it's the THATCHER, speak up." No answer.

I said, "Captain open up." He again protested. I said, "Captain open fire." He opened fire, and as soon as we opened fire it opened fire at us. It was just waiting hoping we would be confused enough to think he was one of our people. But he turned out to be a true enemy. We were able to get it on fire.

Then the Captain reported to me, "Sir we're running out of ammunition. All we've got left is star shells." I said, "Captain, it's a hell of a way to use star shells, but if that's all we've got, shoot him with star shells."

We were closing all the time, so it was point blank range. The star shells did pretty good work. They helped to get the fire going.

Then Arleigh Burke's division came barging down and started shooting at the same ship. So we really polished that one off.

Incidentally during the period when I was chasing that group up to the northwest, Arleigh's division came back in and started straddling us. Which showed that we weren't the only ones having trouble keeping track of friend and foe.

I knew it was Arleigh's division that was shooting at us, so I called him on the TBS. I said, "For goodness sake, Arleigh, stop shooting at me. I'm trying to help you out here."

He always had a pretty good sense of humor, even in battle. He said, "Okay Count. I won't shoot anymore, but excuse the four salvos that are on the way."

Q: Why didn't you use the same tactic, when you were chasing the three cruisers, with the CIC man? By asking them to identify themselves?

Austin: Frankly, I don't think it was feasible because I was not up where I could see ships. I was down in the CIC at the time. I frankly don't think we had time.

8 Austin - 257

As Admiral Merrill told me when we got back from this battle, he said, "Count, God bless you. The next time we get in a night battle, don't get as close as you got to those cruisers of the Japs. I checked you and your whole division off. If they'd ever opened up, they could have blown you out of the water."

We were within 1300 yards of them, at the time that I had to make the fateful decision as to whether or not to shoot. That was sitting ducks, as far as we were concerned, with torpedoes 1300 yards. If you fire a salvo at a whole division, you can't miss, or you shouldn't miss. We would probably have lost some of our ships, if we had fired. But that's the name of the game.

I look upon it as one of my errors of the war, because I had to make a quick decision. You don't keep plowing in at 30 knots very long before you've eaten up 1300 yards. We were going in from the bow of this formation, so they were closing us. So I had to make an instant decision as to whether or not to shoot or turn away. In view of the strong protestations on the part of the CIC officer, I decided to not shoot.

You don't stay on a steady course for very long in a battle like that, because if you do you're a sitting duck. You do vary your course. In doing so, it was possible that if we'd worked our way back to our own cruisers or that they had worked their way towards us, while we we had been maneuvering, it was possible.

I was pretty certain I was right, but I wasn't dead certain. I frankly didn't think of testing them out with a voice message. With a whole division of enemy cruisers that close, you don't advertise your presence too much. They probably were on our voice circuits.

Q: That is odd that they didn't think about it, that they didn't open fire on you before you got that close realizing that you were probably trying to get in, or they thought you were going to get in, to shoot torpedoes.

Austin: It is, but it was a situation where they may not have known we were there. They didn't have as good surface radar in those days as we had. This was one of our big advantages over them. We had the SG radar and they didn't have anything comparable to it. They were depending on the old eyeball.

Q: Under the circumstances, from what you've said, they probably would have preferred to remain undetected anyway.

Austin: They would have preferred to have gotten past this task force intact. And been able to shoot up our landing force ships, the transports, cargo ships, and all.

Fortunately we were able to keep them from getting to their objective, which was our landing forces.

It was a successful encounter from our viewpoint. We didn't actually lose a single ship. One of my ships had to be towed home, because of damage it had gotten. The flag ship that I was in had to repair a hole in it's side and piping, but we were able to get back under our own power. So from our viewpoint, it was a very successful engagement. We were able to sink a few of the enemy, and we lost none.

We had some pretty unhappy moments on the way back the next day, because my particular ships were so low on fuel that we had to limp along at a very slow speed in order to get back to port. We had not been able to go in and refuel. The Japanese air took full advantage of this and hounded us pretty much on the way back. We had as many as 60 planes at a time coming at us, going right along straffing at bridge level. We were able to shoot down several of those.

Q: Our anti-aircraft aboard ships at that time were efficient, weren't they?

Austin: I would say reasonably so. When they came right down your gun barrel, you got them. But otherwise you shot lots of shots. At least it made it uncomfortable for them to get too near you to get the accuracy that they needed to do damage to you. Actually, I wouldn't say that our anti-aircraft capability was of the highest.

Q: It greatly improved during the war.

Austin: Oh yes. This was fairly early in the war, from our viewpoint. The first part of the war we were just recovering from the terrific blow of Pearl Harbor. And then getting ships out of builders yards at as quick a pace as possible, and not always properly put together.

Q: In fact, a lot of them were almost pasted together.

Austin: I had no complaint with the ships that I got from Bath, Maine. They were well built ships, but they had been started in time to get pretty good quality workmanship on them. They were the first of the 2100 tonners, among the first. Not the very first ships, because there were several ships that preceeded us. We were among the initial batch of 2100 tonners.

So much for the battle of Bougainville. Unless you have some questions —

Q: I think it would be interesting Count for you to describe what happened, if you will. For the simple reason I suppose that no two people's account of a battle always jive. I've read various accounts that Morison and various other people have developed about the battle. I think it would be rather interesting from your standpoint.

Austin: Of course, I only saw what I saw from my ship. I've given you a pretty good overlay of that. The various countermarches and all of the cruisers all this time, I wouldn't have first hand knowledge of it. I'd be repeating to you what I've read, and I don't think that's in the best interest of history.

Shall we go on to the night we intercepted the Japanese task force off Buka?

During war many operation orders are pretty involved and rather long. I look back upon the order that we got sending us to this battle as probably the optimum in brevity of wartime orders. It came from Admiral Halsey.

Substantively it was as follows: "Highly reliable intelligence reports indicate enemy will attempt to evacuate 800 aviation personnel and technicians from Buka tonight. X-ray, you know what to do." End of operation order.

We received this in the middle of our taking on board fuel and ammunition to replenish what we had used up the night before. Arleigh asked me to come over to his ship and talk it over. He wanted to know first how the rearming and refueling was going on my ships, and I gave him a curb stone estimate.

He said, "Let's pick an hour that we'll get underway here. Let's take the chart and step this off."

So we took the chart and stepped it off. Then he said, "If we leave here by such and such a time, we ought to be able to get up there all right. Then we'll have better fuel status and ammunition status." So that's what we did.

We set a time to get underway. We worked pretty much like the beavers that we were called getting stuff aboard in the meantime. You can always speed things up a little bit you know, if you have to.

When we got underway, we were pretty close to but not fully rearmed and refueled. We were safely on the good side.

On the way up Arleigh sent to me his detailed plan for the night and asked for my comments. I always tried to be as good a kibitzer as I could. I felt that that was one of my main functions, to be the devil's advocate. So I tried to find some flaws with his plan and I couldn't. So I told him so.

It turned out that he was pretty accurate in his planning. We set a point at which we would intercept this task force, and we set a time. I believe the time was midnight.

Believe it or not, about a quarter of twelve we made contact by radar with the task force. We both went in for torpedo attack. We were cruising in two columns. So when he gave the word, we went in for torpedo attack in accordance with previous doctrine .

We had some luck with a couple of ships in the first foray. And then, of course, the enemy task force split. Arleigh told me to take one part, and he took the other part of the retreating ships.

One of the ships that I was chasing, I got on fire and dead in the water. Then I started after the second one.

Arleigh, in the meantime, saw what I was doing. In fact, I reported that I had one ship dead in the water and on fire and that I was taking out after the other one. He said, "No you don't. You stay and see it sink."

I made my views rather clear in a few words, and implored him to let me take out after the fellow that was still unharmed. He reiterated in a most emphatic manner his desire that I see the ship sink.

I had to turn around, because I was already on my chase. I turned around, I went back to take this ship under fire again. During the time that I was firing at this ship that was disabled, I received a torpedo hit in the engine room. It, luckily, didn't explode. But it did bend the frame in the engine room and put a little dimple in the side of the ship. But luckily, the Japanese had some torpedoes that didn't go off, the same as we did. Or I wouldn't be telling you the story probably.

When I saw my enemy ship sink, I took off as quickly as possible. I used a little imagination on the last bit of her sad end.

I took out after the ship that I had been chasing but it was too late. She had gotten quite a head start on me.

Arleigh, in the meantime, had had pretty fair success with the ships that he was chasing. He had gotten one of them. The other one was away toward Rabaul, where their home port was.

So we chased these two ships the rest of the night. We had Rabaul on our radar, when Arleigh with his usual enthusiam came up on the TBS and said, "If necessary we'll chase them right into Rabual harbor. They'll stop there, by george." I said, "Arleigh, if we do I hope that those Japanese fuel oil fittings fit our hoses, because I'm going to be out of fuel by the time we get there. I expect you will be too." Arleigh said, "I get it, I get it." Then he gave the order to reverse course.

The Japanese missed a golden opportunity the next morning, because when we were able to get our fuel soundings we had so little fuel left that we had to proceed at a very slow speed all the way back to our base. Arleigh requested air cover at dawn, because we were right under the guns.

The air cover didn't arrive at dawn, but I think the Japs thought it was a trap. I think that they thought that we were ordered to poke along out there just to entice them to send out air which would then be shot down by high air cover that they thought we had.

Anyway, we were able to limp back in at slow speed. But it was a pretty uneasy time, knowing that you're out of ammunition, that you are out of fuel oil, and that you are so far from home. If they had sent out an air attack on us, it would have been pretty sad.

Admiral Halsey was very pleased with the results of his very brief operation order. I went through his headquarters, while on leave for rest and recreation to Australia, with my division, not long after that. He received me and spoke of the battle in very praiseworthy terms. In fact he said he considered it the Trafalgar of the present war.

It was a gain, a successful battle from our viewpoint. Because we lost zero ships, and we did impose pretty severe penalty on the enemy because the personnel that they had on those ships that night were high critical to them at that time. It's always valuable personnel, highly trained technicians in the aviation, and pilots. It was definitely a good show.

Q: I've oftentimes wondered if the situation could not easily arise where a ship would practically have to sit still in the water because it was running out of fuel.

Austin: Oh yes.

Q: Could it get down to that really?

Austin: You try not to.

Q: In the midst of a battle, and a long chase, and then back home might require more fuel than you estimated would be needed.

Austin: We were so low on fuel that morning, if we had run at a speed of 12 knots we would have been out of fuel before we got home. That's how low we were. Fortunately, the slower you run the less oil you use per mile in a ship. So you can go a long way on a little bit of oil if you can go slow enough. Going slow, when you're within reach of the enemy's air, is not a comfortable situation to put yourself in.

Interview # 9

Vice Admiral Bernard L. Austin, USN, Ret.
Rockville, Maryland
by Paul Hopper
March 28, 1970

Mr. Hopper: Count, would you like to continue on from where we left off last time?

Admiral Austin: Paul, I believe we left off with me going with my division to Sydney, Australia for a leave and recreation period of ten days.

The night before we arrived in Sydney, I received orders detaching me immediately on arrival and directing me to report to Commander Destroyers Pacific for duty as a squadron commander of squadron 14. The orders read to Captain B. L. Austin.

At that time, so far as I knew, I was a Commander. So I questioned the receipt of the message and was assured by the radioman that it was plainly spelled out, C a p t a i n.

When I went ashore and reported to the senior officer present of the U. S. Navy in Sydney for transportation to Pearl, he informed me that he did not have any indication of my having been promoted to Captain, although my orders read that way. He, therefore, expressed a great regret that he could not assign a car and driver to me during the short time I was to be there before my transportation took me out.

Fortunately for me, I did get a couple of days at Sydney because the air transportation was a little fogged up. My turn didn't come until Christmas Eve.

I spent Christmas Eve and Christmas in a rather crowded plane with many other military personnel, all ratings and ranks, heading toward Pearl Harbor. The plane was so crowded that we took turns sitting down and lying down on the way up, because it was not what one might call a plush configuration.

On arrival in Pearl Harbor, I reported to Commander Destroyers Pacific. He expressed a great concern over the fact that I had been assigned to a squadron commander's job and not been promoted to Captain. He showed me a dispatch which he had sent to the Bureau of Personnel on the subject.

A few days later he received a reply, which simply referred him to a dispatch which they had sent to him some three months before, naming me among a few others who were to be promoted to Captain if the Commander Destroyers Pacific concurred. This, in some way, had found itself a little secluded nitch in Commander Destroyers Pacific's files and had never been shown to him.

So I was forthwith promoted to Captain, but I don't think I ever got the back pay. I think the rule at that time was you didn't get on the paymaster's roles until you actually were promoted.

As you know, the promotion system was somewhat discomboluated during the war.

I went to my little flag ship, which was then in the Navy yard getting ready for the next operation. Very shortly that operation commenced.

My assignment was to escort a cruiser group that was assigned various bombardment tasks. Then, on the actual assault on the islands, I was assigned to the Kwajalein end of the show and given a direct control of our little missile ships. This was probably among the first, if not the first, use of missiles by our Navy in a real assault.

We had these little ships just loaded with missiles, but they didn't have very much room left for communications equipment. So at the conference prior to sailing, I raised the question with the task force communication officer as to how I was going to communicate with these little ships.

He said, "By flag hoist, I guess." I said, "In the heat of battle there, flag hoists may be flying the wrong direction. We're going to be operating those little fellows within stone's throw of the beach, because that's the only range that their missiles have got. I wonder if we couldn't equip each one of them with a walkie-talkie."

He thought that wasn't a bad idea. So I got myself a walkie-talkie and got each one of them a walkie-talkie installed.

So that, when they came steaming down in column and I wanted to turn them to have their broadsides to the beach all I had to do was to give commands over the walkie-talkie and they all got it beautifully despite the bang bank bang of the bombardment from the other ships.

We took those little fellows within a thousand yards of the beach. Actually during this show I had to be in close enough to talk with the walkie-talkie to them. So I was in very close for a destroyer's draft. The flag Captain was a little concerned about running aground.

Actually we took enemy lines under fire with 40 milimeter guns. So it was a close bit of combat. Without binoculars, you could see the enemy moving around over there.

According to plan we weren't supposed to fire at individual groups of the enemy soldiers. We were given bombardment assignments, but not targets of opportunity on the ground

So the Captain asked for permission to fire at these enemy groups that he could see setting up machine guns to fire at us, he wanted to fire first. So I gave him permission. It was all right, no one criticized me for it because they were obvisouly enemy troops, our troops had not reached that point yet. We were so close that we could see very well how the battle was progressing.

Then after the assault was completed and we were consolidating, Admiral Turner assigned me the task of commanding the screening operations around that part of the atoll. In other words, assigning ships to take their turns reguarding the various passes.

I was doing all right, until I found that he was grabbing off some of my destroyers without telling me about it. I improvised for awhile, then I saw this just wasn't working too well.

So I went aboard his flag ship and spoke to his chief of staff about it. He said, "Oh yes, I know. Admiral Turner gave you a job to do, and now he's taking the ships that you've got to do it with. You'd better not talk to him, he's not in a good mood today. He does that you know, from time to time."

I said, "I will talk to him, because this show won't run this way. I'm going to think somebody's on a station out there, and he's not going to be there because Admiral Turner will send him some other place and I haven't got the news."

With some reluctance, I was allowed to see Admiral Turner. As soon as I pointed it out to him, he was very nice about it. He said, "Why sure, you're darn right. It won't work, my taking ships off that you think are working in your schedule. I want you to keep the job of being responsible to me for all these entrances being properly guarded. I'll tell you when I want a destroyer sent some place, and then that way we won't have them supposedly in two places." So we had no problem.

Chiefs of Staff sometimes, I think, tried to protect their boss from frequent callers and people that they think will annoy him and will raise his blood pressure.

This was Admiral Kelly Turner, the one who was in charge of the amphibious operations pretty well up the line. He was the overall amphibious poncho and he did a good job. I think he probably tried to do more than any human is capable of doing, yet he was quite successful.

After this operation, I was back in Pearl Harbor getting ready for the next operation. The Chief of Staff Commander Destroyers Pacific, called me and said the Admiral would like to see me and was sending his car for me.

I thought they had a little board of investigation that they had to toss in somebody's lap. Because when they send their car for you, they want to hand you something that may be slightly warm.

When I got over there, I misguessed this. Admiral Kauffman told me that he wanted me to come to his staff as his operations and training officer. I tried to beg off.

I said, "Admiral, I don't think this is fair. I've worked my way up from Commander of a destroyer to division commander and now squadron commander. I've only had one operation and I don't think it's quite fair to pull me off and foreshorten my tour."

He smiled and said, "I thought you'd take that attitude. I've got a proposition to make to you. You've got an old squadron. How would you like to have a brand new one? With your seniority it would take you a long time to work up to a new squadron. You've been out of the states for a long time and you need a chance to get reacquainted with your family. If you come on my staff as my operations and training officer for six months, I'll send you back and guarantee you that you'll get a brand new squadron."

I said, "Sir, your offer is very generous and I'll be happy to accept."

About three months after I'd gone on his staff as operations and training officer, he came back one morning from Admiral Nimitz's morning conference and called me in. He said, "I made you a promise in all good faith. I know that you've been looking forward to going back, getting a chance to see your family, having a few weeks or maybe a month or so in the states before you bring out a new squadron. Admiral Nimitz told me this morning he wants you on his staff Monday morning. There goes this promise, and there goes the new squadron."

So I went up to see my friend Preston Mercer, who was the one that I was to relieve, a classmate of mine and a good friend. I asked him if there wasn't some way to get out of this gracefully. I told him that I'd been promised this new squadron and this came as kind of a shock, and I knew that if I came on the staff there I wouldn't get back to any other duty for a long time.

He said, "No. Frankly, Count, Admiral Towers doesn't like me, and has put the heat on Admiral Nimitz to have me replaced. Admiral Nimitz asked for nominations for my relief from BuPers. Yours was one of only two names that Admiral Towers would accept. And that he'd be happy with. The other one is Everett Abdil, who's in the middle of an operation as Chief of Staff to Admiral Struble in the Philippines, and Admiral Nimitz won't pull him off the job right in the middle of an operation. So you're it."

So I moved to Admiral Nimitz's staff at that time. When I relieved my good friend, Preston Mercer, as assistant Chief of Staff for administration to Admiral Nimitz, he pointed to his incoming basket which was heavily laden and warned me that things flowed through that basket and it was very difficult to ever see the bottom of it.

The first night in the job I saw the bottom of the basket at about 3:30 in the morning. So I started off with a clean basket the next morning, but it wasn't for long that it stayed clean because it came in faster than I could handle it.

One of the things that Captain Mercer impressed upon me was that Admiral Nimitz was very much opposed to increasing the size of his staff. I made a sort of study of my areas of responsibility. Personnel management was handling every single man and officer in the Pacific Ocean area and in the Pacific fleet. They were cramped into a rather small area. They had built a mezzanine in it and had people typing right over other people. It was not what an efficiency expert would call the ideal office arrangement for maximum efficiency.

The first day two yeomen brought in the personnel documents that I had to sign as Assistant Chief of Staff for administration, according to the then existing staff regulations. These stacks, that the two yeomen brought in, approximated about a foot and a half high each.

I found out quite soon that I wasn't able to even peruse, or swiftly find out, what I was signing and get through all these in time to be ready for the next onslaught.

So despite the warning of Captain Mercer, I had the personnel officer in and discussed the situation with him. I studied his personnel allowance in his division. I then made a recommendation to Admiral Nimitz.

That recommendation in essence was, "We should not handle all the personnel papers for the entire fleet and the Pacific Ocean areas on his staff if he wanted it done properly and if he wanted his staff kept small."

He was very reasonable. He said, "I think you have a good point. Now tomorrow, just bring in your daily take of personnel papers and let me see what the nature of them is."

So the next morning the two yeomen came in and their stacks were a little higher than usual, I guess, because they were about two feet high apiece this time.

So I told them not to put them on my desk, just hold them, and I'd see if Admiral Nimitz was free. He was able to receive us, so I took them right on in.

Admiral Nimitz just took one look at them and said, "I think your point is well made. Draw me up a specific recommendation as to what you want to do about it."

So I gave him a specific recommendation and a memorandum promptly before he changed his mind, before somebody else might get to him.

My recommendation was that we transfer all enlisted personnel administration to the service force and equip them with the necessary business machines to facilitate the handling of the personnel papers. And that we also transfer to the service force the routine orders and other personnel matters having to do with all officers below the rank of Captain.

Admiral Nimitz read my recommendation and he said, "I think this is all right, except for one thing. I want to include Commanders in the category of officers to be handled entirely by my staff."

So we changed that, and transferred the personnel management to the service force. We built them some big quonset huts down in the flat area there. We got some business machines in and got the personnel management on a sort of real modern up to date basis, without increasing his staff.

But there were certain areas where it was not possible to cope with the situation, without increasing Admiral Nimitz's staff. One of those was the direction of the mail.

I made it a habit to take a turn around the headquarters every night when I left my office to go to my quarters. I noticed that no matter how late my walk around was the mail liasion section was always still working. And that all the personnel assigned to it were always there.

One night I was making my rounds about 2:30 in the morning, I went into the mail liasion section and spoke to the officer in charge. I took a deliberately antagonizing attitude. I said, "Why don't you people do your work in the daytime?" I've never seen a more hurt-looking expression come over a fellow's face. This young Lieutenant looked at me and said, "Sir, we work all day. We just can't get our work done just during the daytime."

He pointed to these stacks of dispatches that they had to go over to glean out their information for their daily mail dispatch to all the post offices telling them where to send the mail to different ships and units.

I said, "Why can't you get your work done in the daytime?" He said, "Sir, look at the dispatches we have to go through. It's no good for us to tell them to send the mail to the wrong place." I said, "When you get your mail dispatches made up for the day, then do you go back and check it?" He said, "No sir, we'd never get to work on the next day, if we did that."

I said, "So mistakes are made." He said, "Yes sir, I guess so." I said, "It looks to me like you need some help." His face brightened up a little bit and he said, "Yes sir, we sure do." I said, "Well, you have three people working in here don't you?" "Yes, sir." I said, "Well, I think you need some help."

So the next morning I went to Admiral Nimitz. I told him I thought he wanted the mail to go where the men were, and not where they'd been. And that I had made these observations the night before, and they were backed up by my previous observations as I had made my rounds of headquarters. Therefore, I recommended 100 percent increase in staff of the mail room. In other words, add three more.

He didn't even hesitate. Always when I made a recommendation to him, I had a written memorandum that he could either approve or disapprove, by initialing opposite, "approve" --- or "disapprove" ---. He reached for his pen and wrote, CWN opposite "approve" and handed it back to me.

Another area of the staff that was very much undermanned, and which had become a concern of the Secretary of the Navy, was the public relations part of the staff. Captain Waldo Drake was the head of the public relations division. This also came under my overall responsibility.

So I got Drake down in my office and discussed the problem of public relations with him. He gave me the same story that Captain Mercer had. He said, "Well, I have to do most of it myself, because Admiral Nimitz doesn't want to increase his staff." I said, "That's true, Admiral Nimitz doesn't want to increase his staff any more than is necessary. But I'm sure that Admiral Nimitz wants us to do a proper job of public relations. I notice that there is some correspondence with the Secretary of the Navy about this, pointing out the lack of coverage of the fleet activities out here compared to the coverage that is given other facets of the war, and pointing out that the American people are interested in the Pacific fleet and their activities in the Pacific Ocean area. And many of them have sons out here, brothers, cousins, fathers. I feel that we have to do a proper job. I deduce from our conversation that you recognize that we're not doing as much as we should."

He said, "That's right. If we had proper organization we could cater to all these different media."

I said, "You draw up for me, with the help of your staff, the organization that, in the light of your experience here, would be able to cope adequately with the need to know, and the desire to know on the part of the various media, and bring it down to me."

A few days later he came down with a large piece of paper which had quite an organization. Of course there were different sections of his division, the spot news, background information magazines, and various catagories. It was a little overdone, I felt. I said, "This is fine, you've done exactly what I told you. Now let's sit down, roll up our sleeves, and get practical. We know that Admiral Nimitz would not be too happy to authorize this sort of an organization. Let's hold down to one magazine media type section, one picture section, one news section, and so on."

He was quite agreeable to this. He said, "I agree. I just did what you told me to."

So after we had revamped it and he had redone it, I took it in to Admiral Nimitz with my fingers crossed a little bit. Because it was a sizable increase over what we then had.

I showed it to Admiral Nimitz and he looked it over very carefully. He asked me if I had thought this all through, and I said I had. He wanted to know if I recommended it, and I said I did. He reached for his pen, and wrote on it, 'okay, C.W.N."

I took it back out and gave it to Drake. Drake was so used to running a one-man show, that even after I got him the 'okay, C.W.N.' on that organization chart, things didn't change much. He couldn't delegate.

So I had him down and we discussed this. His reason for not proceeding faster with the reorganization was that he was very anxious to get just the right people in all these spots. He had been negotiating for them, but just hadn't gotten the right people yet.

So I said, "Admiral Nimitz's staff has pretty high priority with any personnel organization. We have lots of personnel flow through our hands here every day. There is no excuse for his staff not getting the number of bodies we need, and getting them quickly."

He said, "You know, we've got to get somebody that has a background in these areas." I said, "That's desirable, yes. But I think there comes a time when it's more important to get someone in there doing the job than to wait for perfect men."

To make a long story short - Waldo was moving a little slowly. I heard about a classmate of mine named Min Miller, who had done a very fine job on the picture side over in the European theater. So I requested that he be sent out to head up our picture section. I discussed it with Drake first.

Yes, he'd heard of him, and thought the'd be a man of the right background. So I got BuPers to send Miller out to us.

Shortly after Miller arrived, Drake went off on an operation to handle the news of the operation. That left Miller as the senior officer left behind.

Miller was not a shrinking violet, he was an aggressive type of individual. So while Drake was away he was sort of moving in to number one position, not entirely on a temporary basis.

He came down to me one day with papers that he thought demonstrated that Drake wasn't quite the guy to head the organization. I said, "Where did you get these?" He took them out of Drake's personal safe.

I said, "We don't play ball that way. These are private and they're somewhat of a personal nature. Drake is doing his job all right. We don't intend to use this against him."

Miller was in high favor with the Secretary of the Navy, and knew it. In fact, I think he was probably corresponding behind the scenes without doing things through the channels.

So I tried to give Drake a good chance to keep his head above water and in control, but with Miller there it was very difficult for him. Miller was a faster operator than Drake.

Admiral Nimitz got pressure from the Secretary of the Navy to put Miller in charge. Admiral Nimitz called me in and discussed it with me.

In fact, one day when we were discussing the situation, he said, "Are you trying to get rid of Drake?" I said, "No Admiral, I'm not trying to get rid of Drake. Waldo is a very fine man and a good news man. He's certainly loyal, he works hard. But he's a one-man show type. I haven't found that he is as adept at delegating authority and holding people responsible for the use of that authority as he should be to head up an organization such as your public relations organization."

Then he wanted to know what I thought about Miller. I told him that I thought Miller was an aggressive type of chap and that he was one that would run a pretty smart operation. I didn't tell him about the filching of Waldo's papers, that was just between Miller and me and between Miller and Drake.

This resulted in Admiral Nimitz finally agreeing to Waldo being given a job in Washington in the office of public relations, and making way for Miller to take over.

We did have a more modern up to date organization in the public relations field after that. It was a situation which I think had been left behind as the Pacific fleet and the Pacific Ocean area expanded. The public relations organization had not expanded with it. So it would have been not easy to get it caught up with the rest of the organization without some upheaval.

The overall situation on the administrative side was in very good shape. We had a very fine and able young reserve officer who was in charge of the detailed handling of air priorities in the Pacific. That also came under the administrative Assistant Chief of Staff.

Very seldom did the assistant Chief of Staff of Administration have to personally make a priority decision, because he had daily contact with his air priorities boss and he established policies and varied the policies to the varying conditions.

But every now and then a situation would arise that required the personal decision of the Assistant Chief of Staff for administration.

One of those occasions was when a Marine General, who had been a neighbor of mine in Belle Haven, appeared at the air priorities office and represented that he had great need of so much cargo space for front line equipment right away.

When the air priorities officer came up to see me about this, he said that the General was so convincing that he didn't stop to question him about the itemization of this front line equipment. So he was a little bit shocked when he happened to be walking out where they were loading this plane that he had made available, and one of the boxes of equipment was leaking. So he got in touch with the General and told him that he was awfully sorry but he couldn't put liquor on a front line overriding priority basis.

The General was very embarrassed. Yet the General had insisted that this was needed urgently by the troops, it was on Okinawa I believe. So the air priorities officer had no recourse than to say, "I'm sorry, but you'll have to see Commodore Austin."

So up came the General, very much embarrassed. I told him that I had to back up my air priorities officer because he was right. But I said, "General we can get your liquor out there for you, but we just can't give it an overriding priority. For example, right now we're shipping 81 millimeter howitzer ammunition by air. That's how tight things are there on air transport. We can't give an overriding priority to your bottle goods. We will top load it as we have space to carry it. We'll get it there. You know, they can't drink it all at one swallow anyhow." He said, "Well, they can drink it pretty fast."

Even some times, it was necessary to go to Admiral Nimitz. Because after all, we were just acting in his stead.

We had one application for civilian priority back to the mainland. The air priorities officer turned it down. It was appealed to me. I got in touch with the company of which this fellow was nominally the president. The officer of the company, to whom I talked, said, "No, we do not request that an air priority be granted for him in the name of this company. In fact, we don't want him back in Washington. He gums up our works more than he helps."

So this fellow went to Admiral Towers and Admiral Towers went to Admiral Nimitz. Admiral Towers was pretty easy to work with. He would have come to me on something like this, but this was a personal friend of his. So he wanted to be sure he got it, and he'd been told that I'd turned it down. So he went directly to Admiral Nimitz.

Admiral Nimitz had me in and wanted to know why I'd turned this man down. He was president of this company, the company did business with the government, and he had a legitimate excuse for going. Why did I not give him priority and get him on a plane?

I told Admiral Nimitz what I'd found out when I had looked into it. Then Admiral Nimitz got angry and wanted to write a letter to this guy and tell him off, because of his having misrepresented things to Admiral Towers, also to the air priorities officer in the first instance.

But it didn't come to that. Admiral Nimitz just backed us up, and the fellow just had to find some other way to get back to the States, if he got there.

It was, I'd say, one case in ten thousand that had to be referred to me, and one in a million that had to be referred to Admiral Nimitz. Because this air priorities officer did an honest and objective job, he didn't play favorites. After all, in a job like that the last thing you can tolerate is favoritism. Regardless of whom, you can not play favorites. Because there was so much demand for air space, both cargo and personnel, that whoever ran it had to do it honestly and straightforwardly.

I remember one time the head of the Red Cross came to my office. And he was really fit to be tied. He was a personal friend of President Roosevelt's. He had been partially turned down by the air priorities people on what he wanted to send to Guam.

I said, "Sit down sir, and let's discuss this." He was a high pressure type and he didn't want to discuss things. He just wanted me to overrule these people and get this stuff going. I said, "Well, we don't do business that way."

He wanted me to know that he was the very close personal friend of President Roosevelt's. And if he couldn't get action here, he'd go all the way to President Roosevelt.

I said, "I don't think you need to bother the President. He's got lots of things on his mind these days. He's never reversed us yet and I don't think he's going to start reversing Admiral Nimitz. Admiral Nimitz does a pretty good job here, and we all take pride in doing our little part of it for him."

To make a long story short - he sat down finally. I said, "Let's go into what you want given this high priority and sent out to Guam." It was a long list. Some of the things I could conscientiously agree we should get on out. Other things, such as doughnut wagons, I didn't think needed to be air lifted to Guam. I said we'd get them on a fast ship, top loaded,

So at the end of the conversation he was fairly happy. He thanked me for what I had done, and everybody left smiling.

The next time I saw him he was on his way back from Guam. He came in with one of these MacArthur cob pipes and said, "I've only given one of these away before. That was to General MacArthur. I like the way you do business, I'm going to give you one of them." So he gave me a MacArthur pipe.

It was just that he was used to doing business that way. He was the executive type, but we simply had to avoid favors, and that's the way we did it.

Q: Generally speaking, I suppose that during your experience there you found more people rather reasonable in their requests.

Austin: Yes. The greatest difficulty was usually with the fellow who had not gotten too high, but he had gotten just high enough to make lots of noise.

For example, I'll cite one little instance. A Captain came into my office one day. He planked his fist on my desk in a most unbecoming manner and demanded that I see that his mail got to him quicker.

I said, "Captain, what seems to be the trouble?" "Well, it just takes too long for my mail to get to me."

He was a unit commander of a division of mine sweepers, I believe. These were not always in the same port. They were used where they were needed.

I said, "If I recall, your flag ship is such and such a ship, I believe." "Yup, that's the one they told me to use as my flag ship, but I'm not in that one."

I said, "Have you told the mail authorities that you aren't in the ship that is supposed to be your flag ship?" He said, "No, that's their business, let them find out."

I said, "I've got news for you. It's not their business. They go by the dispatches that indicate where people are, and by the organization of the fleet. If you're not where you're supposed to be by the fleet organization, you better let the mail liaison people know which ship you're in if you want to get your mail on time."

That's what I mean by sometimes you got some flak by people like that. But generally speaking, as you say, the higher they were and the more responsible positions they were in the more easy to deal with.

Q: Did you find that generally Reserve Officers were hard to get on with?

Austin: I would not be able to agree with that.

I found that some of the most able people that I ran into, in the whole war, were reserve officers. We had some, just like some regular officers, that were not outstanding.

For example, the flag secretary on Admiral Nimitz's staff was a young man who had been the youngest president of a big eastern bank before he came in. He was an able flag secretary, very able. And yet he had trouble with Admiral Nimitz's flag Lieutenant and personal aide. So much so that the matter came to my attention as a matter to be looked into.

I had Lieutenant Commander Thorne in and talked to him, I got his side of the story. Then I had Lieutenant Commander Lamar in and got his side of the story. It sounded entirely like too petty a thing to ever get up to Admiral Nimitz.

I told Lamar, "You're acting about as much like a little boy as I've ever seen a Lieutenant Commander in the Navy act. I am not going to put up with it. If you don't stop your heckling of the flag secretary, that's what it boils down to in my humble opinion, I'm going to take you by the ear and take you right to Admiral Nimitz. I don't want to have to take his time to spank you, but if you don't start acting like a grownup instead of making it more difficult for the flag secretary to do his job that's just I'm going to do."

Q: That's a difficult job, at best.

Austin: That's right.

So Lamar got the news. This was at night that I was talking to him. The next morning he came through my office very smiling and said, "I'm going down to see Oakleigh Thorne, but I won't be a little boy." So they got along better after that.

But Lamar was a difficult chap. He had been with Admiral Nimitz since Admiral Nimitz went out to the job. He'd been in the Bureau of Personnel, I believe, before that. So he did what aides some times do. He sort of assumed the reflected authority of his boss. Admiral Nimitz was not the kind to have his flag Lieutenant throw his weight around.

As a matter of fact, I was talking just the other day in North Carolina, where I was stopping in Greenville to see my youngest sister. I was talking with an officer who had been an aide in Pearl Harbor at the time that Lamar was an aide.

He asked me if I had known Lamar. I said, "Oh yes, you mean Stinky." He said, "That's him. He was a tough guy for the rest of us aides around there. We all dreaded him. One day my boss was invited to a party that Admiral Nimitz was giving and he didn't go, because he didn't get the invitation. So Admiral Nimitz asked Lamar why so and so wasn't there. Lamar said he didn't know, but he had given the invitation to me, his flag Lieutenant. It just happened that I hadn't been in Pearl Harbor for five days, because I was over on one of the other islands on leave. Stinky got stuck with that one. I didn't get it, but that was just the sort of thing he'd pull on you."

One day Admiral Nimitz sent for me, he was a little stern in his voice, he said, "Lamar tells me that since you have come to the staff, you have added 60 officers to my staff." I said, "Admiral, Lamar has informed you incorrectly. I have, in the first place, added no officer to your staff that you have not approved in writing. It won't take me long to go out to my office and add those up. I think the number, sir, will come out to be about 27."

It was one or two off from that. I'd kept very close tabs of how many I'd added to his staff, because I knew from Mercer's advice how much he wanted to keep from having his staff any larger than was absolutely necessary to do the job. So every time I'd asked him to add somebody to his staff, I'd previously determined in my own mind that it was absolutely necessary. So I went out and came back with the right figure.

What Lamar had done was that he had taken the total numbers, enlisted and officer, of personnel charged to Admiral Nimitz's staff. That included all itinerants in Pearl Harbor, while they were there awaiting further assignment. He hadn't told Admiral Nimitz this. It happened that there were about 30 itinerant people in his own division. In addition to being the flag Lieutenant to Admiral Nimitz he was the division officer of the administrative personnel, such as the signalmen, the drivers, and that sort of thing. So he had about 30 people there on temporary assignment that I hadn't had anything to do with at all. They were just floaters coming through and he'd nabbed onto them to augment his own services. Then he went in and told Admiral Nimitz that I'm loading his staff.

Admiral Nimitz, I think, knew before he confronted me with this that he was being given misinformation.

Q: I'm surprised he'd put up with a man like that.

Austin: Lamar was very good at catering to Admiral Nimitz. You've seen them.

Q: It takes just the right kind of a guy to do that.

Austin: That's right.

Admiral Nimitz knew Lamar wasn't popular with the other flag Lieutenants in the area. But Admiral Nimitz was a great protector of those who were loyal to him. Lamar never gave Admiral Nimitz any reason to feel that he wasn't looking out for Admiral Nimitz's interests, his comfort, his health, his happiness 24 hours a day seven days a week.

It's some times difficult for the boss man to see one of his close aides as others some times see them.

Mercer had warned me about Lamar. He had told me that Lamar had the Admiral's confidence. And that he would put his oar into things that he shouldn't put his oar into from time to time, pretending it was what the Admiral wanted. But you'd usually find the Admiral hadn't indicated any desire in that direction at all, that it was what Lamar wanted. So I was forewarned and really had no trouble with Lamar, except little things like that that were easily corrected.

With the Thorne-Lamar controversy, I had no problem there. I think Lamar realized that Admiral Nimitz had enough confidence in me that if I took him by the ear and took him to him it would make it a little difficult for him.

Q: Stassen was flag Lieutenant for Halsey.

Austin: At one time, yes.

Speaking of 'the higher they are, the more easy to deal with', I very often had a queue of people to see me most of the working day, because of the diversity of my areas of responsibility. I was sort of the buffer between Admiral Nimitz and all the administrative headaches, between the Chief of Staff really.

The Chief of Staff was old Sock McMorris. He never wanted to be bothered with administrative matters. Sock was quite a character really. They called him by various nicknames. He was not a handsome man, but he did have a lot of strength and character in his face. I think one of his nicknames was 'the phamtom of the opera.' I'll try to give you a little insight into Admiral McMorris's aversion to administrative details.

One day Admiral Nimitz called me in and he said, "I want you to write up for me a staff regulation that will require that every flag officer's fitness report, that comes to this headquarters, will be on my desk for my signature within one week of it's arrival. If we are to prepare a report, it will be on my desk within one week of the day it's due to be prepared."

So I went back to my office and I drew up this memorandum. Knowing that the Chief of Staff was involved in this, I went down and told him that Admiral Nimitz had directed me to draw up the memorandum and that I felt he should know about it and have a chance to see what I was proposing to the Admiral.

Well, he hit the ceiling. He reached down in his lower right-hand drawer and he pulled out a whole handful of back reports. He said, "My God, I can't get all these done in a week. Make that two weeks."

I was able to sell Admiral Nimitz on the additional time to be allowed for Admiral McMorris, who was one unhappy person because that made him clean out that bottom drawer.

When Admiral Nimitz moved to the forward headquarters — there're some interesting things about the development of that headquarters which I'll cover at a later time, but this pops in my mind. The plan was that I should move out there with him, and that Admiral Towers would be in charge of all administration back at the Pearl Harbor headquarters. So he didn't need the assistant Chief of Staff to the Fleet Admiral for fleet and overall administration.

I was all packed. I'd been out on a final inspection trip a few days before to make sure that everything was ready out there. It was ready when I got there, but in the middle of the night while I was there it was unreadied in a hurry. Someone woke me up and said, "A bulldozer has just gone through the main cable to the communications center."

Q: Where was this, Admiral?

Austin: This was on Guam.

I said, "I'm sure they're doing all they can to repair it." "Oh yes sir, yes sir. The head of the Seabees is out there right on the job with them." So I turned over and went back to sleep. There was nothing I could do about it, and there was no use to send word back to Admiral Nimitz and get him all perturbed until I saw how well they were able to patch the cable.

9 Austin - 297

So by the time I had finished my breakfast the next morning, they had a good report to make to me that the communications center was back in commission. The cable was repaired and it would be all right.

So I went back and reported to Admiral Nimitz that the headquarters was ready for occupancy. We had our very elaborate shift plan to put into effect, whenever Admiral Nimitz desired to put it into effect.

So I was all packed and ready to go as plans indicated, when Admiral Nimitz sent for me. He said, "Well, you'll have to stay behind." I said, "Aye aye sir. In that case, I'll send my number two out there." He said, "All right." So I sent my assistant out and I stayed behind.

Admiral Nimitz then indicated to me, he said, "I want you to move into my quarters here. You will be my alter ego for entertaining here. There is a closet full of liquor. The flag Lieutenant will turn all that over to you. You'll keep my quarters here and act as my represnetative for extending hospitality to people that should have it extended to them as they come and go to my headquarters."

This had gone on for a couple of months. Admiral Sherman, on a trip to Washington, came through. In the meantime there had been several, what we call, telly-memos back and forth between Admiral McMorris and me.

The first one directed me to proceed to Guam immediately. Admiral Towers, of course, got a copy of that and was reading it when I took my copy down to show it to him. He hit the ceiling. He said, "I told Admiral Nimitz that you had to stay behind here, that I was not going to be left with all the administrative headaches without the assistant Chief of Staff of administration being here. I'll send McMorris a reply to this. You don't have to reply to it, and you don't go." So I didn't go.

A few weeks later Admiral Sherman came through on his way to Washington on a mission for Admiral Nimitz. Sherman told me, "When I come back through - this isn't just McMorris' order now, it's Admiral Nimitz's - you get on the plane with me and go back to Guam. Admiral Nimitz will take care of it with Admiral Towers. You just have your bag packed when I come back through here. You get on the plane with me."

When I got out there poor Sock welcomed me with open arms He said, "My God, I didn't realize how many headaches are involved in administration in an outfit like this. I just don't have time for all these picayunish details. People get more crazy ideas, in your areas of responsibility, than in the whole fighting area of the Pacific war. You take it all over. Don't let any of those people get near me that have their complaints about this or that or the other and what they want to see me do next, and so forth." So I set up my little office.

The head of the Seabees outfit out there had been given some instructions, before I got there, about the building of an officers club out there. I sent for him and asked for a sort of progress report on this project.

He said, "I deal with Admiral McMorris on this. I received my instructions from him and I'll continue with him." I said, "Captain, just wait a minute. That's not the way Admiral McMorris wants to run it. This is an administrative matter. I'm sure that you and I can handle this together. You just let me know of anything that has gone on before and we'll be able to work it out."

He was a little bit proud, I think, of dealing directly with the Chief of Staff, and he wasn't about to deal with a flunky under him.

So despite my warning that he shouldn't see the Chief of Staff he went to see him. Admiral McMorris tossed him out on his ear and told him to come back to see me.

So we got everything on an even keel. He and I got along fine. We got our officers club built, and didn't have to bother Admiral McMorris anymore.

Admiral McMorris was a very hard working individual, I don't want to give you the impression that he wasn't doing his work. It was just that he kept such a finger on the pulse of all the operations that were going on that he just couldn't be bother with the little picayunish things -- like somebody wanting an air priority for something, or somebody wanting an officers club this way or that way, or in this location or that location. That's what he had an assistant Chief of Staff for administration for.

9   Austin - 300

This is where, I think, the average Chief of Staff would have wanted his assistant Chief of Staff for administration to work through him to the boss. Actually the way McMorris was constituted and the way Admiral Nimitz knew Admiral McMorris was constituted really resulted in my working directly for Admiral Nimitz and keeping Admiral McMorris informed on the major things. He didn't want to even know about the minor things. He just wasn't going to be bothered with them. In a way it wasn't a bad thing.

Q: You would think that Admiral Nimitz might have thought it quite appropriate for him to be more involved in all the details.

Austin: Every now and then you had an administrative matter that was in the non-picayunish category.

For example, there came up a problem about a Catholic Chaplain directly disobeying the orders of General Erskine. This raised quite a little wave, shall we say.

That's the kind of thing that even Admiral Nimitz had to get into, but Admiral McMorris really didn't get involved. Because when the controversy was presented to CinCPac by dispatch, Admiral Nimitz sent for me and told me to look into it.

I looked into it. General Erskine was ordered back to Pearl Harbor to tell his side of the story and the Chaplain told his. Having heard the Chaplain, I sent for the senior

Chaplain of the Catholic faith in the area.

I said, "One of your boys seems to be acting a little differently from all the other Catholic Chaplains. He refused to participate in a joint ceremony in General Erskine's division. He insisted that General Erskine give him orders in writing and then he flatly disobeyed them." This was Father Sheedy.

He said, "Well, you know, he's technically right. But he hasn't read all of his instructions from the Church. We recognize that in a military situation there are going to be such things as Memorial Day ceremonies that aren't going to vitiate the Catholic Church's law if a Priest is sitting on the rostrum and maybe says a prayer during the ceremony. If he had informed himself a little better, he'd know that he is allowed to do this. He's wrong. He's really not on a good wicket. The Church has a way of handling disciplinary matters. If you want us to handle this one, we'll handle it. It will result in his being transferred and it will result in his being admonished as to how he should act in a similar circumstance in the future, and he may go to a place that he won't like as well as his present duty. We can handle this, if you want to avoid having a court martial and trying him for disobedience of orders and all that. Frankly it wouldn't look so good for the Church. If you court martial him, he is not in a very good wicket. So I think I'd recommend to you that you let us handle it."

So I told him that I thought that would be a good idea. I told Admiral Nimitz what I had done, and he was happy with the solution.

And General Erskine was happy with it. After all, he had to report the guy after he refused duty. He had nothing against him personally, and didn't wish him any harm, but he had to do his duty.

Admiral McMorris knew about that, because he saw it in the dispatches. A thing of that nature, if he were interested enough, if I hadn't already told him what was done about it, he'd ask me, "What did you do about Erskine and his Chaplain?"

That was about the degree of overseeing of my bailiwick that he did. In other words, things such as discipline and all are so much a matter that is pertinent to the commander himself that there isn't too much gain by having a full staff on some of these things. Lots of them are of a rather sensitive nature too.

For example - this is sort of on the ludicrous side - one day Admiral Nimitz buzzed me and I went in. There sat one of his flag officers, a very good personal friend of his. In fact, I think he was a classmate. (I won't mention the name here.) He turned to him and said, "Admiral so and so, you know Commodore Austin." "Oh yes, yes indeed." I'd been to his house for dinner a couple of nights before.

Admiral Nimitz said, "I'm sure that Commodore Austin is quite capable of taking care of the problem that your Captain so and so has with his mess boy. I don't think that is a matter that requires the fleet Admiral's attention."

This is about as close to a bawling out of a flag officer that I heard Admiral Nimitz give. That flag officer's face turned red, and he knew he had overstepped the bounds of intimacy with his boss. Because this Captain of his had complained to him that his mess boy didn't show him the proper respect.

Can you imagine a flag officer being so lacking in proper evaluation of things as to take that to a fleet Admiral?

As a matter of fact, this same Captain had on a previous occasion come to me with a complaint.

Admiral Halsey and Admiral Spruance alternated in command of the fleet at sea. When it was Halsey at sea, it was the third fleet. When it was Spruance, it was the fifth.

When this setup was established, Admiral Nimitz told me he wanted a set of quarters for the fleet commander who was in port and planning for the next operation. So I had to move a group of Captains out of their quarters to make way for the fleet commander to have a set of quarters, for himself and his Chief of Staff and the few officers of his staff that he wanted in the same set of quarters.

I personally looked into this myself, instead of just telling the quarters chap to just transfer these Captains to some other place, because all of these Captains were very senior Captains. Actually if I hadn't been a Commodore, they'd all have been senior to me, because they went through the Academy ahead of me.

When this fellow came in and complained about the quarters to which I had reassigned him, I asked him to sit down. I said, "Captain, what's the complaint? That's a perfectly nice set of quarters. What's the complaint?"

He said, "Well, my house mate (he named him) who is several numbers junior to me got a better room when we moved than I did. He's in a separate house now, that due to it's location on that curve, has more sun in his room than mine has during the day."

I said, "Captain, they're identical rooms in identical floor plans. I didn't take into consideration the curve of the street there. Captain, if you are so concerned about the amount of sun in your room during the day, my room has lots of sun during the day due to it's location and I'm never in it in the daytime. If it'll make you happy, you move into my room and I'll move into your room." He said, "That's fine."

About that time it was time for lunch. Forest Sherman usually stopped by my office and picked me up to go up to the mess for lunch. On the way up Forrest said, "Count, you look all whooped out. You never have any real problems, do you?" I said, "No Forrest, I never have any real problems. But it's the picayunish ones that get me down." He said, "For instance?" And I told him this story.

He laughed and said, "You've been a Commodore now for several months. I've been intending to invite you up to share my quarters with me. I've got a spare room up there that every now and then Admiral Nimitz uses for an overflow for his guest cottage. I told him the other day that I wanted to invite you to occupy that room. Why don't you just move up there instead of moving into Captain so and so's room?"

So that's when I moved up with Admiral Sherman.

Some of these little things that I'm telling you about are almost in the category of being unbelievable. But it does illustrate how frustrated people can get very picayunish.

This Captain probably felt that he should be given a more responsible job than he had. He was fairly senior as a Captain. He was the assistant to the Inspector General of the fleet. As such, he did paper work day in and day out. I guess he got a little frustrated and he got perturbed by such things as his mess boy not showing him enough respect and so forth.

Interview # 10

Vice Admiral Bernard L. Austin, USN, Ret.
Rockville, Maryland

By Paul Hopper
April 4, 1970

Mr. Hopper: Count, would you like to take up where we left off before and proceed.

Admiral Austin: Paul, I believe we had pretty much covered my entry of my duties at Admiral Nimitz's headquarters.

Admiral Nimitz was not unmindful of the fact that I had been away from home quite a long time. I suspected at times that some of the official errands that he sent me to Washington to perform for him had to do with things that he could have handled by dispatch or mail if he had really wanted to. But I think he was actually being kind to me to let me go back, at least within telephone reach of my family once in awhile.

One of these errands came toward the end of the war. I had been after Admiral Nimitz for some time to reduce the very heavy censorship that we had in the Pacific fleet and the Pacific Ocean area. I could see no real military security reason for the very great limitations that we placed upon the personnel, at that time, as to what they could say back to their people back home. I felt that it would be a great boost to morale, if we would take advantage of the more secure position which we then had in the Pacific and allow them to be a little more talkative in their letters. I finally got a draft that Admiral Nimitz agreed to.

It was a fairly drastic relaxation of our censorship rules, and I expected it to meet with some opposition in Washington. But I was a little surprised when I got back on one of these trips and Howard Orem, who was then flag secretary to Admiral King, told me on arrival that Admiral Edwards wanted to see me right away.

Admiral Edwards was Admiral Kings' Cominch's Deputy I believe at that time. He was a rather firm individual, sort of pleasant but firm type. As soon as I entered his office he got up and started pacing up and down and said, "Why in the world did you get Admiral Nimitz to sign that letter about relaxation of censorship?"

I said, "Admiral, I am guilty as accused. I did get him to sign it, in fact I wrote it. Admiral Nimitz did not sign that letter lightly, nor did he sign the first letter I asked him to sign on that subject. He thought the matter through very carefully and he listened to the arguments on both sides. Admiral Nimitz just feels that it is time to relax the very stringent censorship rules that we have in the Pacific Ocean areas and the fleet now."

He said, "Do you realize that if I recommend to Admiral King, and if he approves of this relaxation, that many mother's sons may die as a result of the relaxation of security?" He was very strong in that.

I said, "Yes, Admiral, I realize that there is a possibility that the relaxation that has been recommended could, in some conceivable way, result in a breach of security which could be said to have caused the loss of some mother's son. Admiral, I am far more firmly convinced that more mothers' sons will be saved if we put these relaxed rules into effect. Because the morale of the people will be better. They will be able to say more than, 'Well, mom, I'm still alive.'"

He kept playing the devil's advocate, very effectively, and really took me over the coals. Finally when he had heard all of my answers, he smiled and said, "Well, I've just been giving you a hard time because I've got to have the answers to the kind of questions I asked you, when I take this in to Admiral King. I, frankly, agree with you. I've just wondered why the heck Admiral Nimitz didn't recommend it sooner."

So with his support, Admiral King did approve the relaxation. I don't know of any specific instances of mothers' sons that died because of it.

Q: I should suspect none.

Austin: One time when I came back on one of these errands for Admiral Nimitz, as soon as I got into the flag secretary's office with my orders he told me that Mr. Forrestal wanted to see me.

So I chop chopped up to the Secretary's office. When I was let in the Secretary greeted me in a very friendly manner. He said, "Sit down, I want to ask you a question." So I sat down.

Out of the clear blue sky he said, "How is Admiral Calhoun performing his duty as Commander of the Service Force?"

I said, "Mr. Secretary, I'm not the person to ask that question of. Why don't you ask Admiral Nimitz" He's his boss. Admiral Calhoun is senior to me by far." He smiled and said, "You've given me the answer I needed."

Lots of people had been sort of undercutting Admiral Calhoun, I think, to the Secretary. I think the Secretary had intimated to Admiral Nimitz that maybe he might get a more gung-ho type in there as his Commander of his Service Force than Admiral Calhoun.

But Admiral Nimitz was a very loyal person. Admiral Calhoun was very loyal to Admiral Nimitz. Admiral Calhoun's organization was performing in a very satisfactory manner. You couldn't really fault the performance of the logistic forces in the Pacific during that war. And so Admiral Nimitz just simply didn't accede to the demands for replacing Admiral Calhoun

Admiral Calhoun, like all mortal men, had his faults and his failings. But full and by, he made a good head of that particular organization.

He had a good Chief of Staff, who frankly I think carried the load pretty well for the old gentleman. But after all, he gave the necessary guidance and leadership. You have to give him credit for it. Because if his organization hadn't produced, you would have blamed him for it.

Whether he personally was carrying the whole war logistically on his shoulders or not was not the point, I don't think.

Evidentally Mr. Forrestal had been given some stories about Admiral Calhoun, which caused him to take this unconventional way of finding out how he was performing.

Q: Did you know Admiral Burt Biggs out there?

Austin: Oh yes.

Q: He was the big oil man of the Navy, I suppose.

Austin: My relations were never very close with Burton Biggs. All that I ever knew of him, he was a very able and a very charming individual, and one who could cooperate with other people in a very remarkable way. When everybody wants the same commodity at different places at the same time, that's a good kind of fellow to have around.

Q: Are there any other incidents that you can think of Count that would be appropriate in this kind of a memoir, before you went back to the States and became associated with the Chief of Naval Operations office?

Austin: I might just give you a few words on one of the little duties that Admiral Nimitz asked me to perform for him.

We had a large number of wounded from Iwo Jima in the hospital. A ceremony had been scheduled at which Admiral Nimitz was to present decorations to those of the men in the hospital who were being decorated. At the last minute something important came up. Admiral Nimitz called me in and sent me to do this in his stead.

I had been pretty close to the unpleasant parts of the war for a good bit of the war, but I must say that I think the experience that morning got next to me about as much as anything did during the entire war.

Some of these men that were being decorated, of course, had lost a leg, an arm, both legs, both arms. The spirit they showed in their faces and in their words as I went along that line and pinned these decorations on each man was something that I wish many of our young men today, who are renouncing their citzenship and renouncing all that this country stands for, could have been with me that morning and see the patriotism that exuded from the eyes of those men who had given something to their country and who were proud to be recognized, even in a small way, for what they had given.

It really brought a lump to my throat and tears to my eyes. I shall never forget that morning. It was one to remember.

I might tell you a little bit about George Hallas, the Chicago Bears man he's known as. George was sent out as the athletic officer on the staff. He's a very energetic and enthusiastic type. I liked him very much.

He came to me with an idea about publishing a booklet (which could be self-liquidating in cost). So that people in the fleet, when they got to these various way stations in the Pacific, would know immediately what facilities for different types of games were available.

We had the booket format worked up. Then we started running into the usual red taype difficulties - where to get the money to publish it, and BuPers wasn't too enthusiastic about it. While I was communicating back and forth with BuPers about their financing it and having it self-liquidate itself through the charge for the copies, one day in came George with a smile on his face. He said, "Here's our booklet, published."

10 Austin - 313

I said, "My goodness George, I'm still arguing with the people in Washington as to who's going to pick up the tab." He said, "Oh I know. I've been looking at the situation and I just got tired of waiting. So I wrote a check for it myself and had it published."

Of course I had to spank him for doing it but you had to admire his enthusiasm for the athletic side of things in the fleet. He really was a great help to me, because with someone like him looking out for athletics I didn't have to worry about it too much.

Q: He was commissioned?

Austin: Yes, he was a Commander.

Q: When you came back to the States Count, you were assigned to the Chief of Naval Operations office, weren't you, as a Commodore? You might refer in here about your promotion and so on.

Austin: I had been working member of the staff to draw up the phasing down of Admiral Nimitz's staff once the surrender had been signed.

Q: Incidentally Count, were you present at the surrender?

10 Austin - 314

Austin: No, I was not. Admiral Nimitz called me in and said, "I'd like to take you with me, but you'll have to stay and keep the store." Admiral Sherman accompanied him, and a number of other flag officers who had been prominent in activities - like Admiral Hill, Admiral Turner, and those. But I was not senior enough, or important enough, to be taken.

Q: He must have thought you were important enough to stay behind and take over for him.

Austin: That was just his kind way. I didn't really take over for him, actually there were others senior to me that were left behind. He meant that I had to stay and keep the store, running the mundane little things that I usually ran for him.

We had worked on this plan of phasing down his staff, before the surrender ceremony. It was Admiral Nimitz's desire that we should phase it down as quickly as possible, without undue reduction of efficiency.

When I took this plan to Admiral McMorris, the Chief of Staff, I had opposite the name Austin, B. L. that he could be relieved by his number two immediately after the surrender had been finalized. That was one of the points of demarkation in this plan.

Admiral McMorris reached over and took a crayon and scratched out that opposite my name and wrote 'indefinite.' He approved the rest of the plan though. I took it up to Admiral Nimitz and got his approval on it.

Almost as if by design, about a week after this act on his part, scratching out my name as one of those to be relieved forthwith, in came a dispatch from the Secretary of the Navy. It said in effect, "Request that Commodore B. L. Austin be made available to the Secretary of the Navy for an important assignment."

Admiral McMorris, as soon as he saw this, sent for me. He said, "So you know the Secretary of the Navy, do you? You've had just time for him to get your air mail letter and this dispatch to get back here." I said, "Now Admiral, you know good and well I don't know the Secretary of the Navy a bit more than anyone else does. Furthermore, you know that I wouldn't do such a thing as to go behind your back and request detachment." He smiled and said, "No, but it does look that way, doesn't it? You've just had time for an air mail letter to get back there, and here you're being asked for in an important job."

Admiral Nimitz couldn't very well say that he couldn't spare me, and so he answered the Secretary to that effect. That I could be made available, and asked for information of the assignment contemplated for me.

10   Austin - 316

Then it came back that I was to be assigned as the Navy member of the secretariat of the State, War, and Navy Coordinating Committee.

I learned after I got back to Washington that the poor officer who had had this job had been caught up in a situation which probably was not as much his fault as it was the system. As the Navy member of this secretariat, it was his duty to get the Navy's approval on finalized positions that were to be proposed to the undersecretaries of the three departments at their next meeting.

Q: They were the members?

Austin: They were the members. They had the authority delegated from the secretaries to take final action on matters that did not require secretary level decision.

This was really a very good organization. It relieved the secretaries of a great deal of minutia. Some things were not quite so minute, but they were still capable of being properly handled at the under secretary level. They didn't need to get up to the secretary level to be finalized.

This poor fellow, who had preceded me in this job, had gone over and left a paper in Admiral King's outer office. He had gone back and gotten it with the indication that Admiral King had seen it and agreed with it, but evidently there'd been a slip.

When Admiral King learned that this paper had been presented, and that he hadn't ever had his say about it, he hit the ceiling. He went to the Secretary and demanded that this officer be relieved forthwith, and be replaced by a proper officer. My name got in the hat.

Then came the matter of my rank. I'd been spot-promoted to Commodore as Admiral Nimitz's assistant Chief of Staff for administration. As soon as I left there that spot-promotion was in jeopardy. In fact, it was null and void. But the Chief of BuPers directed me to retain my rank and continue to wear my Commodore's uniform in my new job.

I kept checking with his office, from time to time, for the next several weeks. This put me in a sort of uncertain position.

There was a matter of relative seniority between me and my Army and State confreres on this secretariat. I was the only Navy member of the secretariat. So it was a matter of who was senior over there. As long as I was a Commodore I was senior. But if I dropped back, this career diplomat and the Colonel in the Army, it was a matter of who was going to be the top guy.

So I kept heckling the Chief of the Bureau of Personnel's office. Finally one day he called me in. He sent for me and asked me to come in.

He said, "Now we've been having a little difficulty. I told you to wear your uniform and to keep your rank. That

ought to be enough for you. Stop heckling my office."
I said, "Aye aye sir. That's enough for me."

Here's what had happened: The Chief of the Bureau had sent a nomination of three people to be spot-promoted in their particular jobs for the job that they were doing and because they had been selected for the job and etcetera. You know, the usual arguments. One of them was Denison, who had been put into the job of Director of the Political Affairs Division of the Navy Department. He was still a Captain at that time. They wanted him spot-promoted.

Just about that time somebody up on the Hill made a speech about there being more flag and general officers in the armed services than there had been at the height of the war. So this nomination lay in the President's basket for some time, and his aide couldn't get it sent on up. In the meantime, by the time the thing finally did get sent up the climate had changed and they refused to acquiesce in the promotion.

So then I had to take off my broad stripe, and go back to being a Captain.

Q: Didn't they, many times during the war, spot-promote a Captain directly to Rear Admiral? Or did they always go to Commodore rank?

Austin: Oh yes, there were a number of promotions from Captain to Rear Admiral, that's the normal thing. Captain to Commodore is the abnormal.

The reason they chose Commodore for me was, I think, the fact that I had no one working for me other than Captains and Colonels. So Commodore was plenty senior to take care of my situation. Furthermore, I was a bit young. As a Commodore, I was the youngest flag officer of the line in the Navy. There was a younger fellow in the Supply Corps who got spot-promoted to Commodore.

Q: Was that Commodore Wallace, of the Supply Corps?

Austin: He wasn't the one I was thinking about. I forget his name, but he was really a hot shot. They promoted him at a younger age than I was promoted.

Q: Commodore Wallace's daughter is my daughter's Godmother.

I was going to make this observation. You speak about the fact that as a Commodore you were senior to the other members of the State, War, and Navy Coordinating Committee. That situation was not the same as it was earlier in the war, as I remember, in many instances. On lower ranking committees, on most occasions, we found that the Army always outranked the Navy man usually by one or two ranks.

Austin: Yes. Generally speaking, I think the Army did outrank the Navy people on all of the committees of this organization. But I was on the secretariat, not on one of the sub-committees.

I might say a few words about this. When the Security Act of 1947 was enacted, I was just finishing my tour of duty as a student at the National War College.

Admiral Sherman was then the Op-03 of the Navy Department. He had me ordered to his division as the deputy to Admiral Woolridge, who was the director of the Politico Military Affairs Division.

Shortly after I reported to Admiral Woolridge for this job, the Admiral called me in. He told me to report up to Admiral Sid Sowers as the Navy member of the newly formed National Security Council Staff. In fact, it was just forming.

I said, "Admiral, does this relieve me of my duties as deputy to Admiral Woolridge?" He said, "Oh no, you do both."

I did do both for awhile. It soon became evident that the work load at the Security staff was a full time job. So I asked Admiral Woolridge to intercede and ask for a new deputy, or ask that I be relieved by someone else up there.

Admiral Woolridge was very reticent. In fact, his feelings were hurt. He said, "No. Admiral Sherman didn't ask me anything about this in the first place, and I'm not going to go to him about it. You have my permission to go to him yourself if you want to." Admiral Sherman was Admiral Woolridge's immediate boss.

So I did see Admiral Sherman and he was very understanding. He said, "Yes Count, I realize it isn't fair to Woolridge and it isn't fair to you to have you do both jobs. I promised Sid Sowers that if he would take the job as executive director of that organization, that I would give you to him as the Navy staff member. So I had to carry out my promise. I made that promise when you were still a student at the school. I didn't realize that you'd be here and in a job that can't very well spare you. I'll talk to Admiral Woolridge, and we'll get him another deputy."

And that's what happened. I then continued with the National Security Council as the Navy member until my next assignment.

Q: Admiral Sidney Sowers actually set up CIG.

Austin: Yes.

Q: He was still a Captain, I believe, or just newly been promoted to Admiral at the time it was being set up. I happened to have been one of the three or four people of the Navy who went to C.I.G.

Austin: He was a very fine man to work for. I liked him and I still get a Christmas card from him every year. He was very close to Mr. Truman, which helped in that job.

Q: He's a very successful business man.

Austin: Yes, I know.

He would always send for me, when he'd come back from the White House. He'd tell me exactly what had gone on between him and the President. That gave me a feel for what he wanted us to do much better than if he'd just called me in and coldly said, "The President wants a paper drawn up on such and such." And he'd tell you how it came about.

He was a very easy man to work for, and a very appreciative one.

Q: He was Deputy Director of ONI for a time, before he became involved in CIG. I, of course, worked with him then.

Austin: Actually we, on the staff of the Security Council, had a lot to do with the setting up of CIA. The National Security Council was the legal father of the CIA. So all CIA directives had to be approved by the Council. The Staff, naturally, had to draw them all up.

Frankly in those early days of CIA, I couldn't give any of the service intelligence agencies very high marks for their helpfulness. They were all dragging their feet like nobody's business. To try to get the facts out of them about any situation was just like pulling eye teeth.

Q: I think the State Department was more cooperative at that time.

Austin: I believe they were. Although, frankly, they were a little the same way. They were all jealous of any organization being setup that would evaluate their material and give it a relative spot, as it were, in the picture to other sources of intelligence.

Q: There was a lot of competition for the top jobs.

Austin: Yes. So, we on the staff had to content ourselves with the real intent of the law, the needs of the separate services. We had to stretch our thinking quite a bit to get the directives out that would not cause the whole thing to blow up.

Q: I'm sure you did.

I lost track of much of the inside maneuvering after CIG became CIA. I was with Sowers with that group when they occupied offices in the new State Department.

Austin: You knew Jimmy Lay.

10   Austin - 324

Q: I had lunch with Jimmy about seven or eight months ago. I had suggested to the people in New York, not to Mr. Mason over at the Naval Institute, to his wife at Columbia that it might be interesting to get Jimmy to talk about the setting up of the CIA and some of his experiences.

He was understandably, I think, quite hesitant to go into things to any extent for the risk of repeating something that he shouldn't. He's with CIA now.

Austin: I didn't know that.

Q: He left the National Security Council at the time of the beginning of the Kennedy administration. Not too long afterwards, he went with CIA, and he's still with them.

Austin: I have a very high regard for Jimmy. He's very able and a very hard working type.

Q: That is my feeling too.

Austin: He has a good mind. He was Sid Sowers' real right hand man.

Q: Really his protege.

Austin: Yes, and when Sid left he fleeted up into the job.

We had a very fine working arrangement on that staff, and what brought us to this point in our talk here, that I'll finally get back around to.

When the National Security Council Staff got to functioning, the question was raised," What about the old State, War, and Navy Coordinating Committee?" It had then become the State, War, Navy, Air Force Coordinating Committee. So they changed the name from SWNCC to SANAC - State Army Navy Air Force Coordinating Committee. This became a subject at a cabinet meeting.

In those days the Secretaries of the military services sat in the cabinet meetings. The Secretary of the Navy came back one day and called me to his office. He asked me to brief him on the State, War, and Navy Coordinating Committee and to tell him what my thoughts were about it's being disbanded or phased out.

I explained to him how it came about, what it had done. Then I expressed the view that it should be retained and continue to function as a coordinating committee at the under Secretary of State, War, and Navy level, and that it would insure that many things of a minor nature, which would otherwise take up the time of the Security Council and it's staff, would be handled at the lower echelon by the coordinating committee.

He liked the sound of my argument. So he went to the next cabinet meeting, and he gave it evidently, and it was very well received.

10 Austin - 326

So he came back from that cabinet meeting and called me up. He said, "I want you to go and give the same briefing that you gave to me to the Secretary of the Air Force and the Secretary of the Army. They both asked me this morning where I got my information, and I told them that Captain Austin had given it to me. They both asked if I could send you over to them and let you brief them."

I made appointments with both the Secretary of the Army and the Secretary of the Air Force. The Secretary of the Air Force at the time was Mr. Symington. Mr Symington was very receptive and very keenly alert all during the time that I was briefing him. He called in his assistant and everytime that he'd ask a question, Mr. Symington would pipe him down and tell him that it wasn't pertinent. When I got up to leave, Mr. Symington was extremely kind. He thanked me very much for my time and my briefing. He said, "Do you have a car to take you home?" I said, "No sir, but I'll call for one when I finish my next errand which is to brief the Secretary of the Army." He turned to his secretary and said, "Have my car standing by. When Captain Austin finishes, have him taken back." I was from across the river, and he was very considerate.

I went down then to the Secretary of the Army. He evidentally had just finished his lunch. I hadn't had any, because I had to do this when I could get appointments with them. So all during my briefing, he snoozed. I don't think he heard very much of it. At one point he kind of waked up and said,

"What organization are we talking about?" He didn't get much of what I had to say. (I think his name was Royal.)

Q: Speaking of that sort of a committee, Count, it would seem to me that a committee of that type could be very useful in many fields other than intelligence to take care of various kinds of things.

Austin: It dealth with many things that were not intelligence. Oh yes, this was not an inter-agency intelligence organization. It was an inter-agency organization to handle all matters that could be handled at the under Secretary level. It had quite a structure. There was an intelligence committee of this coordinating committee. There was a committee on the Philippines, because at that time we were in the hassle of turning over the Philippines and giving them their independence. So there was a sub-committee just on that particular problem, because that problem cut across State, War, and Navy area of responsibility and concern.

I'm sure there are many committees between those agencies. But with the old State, War, and Navy Coordinating Committee you had a sort of framework within which they could be made to operate efficiently.

For example, one time the under Secretaries had approved the preparation for tuning over the Philippines to the Philippine government. It involved the drafting of a pretty long dispatch to General MacArthur to accomplish the things that had been agreed upon. This is where the secretariat came into play, we did the drafting of the dispatch. Then after we drafted it, we had to get it approved by the three members of the organization, the under Secretaries.

We drafted this dispatch. We got it approved promptly by both of the military members, but we couldn't get the State Department's approval or suggestion for changes.

Days went by. I kept checking on this with the State Department senior chap each day. Finally one day he said, "Tell me, you military chaps really amaze me at times. We're kind of taught to put things off and maybe they'll settle themselves. You fellows, whenever you're given a job, you just put your head down and you won't let up until you get there and get it done. To be perfectly frank with you, I think you might as well cease and desist from bothering me about this every morning. I've found out where it is. It's up in the State Department. It's in the basket of a fellow who has to initial it before the under Secretary will act on it. That fellow is not here."

I said, "Where is he?" He said, "He's on leave. He's out in Minnesota hunting and fishing." I said, "You know how to get in touch with him, don't you?" He said, "Yes, they know how to get in touch with him. You wouldn't call him back from his leave, would you?"

I said, "I would. After all it is not fair to General MacArthur, to the Philippine people, or to the United States interest to have this thing delayed until it will do no good. The purpose of it was to give General MacArthur guidelines that would enable him to get his ducks in a row. Your fellow is out duck shooting instead of getting General MacArthur his guidelines out there, so he can get his ducks in a row to perform an important function here. And that is to give a country it's freedom and it's independence."

Q: Why couldn't this chap's next in command do it?

Austin: No, they weren't organized that way.

Actually what happened was that they called him back from his leave. This fellow saw that I was going to continue to make an issue of it, so he evidently spoke to someone high enough up in the State Department that they called this fellow back. It got to the under Secretary and got cleared within a couple of days after that.

Q: This matter of letting the dust settle has sort of a classical connotation.

Austin: Yes.

Q: You remember Mr. Atcheson's remark about China.

Austin: Yes.

This fellow was not a lazy sort, that I was dealing with. He was perfectly energetic and intelligent. He said, "It's just the way we're brought up. We're brought up to sort of put things on the back burner and let them simmer, and maybe the problems will go away."

Q: I'm afraid that philosophy has permeated the State Department through a lot of it's work.

Austin: Yes, and is partly responsible for some of our not too happy policies.

Q: Count during the Eisenhower administration, there was a comparable line of organization setup as I recall which involved the under Secretaries of the three military services, Defense, and the State Department. Then they had an implementing board which was composed of a large number of committees that delved into all kinds of issues, questions, and projects. That was after you had left the State, War, and Navy Coordinating Committee?

Austin: Yes. During the early part of General Eisenhower's presidency, I was the Joint Chiefs of Staff's director of their staff. This may be an interesting little thing to tell you about.

General Eisenhower was very much interested in the proper functioning of the Joint Chiefs of Staff. He had been a member of it, he knew it's weaknesses, and he felt that something had to be done about them.

One night all of the Chiefs, plus the director of the Joint Staff, were asked to come to dinner at the White House for dinner with the President. It was a very informal dinner.

After dinner, he got right to the point. He asked me to come sit next to him, in the room where we were having our coffee and brandy.

He said, " The reason I've gotten you all here tonight is to try to do something about making the Joint Chiefs of Staff more able to do what the law intended they should do. I feel that the key to the thing is the Joint Staff."

He turned to me and said, "I am willing to promote you and every member of your staff one grade, if that be necessary, to get the kind of staff work that we need for the Joint Chiefs. What do you think of that?"

I said, "Mr. President, it's hard to turn down a fourth star but I don't think it would be a good idea, sir. I think it would generate a feeling on the part of those that hadn't been promoted one rank that here were a bunch of fair-haired boys that were being treated with greater kindness than was required. I do feel that the quality of officers that we have on the staff of the Joint Chiefs is a highly important thing. This is something I have been working on with all of the Chiefs of Personnel. I am frank to admit and I say this with some hesitation in front of all the Chiefs, that despite the fact that they have assured me that they would put the pressure on their Chiefs of Personnel to give me the best people possible from their services, I still get people sent to the Joint Staff who have not had the background nor do they have the natural intelligence for the job they are being sent to. But I don't think the answer is up to the rank of each one of them that come to the staff. I think it would cause repercussions which would be hard to get over."

Q: I'm surprised that he suggested that.

Austin: It just showed how anxious he was, though, to get something going.

I told you about what I told Admiral Burke, about having the Joint Chiefs have offices down alongside each other and so forth.

Frankly, that was the kind of thing that I proposed while I was the director of the staff. I am still convinced that you're going to have to go to this in order to get away from the narrowmindedness that is always going to exist on any service staff.

If an officer has never looked at things from anything except his Army viewpoint, he's going to tend to look at things that way when he's writing a paper for a Chief on a joint problem.

Q: Would you accomplish anything by putting the fellows all in the same uniform?

Austin: No, I don't think that has any effect at all.

While I was the director of the Joint Staff, I had every officer that reported to the Joint Staff come in to report to me personally. This is about what I told him.

I'd welcome him warmly, regardless of what service he came from. I would then say, "I hope that you left your uniform, not literally but figuratively speaking, outside when you came down here to report. We want you to maintain close relations with your parent service, only in this way will you be able to serve us very well. But we do not intend to have you act as an agent of your service. If I ever find that you are so doing, I will ask for your relief immediately."

I meant it, and I almost had to ask for one's relief. Unfortunately, he was a naval officer, but he got the word and changed his ways and he came around alright.

I had a high degree of objectivity, on the part of the people that were there. My main complaint, frankly, was of a lack of talent.

Most of the people sent to the Joint Staff, while I was there, were very able people. But there were a few exceptions, and they were of the type that didn't have to be.

For example, one poor naval Captain. I noticed that he wasn't exactly pulling his weight on a committee to which he'd been assigned. I sent for him and I asked him, "You seem to be working hard, but you don't seem to be able to contribute too much to the working of your group." He said, "Frankly, Admiral, I don't feel that I have been contributing much. I was ordered to a job up in the Navy Department. I didn't know I was coming to the Joint Staff, until I reported up there. They changed my orders, and sent me down here. They had the orders changed of an officer that was ordered to the Joint Staff that they wanted."

Q: I was going to ask you that, Count. Hasn't it been the tendency, not only in the Navy but in the other services too, oftentimes for the personnel people to feel that a staff job is less important than perhaps a job in the field or some place where a man has a more active command?

Austin: Frankly, any shore billet for a naval officer is considered secondary to any sea job, in the years of his training, as it were. Later on, I think that phases around the other way.

I think, for example, that the job of CNO is considered quite as important as being a fleet commander. In fact, he's the senior guy.

But there is a lot to what you've just said. But this does not mitigate against getting good people, because they all are rotated.

What happened in the case that I just told you about was that my pressure on the Chiefs and my personal intercession with the Chiefs of Personnel had resulted in a very able officer being ordered to the Joint Staff. But what happened up in CNO when he reported in for indoctrination?

(This was something that I approved of fully - that they should be indoctrinated up in their department so that when they came to the Joint Staff, if they'd never had duty in Washington before particularly, they would know where to go for what, instead of floundering around wasting their time.)

When this very smart chap that had been ordered to the Joint Staff reported in they latched on to him, because as they started indoctrinating him they found that he was a real smart fellow. This other poor chap, that had been ordered to them, they had his orders changed to send him down to fill the gap left by their taking the good man for their own.

This Captain did all right in the long run. He worked hard, he realized that he was sent there without the proper preparation, but he turned out all right. But I doubt if he turned out to be as much help as the chap would have been who had been picked by the Chief of the Bureau of Personnel and his people to meet the demands that I was putting on them for good people.

Q: How long were you in that assignment, Count?

Austin: A regular turn, it was a two year assignment. It rotates between the services, and I had my regular tour there.

I went from that to command the second fleet.

I found no difficulty really with the service bias on the Joint Staff. The head of the Strategic Plans Division was an Air Force officer, his name was Ollie Pitcher. He was not a West Pointer, he graduated from Harvard. Ollie Pitcher was just as objective as you could ask a person to be. He was a Major General. He presided at the Strategic Planning Committee meetings, at which all the services had their Chief Planners present, and he did a good job. I sat in the back and listened to their meetings, and I know. He'd lower the boom on an Air Force chap just as quick as he would on an Army or a Navy chap, if he got out of line. But, Ollie didn't make himself a hero to some people on the air staff by doing this objective job, as I can show you.

When my term was almost over, Nate Twining, who was the Chairman of the Chiefs at that time, called me up. He said, "Count, who do you think would be a good Air Force officer to relieve you as director of the Staff?"

I said, "General, I don't know how it would affect his career, but Ollie Pitcher, in my opinion, is eminently qualified to relieve me." General Twining said, "I think so too."

I went back down and called Ollie in and told him about this conversation, because I didn't want him to be hit unawares with the proposition as to whether or not he wanted to be considered for it.

In the case of a naval officer having been there for a full tour in one job, to take on another job in the Joint Staff wouldn't work because they wouldn't consider that a proper rotation of duty, but the Air Force does things differently.

Q: They're more flexible.

Austin: Ollie said, "Frankly Count, I'd like the job. I'll never make three stars in the Air Force if I don't get it by relieving you, because the people that pick the three star boys haven't thought I've been enough of a proponent of the Air Force's position while I've been down here. Frankly I'd be happy to be considered for it, if they do think I'm qualified.

A few weeks went by. General Twining sent for me again. He said, "Tommy White tells me that he doesn't think Ollie Pitcher's quite physically able to take on your job. What do you think about that?"

I said, "General, I'm not a doctor, but I do have two eyes and I do have some common sense. Ollie Pitcher's a lot younger than I am. I've seen him stand up under the most grueling sort of schedule. Ollie has a little pink eye, some times he looks like he's not as hearty and robust as he might be, but that's just pink eye. It's not a thing that's going to impair his ability to carry on the task of my job."

General Twining smiled and said, "I think you're right." And Ollie Pitcher relieved me as the director of the staff.

Q: He probably deserved it.

Austin: Yes, and he made a very good director, I'm sure.

Q: You like to see an officer get what is coming to him.

Austin: Yes, and he did retire after that job. So what he told me was probably a correct assessment. He probably sensed that he had not endeared himself to some people in the Air Staff by being as objective as he had been, but this is regrettable.

Q: I was going to ask you this Count: It used to be said during the early years of the war, particularly about the Navy, less so about the Army, and I suspect less so about the Air Force, that unless a man came from the Academy that his chances of going very far were not too good, particularly in the flag rank.

Austin: I don't think that pertains as much today as it did many years ago. It's been a long time now since the Academy has been able to provide us with all the officer input that we need. So I would say that today it wouldn't make a real noticable amount of difference as to whether a man came from the Academy or didn't. I think it's what his service reputation adds up to.

Q: That's the way it should be.

Austin: That's right, that's the way it should be.

In the Air Force, at the time of which we're speaking, when Ollie Pitcher was designated to relieve me as director of the Joint Staff, I don't think it made one bit of difference. Because you had people in the Air Force who had been West Pointers, some from Annapolis, and lots from other colleges other than the two military schools. I don't think that was mitigating against Ollie Pitcher. I think Ollie Pitcher had been too honest, too objective, and a little corrosive when he chose to be. He didn't mince words if he wanted to blow some one down. He was a gentleman and a very stout fellow. I had a very high regard for him.

Q: You must have had a great number of very interesting problems come up in that period.

Austin: Yes, we did.

The big problem really was trying to get answers quickly enough from an organization, such as the Chiefs. You might say, the organization is wrong. I think it is, in that you don't have the Chiefs devoting the major part of their time and effort to the job. You have them spending a few hours each day on their Joint Chiefs jobs.

Q: Don't they have a deputy, perhaps, to do that?

Austin: They have that. The law that setup the JCS as part of the military establishment, under the Security Act of 1947, provided that their duty as a member of the Joint Chiefs of Staff shall be their primary duty. And that their Vice Chief will relieve them, to the extent necessary, of their service responsibilities so that they may give their Joint Chiefs duties their primary effort. This is what the law says. They've never obeyed the law, in my opinion.

Q: It certainly should be one way or the other. They should devote their entire duty to being members of the Joint Chiefs, or they should have a deputy to do this.

Austin: They had, what they call, an operations deputy that is at the Vice Admiral level. Their Vice Chief is a four-star officer, and quite capable really of relieving them of the chores of meeting people that want to see the top guy in the Navy. Let him be the top guy in the Navy, the other guy's down working on the Joint Chiefs.

But you've got to pull him out physically from the Navy Department, or the Air Force part of the building, or the Army part of the building, if you're going to have the Vice Chief see all these people that have to see the top man.

Put him in a room right alongside of the Chairman of the Joint Chiefs of Staff. If people want to see him urgently enough, they'll come down there to see him.

In this way, the Vice Chief could actually take over the matter of meeting delegations and people and running in to hold the Secretary's hand on matters that come up and give him military advice on it.

Then the Chief would still be the Chief, but he would be free to just go up for an hour or so a day and keep his hand in on what his Vice Chief was doing and see if he wanted to give him advice and consent or non-concurrence and hell.

Q: He'd be devoting his best efforts with the Joint Chiefs.

Austin: That's correct. And I think the country's interest would be better served if we could ever come to that.

Q: Certainly if we need unity in any phase of our government, it's in our military outfit. At least, if not unity, we need a type of coordination not always evident.

Austin: Paul, you have in the military a very high order of concern for the security and the interest (I don't mean just military security) of our country. And yet, the military voice in this country has become less and less audible in the councils of our nation since the passage of the National Security Act of 1947. It should be the other way around.

They should not, in my opinion, ever intrude in matters in which they do not have competence. I think it is only at great risk to our nation that they are kept from having this voice heard in matters that do concern their area of competence, and areas in which only experts should advise.

Interview # 11

Vice Admiral Bernard L. Austin, USN, Ret.

Rockville, Maryland

by Paul L. Hopper

May 16, 1970

Mr. Hopper: Count, at our last interview we had covered pretty well your last assignment with Admiral Nimitz in the Western Pacific. You had returned to the States and you had become a member of the Navy Joint Staff. You had previously served as a member of the State, War, Navy Coordinating Committee. You had attended the National War College. You were about to be assigned, as I recall, to the newly formed National Security Council as a Navy representative. Would you like to comment further in this connection?

Admiral Austin: Paul, my service on the National Security Council staff was one that I look back to with pleasant memories. There were associations that were stimulating. I feel that our papers were papers that had some meaning and could be addressed in a meaningful way. They were short, and I take some credit for their being short, because every time we passed page four I would say, "Gentlemen remember if the President is to read this, we've got to keep it short."

Although I annoyed some of my fellow members of the staff some times I think by this continuous watch-dogging of the length of the paper, I think it was an important thing to do, as I will point out a little later.

As you know, the Council itself is only advisory to the President. So that the staff was, in effect, writing policy papers not in granite as it were, not etching in granite the policies that they conceived. They were giving advice in a form of a readily usable piece of paper to the National Security Council, which in turn advised the President on the issue in question.

During the time that I was there we dealt with a number of fairly important issues. For example, one just pops into mind because it's so much before us today and that is the state of Israel's creation.

When we had these problems presented to us, either as a problem of concern to the President, as a problem of concern to the Secretary of State, or as a problem of concern to the Secretary of Defense, who was at that time Jim Forrestal we put the problem on our agenda, not necessarily at the bottom of the list because they came to us with varying degrees of urgency indicated.

So, if it were one that took it's place at the top of the list, we met immediately. If necessary, we met that night. If necessary, we met the next day all day and the next night. And so on, until the problem was ready for presentation to the Council.

This meant pretty hard work and long hours some times. I remember in the case of the Israel problem, we met all one week-end, night and day, just stopping long enough to eat and sleep. There were other problems that caused us late hours and long hours.

We had a small staff. It was not so big as to become a 'Tower of Babel.' It was a real working staff. There was no seniority on this staff, we were all workers. So we didn't have any jockeying for position, as it were, to get promoted or anything. We were all professional officers, including those from the State Department.

In fact, there were two from the State Department, two from the Army, two from the Air Force, and they were allowed two from the Navy. Somehow we never got around to furnishing the second officer, although I requested it a number of times.

The immediate impression would be that this staff is overweighted on the military side. The military men had all been chosen with some view to the fact that they would be dealing with national problems, and not with military problems alone. Therefore, you had people sent to the staff who had politico-military backgrounds in one way or another.

Then in addition to the members from the Departments of the Army, Navy, and Air Force, and State we had regular members of the stuff - such as Dr. Boggs, who was not from any department. He was simply hired because of his competence in the field which was pertinent to most problems that we addressed.

Q: He was a cartographer, wasn't he, primarily?

Austin: Not this Boggs. This one, I believe, had been given his doctorate degree in political science. He acted, usually, as the recorder of our meetings.

We had access to all of the military departments, but we didn't have to call upon them for experts as often as we did Treasury, or Agriculture, or the Federal Communications Commission, or any agency of the government that had expertise that was pertinent to the issue under study. They not only cooperated with us, but they cooperated with us to a very commendable degree. It was in their interest to do so. They didn't know what we were going to ask this chap who was coming over, who was an expert on boll weevils or an expert on tax matters, or what. They wanted to send a man who was sufficiently informed that he wouldn't let them down. So we got top notch advice and expertise that fit into the staff from the various departments as we needed it.

We had to work, usually, against a deadline because most problems that require National Security Council attention are problems which won't wait until you've had a study made, and then a study made of the study. We had to grapple with the problem and come up with an answer against a deadline, as a rule.

As we could, we got around to what we called the country policy papers. These were those that we could take more time with. We could take a country like Greece, where there was a complex of problems, and we could study it in depth and then come up with a reasonably short paper which would outline the general policies that this nation should follow in it's dealings with the problems of Greece, or whatever the country may be.

During this time we produced many papers. They were all reasonably short. They could all be read by a man as busy as the President of the United States. They didn't have to be briefed by a lower echelon staff member, and thereby run the risk of having the lower echelon's bias read into the interpretation of the policy paper.

Years later I came back to the Pentagon as the deputy to Admiral Wooldrich, who at that time was the representative of the Joint Chiefs of Staff on the policy planning board of the National Security Council.

11 Austin - 348

When Admiral Wooldrich sent me to the first meeting of this organization in his stead, I was a bit appalled. I had already noted, from my reading into the current picture when I came to this new job, that the Security Council paper had gotten to be 30, 40, and 50 pages long in some cases. After I had read them, I very often wondered just what our policy was that was being addressed by the paper.

After this first meeting, I no longer had to wonder why the papers were so long and why they were so lacking in concise, clear-cut statementof policy.

Around the table sat 30 or more representatives from various agencies of the government. These representatives appeared to be mainly concerned not with what was best for our country, but with getting into the paper a particular phrase or sentence which was desired by their particular agency.

For example, from Treasurey the representative usually wanted something to the effect that this policy would not cost anything.

That didn't put much vim, vigor, and vitality into lots of papers.

My point here is that in 1947 we had a working organization. We had a workable organization, and it produced papers that meant something to the Council. In only one instance, do I recall, that a paper which reached the Council failed to receive the President's approval, in substance just as it was written.

I won't mention what that paper was, but suffice it to say that it did not meet with the President's approval. In fact, it never got to the Council because he looked at an advance copy of it and ordered all copies burned.

The pertinent thing, I think, in the production of national policy is not to have the ultimate in the 'druthers' of every agency of government, but rather to have the substance of what well-meaning men, addressing themselves to the problem with a minimum of bias, or pre-conceived ideas, can suggest in the light of the conditions existing at the time, our historic traits, and prochivities and with a concern for generations to come.

When we had that small staff, mainly made up of professionals who weren't there to get promoted, but who in fact were probably losing out in promotion potential in their own services because of being on a non-military job, (in the State Department I don't think it hurt them as much as it did the military chaps) we were not there to work our way up in an organization. We were there to serve just as loyally as we'd serve on a battlefield or in a naval battle, during the time of our assignment there. We knew it would only be for a couple of years, so if the going was tough, you could grit your teeth and roll up your sleeves and work like heck for the time that you were there and hope that your labors would help your country go along the right path.

When the small staff gradually escalated into this enormous organization, you arrived at the 'Tower of Babel.' I don't say they didn't turn out any good papers. I'm sure that some of them would pass the test of being good papers, if one could take the time to synthesize from all the dross the real essence of wisdom that may be in the paper.

This reminds me of an old quotation. "Facts are the mere dross of history. It is from the abstract truth which interpenetrates them and lies latent among them like gold in the ore that the mass derives its value." -- Lord Macaulay in his Essay on History.

When Mr. Kennedy became President, he, in effect, dispensed with the advice of the National Security Council, the act was never repealed, but I believe he used it to a minimum. I can understand why he might have arrived at that decision. Because if I had had to sit in his seat of responsibility, I would have found it very little help to me to have the National Security Council sending up to me papers which I had to have briefed by someone else because I couldn't ever have the time to read them.

I think that in our society today, we are seeing a similar over-emphasis on the ultimate in the protection of the individual, just as in the case of the National Security Council we saw the ultimate in the protection of the right of every agency of the government to have it's say. We are seeing the ultimate in the protection of the right of the individual at the expense of the practical protection of the rights of all individuals, of society as a whole.

Q: Count, I believe you were quite close to Admiral Sidney Sowers during the time that you were a member of the staff of the Council. Would you like to comment briefly on your reaction to Admiral Sowers, and how he worked?

Austin: I had never met Admiral Sowers, until I went to work for him on the National Security Council staff. Evidently Admiral Sherman had made him a firm promise that I would be sent as the Navy representative on his staff if he were to accept the job as the executive secretary.

I found him a very easy boss, a very homespun type of character, but one who usually was on top of every problem. He appeared to be very easy going, but I think that he was always well informed and on top of every problem.

He was a very close friend of the President's. The President confided in him a great deal. I don't know whether my being the only Navy member of the staff had anything to do with it or not, but Admiral Sowers would seldom come back from the White House without calling me in and de-briefing me on what had transpired while he was over there.

11 Austin - 352

One time he came back and he said, "Did you hear the President's speech last night?" I said, "Yes, I heard that speech." He said, "What did you think of it?" I said, "I didn't think very much of it. I think he should have read it to himself before he read it in front of the microphone."

He said, "Well, he's very unhappy this morning. He feels that that speech went over like a lead balloon. The reactions are not very encouraging that he's getting in from various sources. I'm a little perturbed because the President asked me for some advice along certain lines. I've been trying to give him the best advice that I could, but I don't seem to be helping him very much."

I said, "May I make a suggestion? When Mr. Truman speaks with his sleeves rolled up and off the cuff, he's impressive. But when he reads these speeches that have been written for him by some speech writer that hasn't quite captured his way of expressing himself, even the good points some times just don't get over."

Admiral Sowers said, "I think you've got something there." So he went back to the White House. A couple of days later Harry came out with his first 'give 'em hell' speeches.

I've always felt a little responsibility maybe for getting him reelected. Although I was born and bred in a democratic country, my own political inclinations are not quite that democratic.

Some times I felt that I unwittingly suggested something that really took off.

Admiral Sowers was very good in the job that he had. He had a very good assistant, Jimmy Lay. Jimmy had been with him over in the CIG organization.

One of the responsibilities of the National Security Council was the issuing of the directives for the setting up of CIA. The willingness to see the other fellow's side of a problem, I think, helped Mr. Sowers put the right amount of authoritarian language in the directives that we prepared for CIA in those days. He, I think, leaned over backwards to avoid treading too heavily on the toes of the directors in intelligence in the services. And in this way, I think, some times their very biased positions were undercut because their own secretaries would not support them, in light of the reasoned language of the CIA directives that came out of the Security Council. Sid had a lot to do with that.

My relations with him were always warm, pleasant, and I look back on them with considerable pleasure.

Q: I suppose Count, due to the fact that you were both Navy men made the cordiality stronger.

Incidentally, speaking of the National Security Council during it's early days working with a small but effective staff, contrasting that with the way CIA has grown recently and then thinking in terms of the British intelligence operation by which they have very few people indeed as a full time staff, but do depend on the other government departments and business people throughout the world and so on who have always been a part of the British intelligence operation — wouldn't you say that, this is an off-hand opinion, perhaps we have almost too many people involved in intelligence today?

Austin: You have hit upon a point which I may be a little less than unbiased on. My training under Admiral Nimitz may have influenced this somewhat.

As you will recall in my discussing my service under him, he was very strict about keeping the number of people to the minimum consistent with the volume of work and the requirements of the job.

I couldn't agree more with the concept that when you get too many cooks you spoil the broth.

As long as you have a meaningful job for everyone, and everyone know his job in any organization, in my opinion, that organization will function better than when you get more people than you need to do the job. And thereby, tend to generate confusion as to who is to do what to whom and when.

I'm reminded of an interesting contact that I had during the time that I was director of the Joint Chiefs of Staff.

I was asked by the Secretary of Defense to come up and brief the then potential presendital candidate, Mr. Rockefeller, on the way we planned on the Joint Staff. He particularly wanted me to cover the Joint Strategic Objectives Plan (JSOP).

So I took the team from the staff up that worked on the JSOP. I led off with a general statement about our planning processes and system. Then I turned the floor over to the briefing team, and they briefed the potential president on the JSOP. When they finished, he was greatly impressed. He thought this was a very important thing.

Then he turned to me and said, "How many men do you have working on this?" I said, "Well, sir, that's not an easy question to answer with a number. The team that has given this presentation is that part of the Joint Staff that works on this problem as their primary job, day in and day out. The individual services are working on this problem all the time. So we have an input from them as far as facts and figures are concerned. Of course, we have various parts of the Joint Staff that make a contribution to the various parts of the Joint Strategic Objectives Plan. For example, the planning committee feeds in the strategy, and the logistic committee feeds in the logistics."

He said, "All in all, how many people work on this?" I said, "If you take a sort of a round figure sir, I think about a hundred people in the staff and in the department address themselves to this problem." He said, "My goodness, something this important you ought to have a thousand people working on it all the time, all the time."

I didn't have a thousand people on the Joint Staff in those days. I know that the Joint Staff has grown to be much larger now.

I knew what everybody on the Joint Staff was working at, and he knew I knew what he was working at. Furthermore, when I needed more manpower on a project I knew the team that was least overworked at the time, and I could utilize my brainpower or manpower in a meaningful way.

But when you get thousands of people in an organization, the degree of positive coordination and control is reduced just about as the cube of the numbers beyond a certain point. There is a certain point beyond which efficienty is not promoted by just more people, in my opinion.

Q: I had raised the point with you because it seemed to me, and perhaps I'm lacking in objectivity in saying it, that even in the early days of CIG that for the number of people involved we produced a lot of effective intelligence. Despite the fact that I served practically four years with CIA after it was set up, even in those days and it was much smaller then,

I began to wonder whether or not it was possible to utilize all the manpower we had involved.

Austin: I think that what I said is particularly pertinent to intelligence organizations.

I have known a little about the British intelligence organization. They may lean too far over on the austere side. But I think in intelligence work it is better to lean to the austere side than it is to ever get overstaffed. As soon as three people know something, it's no longer intelligence, it is then an open secret.

That was one of the laws of the Medes and Persians as observed by the British intelligence. If three people knew it, it was considered no longer a secret.

Then of course you can go too far in keeping intelligence secret. I'll sight you a little experience that I had while with Admiral Ghormly in London.

We had many special naval observers come over to get information in a particular specialized field. Part of our job was to maintain proper relationships with the Admiralty so that as soon as they arrived in England, we could get them on a ship or on a station where they could get the information that they needed and get the heck out, because the British were being very lenient with us in the numbers that they would accommodate in their ships and on their stations.

One day an officer came in to see me. He had just arrived, after some difficulty enroute, and he was not too happy. I asked him what his mission was. When he told me his mission I said, "We've already sent back all there is on that. Surely you should have seen it before you left. It went back months ago." This didn't make him any happier about his unhappy experiences on the way over.

When I had an opportunity I brought this to Admiral Ghormley's attention. In the meantime, I had gotten out the file folder which showed the exact information that we had sent back. I showed him a copy of this fellow's instructions, as to what he was to get while he was over there. The two were practically identical.

Admiral Ghormley was about to go back for the ABC conferences in Washington. He took this case back as illustrative of the fact that what we were sending back was not being disseminated to the people who needed to know it.

In this case, I believe it was the Bureau of Ships that needed the information. I guess somebody in intelligence decided that Bureau of Ships didn't need to know anything that came from the war zone. They were building ships for future use.

Such things as the British experience with cast iron castings vulnerability to underwater explosions was worth it's weight in gold to our people. You could use that immediately. You could stop installations, because you know you're going to change them later anyhow. If you went ahead and put in the cast iron castings, they'd make it highly likely that you're going to lose the ship.

There was a shake up in ONI, as a result of what Admiral Ghormely brought back with him. The shake up came, because when he brought this to CNO's attention, it was found that the standard procedure for handling what came back from London was to put it in a special vault. Then if they got querries in ONI about any of this, they would then consider whether or not to let the fellow go in the special vault and look at it.

So you can overdo the secrecy of intelligence.

Q: That was brought to my attention several times during my experiences in World War II. As I may have told you, I started out in intelligence and later transferred to Procurement and Material.

I recall on several occasions that dispatches would come in from a naval attache, for instance. It would be marked 'secret' or 'most secret.' The actual origin of the information might have been picked up in the newspaper in that country. Instead of sending it through in the clear, it would be sent through under security, and little or not use could be made of it.

On the other hand when I transferred over to Procurement and Material, toward the end of the war, I found that they on the contrary it seemed to me were almost lax about intelligence, the kind that I thought was highly desirable to keep secure. For instance, we were very much concerned with all the plans for shipbuilding at that time -- where material could be obtained for the ships, how much money we could get. We were holding conferences with the War Production Board and people like that. It seemed to me that perhaps we should have taken more precautions in intelligence.

Austin: I think this is one of the reasons why in the military services they try to give an officer a fairly board spectrum of experience. Just as in your case, your experience on the one side helped you to have a better and more practical view of intelligence on the other side. I'm sure that this does pay dividends in many instances.

It's very difficult for a young officer who has a particular inclination toward gunnery, to have to do a trick down in the engine room or the fire room when he's a young officer. But I think, in the long run, the concept is sound. It helps him to understand better what the overall picture is. If he's just in intelligence, for example, all of his life, he is likely to become too security conscious.

The problem of overclassification of information is one that has haunted military services ever since the beginning of military organizations.

I recall that during the battle of Inchon, I was a logistic commander there and was in my flag ship quite a way out from the firing at the moment. I needed to get information through to one of the task force commanders. So I tried by the usual means of communication and found it impossible, because the circuits were just jammed with high priority traffic, lots of it in code. I finally had to resort to putting a messenger in a boat and sending him through to the task force commander in question. That was the only way I could get my message to him.

This was not because we didn't have lots of communications circuits. I was on a task force circuit, because I was a task force commander. But there were just too many people saying too much, and too much of it in code.

Frankly I've always felt that once you start shooting there shouldn't be anything in code.

Q: I suspect that strategic advantages have been lost by coding and encoding.

Austin: That's correct.

People get so much in the habit of encoding certain types of information — such as the dispostion of the enemy, or your state of fuel, or something of that sort.

It may help the enemy to know that you're running out of fuel or something. I can understand that. But by the time it can get used in his organization, he's going to know you're out of fuel, if you are. In other words, time is an important factor.

Q: Just one further thought about intelligence - in brief experiences with the Navy I've always been interested in intelligence.

The idea of having too many cooks involved in making the broth, I think, applies so well to what you've been saying about intelligence and about your experiences on the staff of the National Security Council. That ultimately you have to arrive at some conclusions or decisions based upon information that's being put together, and you simply don't have the time to take into account everybody's point of view. And even if you did, in all probability you'd find that perhaps a good deal of the conglomeration of points of view are not pertinent or could be dismissed in actually arriving at your final conclusion.

Would you like to discuss now your assignment to the Imperial Defense College in London?

Austin: The assignment to the Imperial Defense College came about like this. I was still working on the National Security Council staff. Not having another Navy man with me on the staff meant that I had to do, back in the Navy Department, the usual leg work and all that the number two man did in the other departments.

So I was doing my Navy Department part of my job, seeing that the papers got to the right people and all, about seven o'clock one night.

An officer came into my office and said, "Count, would you like to go to the Imperial Defense College?" I said, "Sounds interesting. How long have I got to think it over?" He said, "You've got until tomorrow morning at eight o'clock."

I said, "As you know, my reporting senior is Admiral Woolrich. Admiral Woolrich is on tour with a group of Congressmen in Europe. I couldn't very well agree to go to some other job without his being consulted."

He said, "We'll take care of that, if you want to go. I've just been given the job of giving Admiral Denfeld tomorrow morning at eight o'clock my suggestion for the job. Your name came up as one that would be considered."

I came home and talked to 'Ice' about it. She was enthused, going to London would be wonderful.

So I went back the next morning and I said, "Subject to Admiral Woolrich's concurrence, I'd be happy to go."

The next day a classmate of mine, who was over in the detail section of NavPers, got me on the phone and said, "Count, what do you mean trying to go to the Imperial Defense

College? You've just been through the National War College. You're educated as far as we're concerned. We can't send you over there."

I said, "Now wait a minute, Joe. Let's get things straight. I haven't made moves to go to the Imperial Defense College. I was asked if I would like to go if ordered. And I said I wouldn't object at all, provided Admiral Woolrich didn't interpose objection. I haven't been drumming this thing up."

He said, "Well, we can't send you over there, Count. I'm sorry, but we can't use an educational billet for somebody who's already been through the National War College."

I said, "Well, Joe, I would think you'd want a student of the U. S. Navy at the Imperial Defense College to have been through our National War College, or to have had a similarly broadening experience, in order to properly represent our Navy at the Imperial Defense College and to make a proper contribution to the Imperial Defense College discussions."

He said, "That's not the way we look at it. It's just an educational billet as far as we're concerned."

I said, "Okay Joe. You're the fellows that do the deciding, so have it your way."

I frankly had practically forgotten about the Imperial Defense College, because of this conversation. After all, he was the detail officer for Captains at that time, and I was a Captain. He said it was against the policy of the bureau. I had given him my views as to the correctness of that policy, but he wasn't impressed with my views. So I just figured it was a settled proposition.

About three weeks later I was in the CNO's outer office briefing his aide, Red Yeager, on a National Security Council problem (I didn't feel it was pertinent enough to take the Chief's time up, but I was leaving this information with his aide to pass on to him at a moment of convenience to the Chief) and the Chief happened to hear my voice out there.

He called out, in a jocular tone of voice, "Count, is that you out there?" "Yes, sir." He said, "Well, come in here." So I went in.

He said, "What's this I hear about your joining the Royal 'Navie'?" I said, "Admiral I don't know what you've heard about my joining the Royal 'Navie,' but I don't know anything about it." He said, "Well, you're going to the Imperial Defense College, aren't you?" I said, "Not that I know of, sir. I was asked if I would like to go, and I said that I wouldn't object at all. I later got called by BuPers, and was told it was against their policy to send anyone over there who had been to the National War College. I happen to be in that category."

He said, "I would think they would want somebody who had been to the National War College." I said, "Sir, I don't disagree with that, but that's not the way they look at it."

He said, "I nominated you for the job. They haven't said a word to me about it." He called out to Red Yeager, "Come in here, Red."

Red came in and he said, "You look into this. My nomination of Captain Austin to go to the Imperial Defense College has evidently hit a snag over there. I want to be informed about it, just what gives."

Red Yeager was never a shrinking violet type and I can just imagine how he took it up with my friend and classmate over in BuPers. He probably called up and said, "What the hell gives over there? Don't you know who's the CNO around here?" (Or something like that.) Red was not adverse to using the power of his boss to carry out his boss' instructions.

I then got another phone call from my friend Joe in BuPers. He said, "Count, what in the world did you go down and tell Admiral Denfeld that we aren't going to send you to the Imperial Defense College for?" I said, "Now Joe, let's get things straight. In the first place, I want you to know just how this came about. I didn't run to Admiral Denfeld." So I told him just how it had happened.

He said, "My goodness, I didn't tell you we wouldn't send you. I just told you it was against our general policy."

11 Austin - 367

Suffice it to say, I did get orders forthwith to go to the Imperial Defense College as a student.

At that time, I was on the Bureau's list for a cruiser command. In fact, I later learned that I was number two in my class on that list. You aren't supposed to know about the list, but when I didn't get a cruiser command I was given that information.

Somehow my name got taken off of the list for cruiser commands. Because when the cruiser commands were given out, I didn't get one. Although Forrest Sherman, who had been the 6th fleet commander in the Mediterranean, had specifically requested that when I became eligible for a cruiser command, I'd be sent to his flag ship as his flag Captain.

In the meantime, Admiral Denfeld had been kicked out as CNO and Sherman had been brought back as CNO.

So I got my Imperial Defense College course, which I enjoyed very much. But I, thereby, I think, lost my cruiser command.

Now for the Imperial Defense College: Our National War College is modeled very much after the Imperial Defense College. It, like our War College, has students from not only all military services, but it has students from all of the main departments of government.

Our War College started out with only State Department non-military students. They now include other departments of government, but I don't believe that they've ever gone quite as far as the British have in trying to have a complete spectrum of expertise trained at the Imperial Defense College.

I think the British look upon that College as a little bit more of a training ground for their future top civil servants than is applicable in our government. We couldn't do the same thing here.

For example, they had a man there from the Post Office Department in my class. He was being groomed as the head of their Post Office organization, and became the head of their Post Office organization. The New Zealand student was a naval student, and he was being groomed as their Secreatary of the Navy.

In other words, they do a little bit more selective training than I think we do or is probably practical for us to do.

The speakers at the Imperial Defense College were really impressive speakers. One of those that impressed me a great deal was Jan Christian Smuts. He had said that he'd never make another speech on a platform. So when Sir Jack Slessor twisted his arm and got him to come and talk to us at the Imperial Defense College, he wouldn't get on the platform.

He said, "I'd be violating an oath that I took to myself. I'm just going to stand down here in the middle of the aisle and talk." And he talked, and he talked, and he talked.

It was a very impressive talk, because it was a man who had seen much of war and of political strife. He was trying to pass on, in this hour's talk to the students of that college the synthesis of the wisdom that he had been able to distill from his many experiences. It just had everybody on the edge of their seats. You could tell that the old gentleman was really giving his all to try to give something that was worth listening to.

Q: He was really an authentic statesman.

Austin: He was. I think, had he lived, you wouldn't have the situation in that part of the world that you have today. He was too much of a realist, he was a practical individual, and yet an idealist with it all.

Another interesting speaker (I've forgotten his name) was the chairman of the communist party in Briton. He used very poor judgement. He gave, to the Imperial Defense College student body, one of the speeches that would have been appropriate on the soap box in Hyde Park. When the question period came, they tied him up so tightly in his own words that the poor fellow was almost weeping when he left the stage. In other words, they pointed out the non-sequitur of the things that he had said. It was a very friendly banter, but he realized that he pulled a 'boo-boo'. And it made him almost cry. He didn't get an converts that day, I don't think.

11 Austin - 370

Another speaker who came over there was our own Secretary of Defense, Louis Johnson, who had fired Louis Denfeld.

Instead of a coffee break at the Imperial Defense College you had a sherry break.

When we had the sherry break the director of the school, Sir Jack Slessor, sent for me. He wanted to introduce me to my Secretary of Defense. When the Secretary of Defense looked at me he said, "Where have I seen you before? From here up (he motioned with his hands over his nose) I've seen you some place before."

I said, "Mr. Secretary, it was when you were the assistant Secretary of War perhaps. Because that's the only time that I've been this close to you before, sir. I, at that time, was a public relations officer in the Navy Department. You called a meeting in your office, because something that the President had given to all of the military departments had been compromised in the WASHINGTON POST. You had Mr. Stetinius, from the State Department, who was in on this secret also. If you recall, sir, I was late arriving. When I got the word I came promptly, but I didn't get the word until a little late evidently, and you had started the meeting."

Actually when I went in, he didn't pay any attention to my coming in. I wasn't told what the meeting was about or anything, until Stetinius got up and came over and introduced himself and told me what the purpose of the meeting was. It was sort of as a slap to Johnson, I think. That's probably why he remembered my face.

After that the U. S. Army student at the Imperial Defense College, who was named Johnson, every time Colonel Johnson had a few drinks at a party he'd come around and put his hand up like the Secretary had right over his nose and peer at me and say, "Where have I ever seen you before?"

All in all, that was a very worthwhile year. We accomplished quite as much as you have accomplished by the students at the National War College, because I'd just recently been there. Yet it was done in a much more 'non-pressure' way.

For example, while I was at the National War College, one day we had snow in the Washington area at night. My particular driving squad was about fifteen minutes late getting into school. General Gruenther met us on the steps and chided us no end for being fifteen minutes late. We were military men, we should make allowances for such things as snow, and he was right. But after all, we were fairly mature people. We did know that the first speaker came on at nine-thirty. So our getting there at eight fifteen, instead of eight, was not quite that important, relatively speaking.

At the Imperial Defense College the lecture room was an old library, beautiful pannelling around with a secret door in back, which they kept well-oiled. When you came there the secretary of the school, who was an old Brigadier of the Marines retired, would show you the secret door. He'd say, "We like you to always be prompt to the lectures, but if something holds you up and you're a little late, this is how you get in without creating any disturbance. We always keep it well-oiled so that it doesn't creak. You can slide in and nobody will know the difference, and you won't disturb the speaker."

Speaking of the secretary of the college - he took great delight in sort of kidding me about my nickname of 'Count', in a nice jovial British way. He seemed to get a certain amount of pleasure out of kidding me about my nickname

One morning when I arrived at the college there stood the Brigadier waiting for me. He said, "I say Count, do you know a fellow in your service named Chandler?" "Oh yes sir. That would be Duke Chandler." He said, "Oh no, you can't do that to us. First a 'Count', then a 'Duke' at the Imperial Defense College from America. You can't do that to us." I said, "In this case sir it's not a nickname. His mother's family was named Duke. His full name is Alvin Duke Chandler, using his mother's name as a middle name. It's not a nickname, but he is called Duke Chandler."

So we had a very pleasant tour in London. They still had fairly strict rationing. This was in 1949, and it was still pretty strict rationing. We were able to get a little food from the commissary in the Embassy, but that was also pretty well rationed.

We were entertained in the home of every British student while we were there. You knew, when you sat down to dinner in their homes, that you were being served their week's ration of meat for the whole family.

So Ise and I decided that all the meat we could get from our commissary would be used in entertaining back our friends who entertained us, and sacrificed their week's ration to properly show us hospitality.

We thoroughly enjoyed the tour there. I've run into many of the students in various places in the years since, and it's always pleasant to see them.

Q: I think it would be of interest Count if there is a contrast, to describe the way the lectures were organized, the type of assignments that you were given at the War College with those that you had at the Imperial Defense College. Generally contrast the two approaches that they used in carrying on their studies.

Austin: The lecture series was very parallel to that at the National War College. The spectrum of experts was very much the same.

I would say that in the case of the Imperial Defense College you got a few more of the top people. For example, the Prime Minister came down to talk. That's like the President coming here.

There was more of an interest on the part of the foreign office and the treasury and the various important branches of the government in the solutions arrived at by the students to problems posed.

For example, the colonial office was very interested in any solution to a problem that had to do with their then colonies.

Very often you would have for a presentation of one of our solutions three or four cabinet members in that small room to listen in. Such interest as that is not evidenced in solutions at the National War College.

Q: I would assume that in the National War College the various heads of our government agencies look upon the lectures as more in the academic field.

Austin: That's correct.

Also they some times look upon it as quite a chore to have to come down to talk to them.

11 Austin - 375

I remember, I think, it was Gordon Gray who blew the whistle on the National War College and the Industrial War College for not coordinating their lectures any better than they did.

Gordon was asked to come down to speak to the National War College. Then a week or two later, he was asked to come down and give the same speech to the Industrial War College.

They have an auditorium big enough for both, and they do listen to some of the same lectures. They just hadn't bothered to coordinate their speaker programs enough to have the rest of the curriculum flexible enough so that they could hear the speakers at the same time.

I ran into somewhat the same thing when I was President of the Naval War College. I couldn't do too much about changing the speaker program that was already set up for the first term, because I went in in the summer. When I looked it over, I was a little shocked to see that they were asking heads of services to come up twice to speak to the, sometimes called, senior course and junior course.

So I got the Chief of Staff in and discussed it with him. He said, "Your predecessor, Admiral Ingersoll, issued an order which had a good effect. But it's one bad effect is that it made these two heads of schools too independent of each other. He ordered that they were to develop their curricula separate from each other and not to allow any compromise to degrade their curricula."

I said, "We don't want to degrade it. I have great respect for my predecessor and I'm sure that he had good reason for issuing that order, but it's now rescinded. Not only is that order rescinded, but any time that we have a cabinet officer or a head of department or a head of service or even a three-star level speaker here, I think it's important enough to have the two schools listen in on the hour's talk that he gives. If they can't make their schedule flexible enough to do that, then they better get together ahead of time and coordinate the lecture program to the degree necessary to obey that general rule."

And that's what we did after that. Frankly. it's an imposition on these people in high places to ask them to come up like that.

We had three courses at the Naval War College. You had the naval warfare course, which is for senior Commanders and Captains. Then you had the command and staff course, which is the level of the Leavenworth course and is more of a tactical training course. Then you had the naval command course. In some cases, when I looked into the records, we had had the same speaker come up to the Naval War College and speak on separate days to all three of those courses.

I not only viewed this with concern from the viewpoint of the speaker's time, but also from the viewpoint of the cost of having the same speaker three times.

I noticed, for example, some academicians were brought there two and three times to give the same lecture. Some of these would come from the mid-west or the far-west, and it's expensive. You pay their way. My budget was tight enough without being careless about the way it was spent.

So I could understand why Gordon Gray objected to speaking on two separate occasions. I had a very high regard for Gordon Gray. I got to know him when I was in several jobs here.

Q: I'd rather you went into this in more detail subsequently, Count.

As I recall you were telling me that when you went to the Naval War College that one of the things that you did — I'm speaking now of when you became President of the Naval War College — was to attend classes in order to see what they were doing.

That reminds me very much of a story that Gordon Gray told me about when he became President of the University of North Carolina.

He went around and attended several courses. In fact, he said that he actually did that for the full first term. He apparently sincerely impressed the professor of psychology so well that the professor asked him if he could possibly take time out the following term and give a few lectures in one of the psychology courses.

Austin: I think that the head of any school will be in a better position to act upon the suggestions that come up to him through his faculty or staff, if he had in fact been there.

I made it a point not to miss a single lecture the first year that I was at the Naval War College. This takes lots of your time, but I felt it was well worth it because then I had a complete feeling for the areas of overemphasis or underemphasis in the lecture program which I couldn't have had other than by attending the lectures. So I did do that. I also went to seminars and sat in on them from time to time.

I think the thing that I did at the War College that was probably most effective was to start, what they called, the president's hour. I had had a certain amount of experience which enabled me to answer questions which naturally came up in the minds of the students at the Naval War College.

So I experimented. I told the planning people to schedule an hour for me just to answer questions. I said, "I'll make no speech. I'll just answer questions." They said, "What do you want questions on?" I said, "Anything the student wishes to ask."

It was a very popular thing. In the sanctuary of a place like that, you can give forthright answers far better than you could if you were not in such a sanctuary. I always tried to avoid maligning anybody by name, but I would give them straightforward answers.

For example if you had such an hour today, somebody might pop us and say, "How did we get in this Vietnam war anyhow?" If I had the answer, in a straightforward way I'd tell them how I thought we did.

After this hour, the Chief of Staff came to me and said, "Admiral, the professors and the students have been streaming through my office all day today wanting you to do another hour like that each month. They want to schedule one every month."

I said, "Oh no. In the first place, I don't have that much wisdom to pass on, or that much knowledge to pass on. It would become non-productive, if we did it too often. I will agree to do it again, but we'll wait about three months and then we'll schedule one. I'll try to pick a time when I think something like the Cuban missile thing or something or that sort is raising lots of questions in their minds. Then I'll schedule another one, but we aren't going to make this on a routine basis."

Q: What happens often times when something like that is done routinely is that you find that the same students ask questions time after time, and many of the others don't participate.

Austin: That is correct. Just the regular questions of the lecturers, there were certain students that always had to get in a question regardless of how pertinent it might be.

Q: A bit of showing off.

Interview # 12

Vice Admiral Bernard L. Austin, USN, Ret.
Rockville, Maryland
by Paul L. Hopper
May 22, 1970

Mr. Hopper: Count, as I recall when we broke off last time you had talked at some length about your experiences as the Navy staff member of the National Security Council, and your attendance at the Imperial Defense College in England. Perhaps now you would like to discuss the continuation of your experiences after you returned to the States.

Admiral Austin: At the Imperial Defense College, toward the end of the half year there (the course is one year duration) the British officers began to be called down to their ministries or Admiralty or this or that or the other, depending on their home base. They were given very fine treatment by their ministries. They would be given a list of those assignments which the ministries thought they might be interested in and they were able to choose from several.

As usual my little wife got to hear that Captain so and so of the Royal Navy was going here or there, or Admiral so and so was going here or there, or Air Vice Marshall so and so was going there.

So finally one day the inevitable question came, "Where are you going, and when are you going to find out?"

I cautioned patience and reminded her that the British did things a little differently from what we found practical in the United States. Usually we were given a little less consideration than they were, and time to plan for our next move.

After several months of this kind of querying by my dear wife, I wrote a letter to our personnel detail and I asked if they could indicate to me whether I would be going east or west or north or south, sea or land. Of course, I preferred to go to sea and a cruiser, which was indicated on my fitness reports through the years back.

I said, "I'm particularly interested in trying to find out whether or not I will go to a duty which will necessitate the releasing of my home in Annapolis, Maryland. If I'm going to be on the east coast, I might want to have my family live there. If I'm going to be on the west coast, I might want to lease it again. And the lease is coming up for renewal quite soon.

I got a very short letter back from the director of detailing of Captains. It said, "It's entirely too early to determine exactly where you'll go. You'll be informed in due time." It then being about two months before I was going to have to go somewhere.

I finally got the news. My assignment was as commander of the Service Force Squadron one on the west coast. I had asked for duty on the east coast, other things being equal. I had two children in college on the east coast at that time.

Shortly after I received my orders I had a letter from my good friend Preston Mercer, who was most unhappy because he had just been ordered to a service squadron on the east coast and he had particularly asked for the west coast.

When I returned to Washington, I went to the Navy Department to see what the status of my service squadron staff was that I was going to be working with. Having been house mates with Admiral Sherman, who was then the CNO, and having been requested as his flag Captain in the Mediterranean when he was the commander of the 6th fleet, I merely stopped by his office to pay my respects and renew an old friendship.

He was most cordial and asked me how I enjoyed my tour at the Imperial Defense College. I told him it was a wonderful year, and I was very happy to have been there. He said, "Of course, you're getting a good sea command." I said, "Yes sir, I am."

I let it go at that because I knew that if I told him I was getting a sea command not to my liking, I would probably start sparks going and I didn't want to do that. That's not my way of doing business.

12   Austin - 384

So I went on over to the Personnel Bureau. I was in one part of it where I could look at the staff situation of my new command to be. A couple of offices away, through the glass partition, the director of Captain's details saw me and had someone come up and ask me if I wanted to see him. I sent word back, "No." The messenger came back a second time and said, "If I had time could I come in, because the Captain would like to see me."

After I'd looked over the situation regarding my staff, and more or less finished my business that I'd come to do, I went in and saw the Captain who was then the head of the detail section. It was not my good friend, Joe, who had been upset because of my going to the Imperial Defense College.

He was very nice. He said, "Count, you know your record rates a cruiser command if you want it." I said, "Well, I do." Then he sent for his assistant and thumbed through some cards and said, "Let's see the first one we can locate for you here." After he had thumbed cards for a bit, it turned out that there weren't any cruiser commands available short of about eight months. In other words, they'd all been just freshly given away, that were ripe.

He said, "We can cancel your orders to the service squadron and order you here to the Bureau to do board jobs and that sort of thing. And pull this skipper off his command at the end of five months. So that in five months, we can have you in command of a cruiser."

I said, "No. In the first place, I wouldn't do that to a Captain of a cruiser. Pull him off three months before the time that he's due to come off, because one year is too short a time. I'll be no party to that. In the second place, I don't fancy hanging from a sky hook here in Washington for five months doing odd jobs, when I could be out doing a regular job. In the third place, all my household effects are already on the west coast. It would be costly to the government to ship them back and cause me a lot of discobobilation waiting for them and wondering when they were coming. Let's just skip it."

He said, "I just wanted to let you know that we in detail here feel that you rate a cruiser command if you want it." I said, "That's comforting to know."

I was sent for by the Rear Admiral who headed that section for officers and men and everything, he was head of the detail in the Bureau. It was my good friend, Frank Watkins.

Frank said, "Count, how do you like your nice new command?" I said, "Well, Frank, you shouldn't have asked 'cause I'm going to tell you. I'm not going to mince words. The answer is, I don't. I asked for a cruiser command, I think my record rated a cruiser command, and there were plenty of cruiser commands that became available. You knew exactly when I was going to finish the Imperial Defense College to the exact day, yet you didn't give me one. You aked me the question, you've got your answer."

Frank said, "Count, you don't realize how fine a command we're sending you to." I said, "Well, Frank, I'm sure it's a good command. I know that you have to have somebody to fill these commands, but I also know that you know that this will be the command that I'm in when I come up for flag selection. You know to be in command of a service squadron, at this point in an officer's career, is not much help to his becoming a flag officer."

He said, "Now Count, we're changing all that. That's one reason we picked you to go to this command. We know you're a shoo-in for flag selection. So we wanted to change the idea that nobody gets selected to flag rank from a service command. That's one of the reasons we picked you to send you to this job. Do you realize that you'll have more ships under your command out there than a lot of Admirals have under their command?"

I said, "Yes, in numbers, yes. But how many of them will I ever see? How many of them will I ever be able to take to sea and maneuver, and advance my tactical competence, and that sort of thing? They're not fighting ships."

So Frank and I parted; he still contending that he'd done me a favor and I still insisting on being honest and forthrigh

I went to my service command and months later, after the Korean War had started, Frank Watkins came out with Admira

12   Austin - 387

Forrest Sherman for a quick inspection of forces in the Far East. Frank got me aside and said, "Count, there's something on my conscience I want to get off. When the MISSOURI ran aground Admiral Sherman, who was then CNO, called up and wanted to know where Count Austin was. We told him that you were on your way, somewhere between the East Coast and the West Coast, to go to your new command as Commander Service Squadron One. So he ordered us to order you to relieve the Commanding Officer of the MISSOURI.

"Count, this is what I've got to confess. I wrote your orders to command the MISSOURI, I put them in my middle drawer and claimed I couldn't locate you until things got so tight that Admiral Hoke Smith was then ordered in command of the investigation down there. He demanded a new Captain right away, and he said he wanted him to be one who had previously served in the MISSOURI. So we sent Page Smith to the job. I still have your orders in my middle drawer back in BuPers."

Q: You'd have been present during the surrender had you been on board the MISSOURI?

Austin: No, this was after the war. This was when she went aground down in Norfolk in Thimble Shoals Channel.

So I not only missed my cruiser command, I missed my battleship command too. But I did go to Service Squadron One, and it didn't turn out to be a bad command.

I was a little appalled when I first visited the ships of my command that were available. The esprit was not good in the command.

Q: There's always a let down after a war.

Austin: Frankly, I think BuPers had used the Service Force a little bit too much as a sort of a dumping ground, convenience in detailing. Where they couldn't find someone that was hollering for an officer, they'd send him to a job in the Service Force.

But, frankly, they have corrected that to a great extent. For example, command of a tanker now is considered just as good a command as you can have before coming up for selection for command of an aircraft carrier. It's called your deep draft command. It's a sort of a qualification for the better commands on the way up.

I found that I had lots of talent, but it was kind of depressed and not enthusiastic.

I had seven oil tankers and they were all swinging around the hook there in San Pedro. I called my chief staff officer and said, "We're going to go out for maneuvers. I will go out in my flag here, the repair ship. All seven tankers will accompany us. We're going to do manoeuvres. I want you to get the Captains over here and I will talk to them and forewarn them about just what we're going to do."

So he picked a time, sent a message, and got the Captains over there and we had the conference. I told them, "Gentlemen, you may think that what I'm going to do is a little unconventional. I want to give you your chance to say whatever you have to say about it before we go out. I will expect you to be able to cruise in formation. This is not to be a convoy type formation, it's to be a closed formation, close order. You're going to be expected to shift to division columns. We'll give the organization, and which division, and so on for tactical purposes. We will also form in a fairly compact formation. We will then execute zigzag by the zigzag clock."

As soon as I said that, I got protests from all skippers. Practically every one of the seven raised cain about it. They said that would be dangerous.

I said, "I will judge the conditions as to when it's dangerous and when it's not. If you all have your clocks in working order, and if you obey the signal when it's given, then everybody will turn in such a way that there won't be any danger. There will be danger if you aren't on the job and don't obey orders, and don't have your clocks working right."

As I expected some of the clocks were not in working order. This was my way of smoking this out. So we got the clocks repaired on the repair ship. We were sure that when we went out we were all going out with good workable zigzag clocks.

We got out and we did maneuvers, night maneuvers and day maneuvers, zigzag practice and everything. During this time, we had fog as you some times do on the west coast.

It was remarkable, we got back in safe and sound. Nobody had been hurt.

One by one the skippers came over. They were pretty enthusiastic about this, they'd like to do it again.

When the Korean War developed, or the police action in Korea as it was officially designated, one of the skippers of one of the oilers came to me one day from up the line. He said, "You know, Commodore, we've gotten lots of pats on the back for how well we've performed out here in the Service Squadron. I was one of those skippers back there in San Pedro that raised so much cain about your taking us out on maneuvers the day you had that conference. I'm willing to eat crow. If you hadn't taken us out on those maneuvers, we wouldn't be able to do what we're doing up the line here now. You made us learn how to control our ships in close situations. Up to that time, we'd just been point to point oilers. We just wouldn't be able to fuel these ships as expeditiously and handle the situation if we hadn't had the training that you gave us."

I'd only had this squadron about three months when the ice-breaker, BURTON ISLAND, which was one of my ships, came back from a pretty grueling experience up in the Arctic.

The Captain came over to call, as was usual. I said, "Captain, I intend to come over and inspect your ship." He did a double take. He told me all about their experiences and I was anxious to inspect his ship. But he was a little taken aback when I told him that I was coming over to inspect. He said, "Sir, when are you coming?" I said, "Tomorrow morning right after quarters I'll be over."

The next morning I went over and I inspected his ship from bow to stern and top to bottom. I had a few criticisms.

After the inspection, we were sitting down in the wardroom having a cup of coffee, the Captain said, "Sir, you don't know how grateful we are that you took the time to come over and inspect this ship." I said, "But I've given you a little hell since I've been here, it hasn't been all roses." He said, "We can take that, sir. This will do us lots of good, morale wise. This is the first time that this ship has ever been inspected by our squadron commander, the first time."

When the Korean unpleasantness developed, shortly thereafter, it was around the end of June that it started, my wife and I had been trying to fix a date with a Vassar classmate of hers whom she'd known a long time. She and her husband had a place up in the Palo Alto area and they'd been trying to get us up for a week-end. I finally had agreed that the long fourth of July week-end would be all right for me.

But lo and behold, I went aboard one morning just before this week-end and there was a message from Admiral Radford, which my chief staff officer had in his hand when I got aboard. It was fairly short. It instructed me to take the first available air transportation to Pearl Harbor, and come prepared to go west.

So I called my wife on the phone and said, "Call off our week-end with our friends. Pack my bag for an indefinite trip."

I went home, got my bag, got in an airplane, and went to Pearl. There Admiral Dennebrink was the Service Force Commander Pacific. He said, "Admiral Radford wants to see you."

So I went to Admiral Radford's office. He outlined to me what he wanted me to do. He said, "We don't have any proper Service Force organization in the Western Pacific. We have only one tanker, one ten-knot slow reefer, two fleet tugs, and the repair ship PIEDMONT, which you can use as a flag ship. I want you to organize the Service Force necessary to support not only the U. S. forces involved in the Korean fracas, but it must be so organized that at any time you can give the logistic support required by any of my war plans for that area, and continue to support the U. N. forces engaged in Korea."

I said, "Admiral, that's going to take lots more than one repair ship, one slow reefer, one tanker, and two fleet tugs." He said, "I realize that. You let me know what you need, and I will personally see that you get it."

After we had finished talking about my new job, he got on the subject of Admiral Sherman. He knew that Admiral Sherman and I were close friends. He and Admiral Sherman had not been on the best of terms. Admiral Radford probably felt that Sherman should not be the one that was made CNO, when Denfeld was given the goby. I think there was a little jealousy involved in this. They were both naval aviators. Admiral Radford had said a few things that I think, in retrospect, he probably had rethought.

He said, "I think Admiral Sherman is doing a very fine job as CNO." I said, "I think so too, Admiral. I always thought he'd make a good CNO." He said, "I didn't think he was the man for it, I'm frank to say that. But the way he's handled it since he's been in the job, I take my hat off to him. He's doing a good job."

I don't know whether Admiral Radford had a suspicion that this may be repeated to Admiral Sherman, or not, but I think he was sincere in what he was saying. And he had his chance later.

When I finally got back to Admiral Dennebrink, I'd been over in Admiral Radford's office about two hours. Admiral Dennebrink is a pretty outspoken individual. He said, "Here you come out as one of my subordinate commanders and you are taken over to the fleet commander's office for two hours and I have a hell of a time ever getting a word in edgewise with him." He was really not happy about this.

He wanted to know what the Admiral had said about my assignment. I told him and he assured me that he too would back me up. That I only had to ask, and if it were at all possible and reasonable, he would put his shoulder to the wheel and help me.

He said, "I've got a staff all picked out for you. We didn't have time for you to do this after you got here. I just went down to the docks and airplanes and picked off people that were under orders back to War College and places like that, and I picked out what I think is a pretty good bag of officers. They aren't too happy. Their families, in some cases, are half way back or all the way back in the States waiting for them at these nice jobs that they were going to. They're all pretty able fellows and I think you'll find that they'll do the job."

Q: Were you a flag officer at that time?

Austin: No, I was a Captain. This was my last command before my class came up for selection.

He said, "We have a special airplane standing by to take you and your staff out. As soon as you can after you get there I want you to give me what you need, then we'll start to work on it." I said, "I'll do that sir, very promptly."

So I went to the airplane and met my staff. The statement about their not being happy was not exaggerated. They had problems with their families. Some of them didn't even know how to get in touch with them, they were in transit and that sort of thing.

I said a few words of sympathy about their problems. I held a conference in the plane as soon as we got squared away at the proper height, when the motors weren't climbing any more and you could hear a little bit.

I said, "Now gentlemen, we're going out to set up an organization. We don't want to have one more ship or one more officer on the staff or one more man than we need to do the job. But we don't want to have one less ship or one less officer or one less man than we need to do a proper job.

"We'll have no warehouses from which to operate. We are an afloat outfit. We have a duel responsibility, the support of U. S. naval forces and also to be ready to give logistic support in the event of any development in the Far East that triggers any CinCPac war plan. You're all experts in your respective fields. I am not an expert in any of your fields, nor am I an expert logistician. I have never before been a logistician until a few months ago when I assumed command of Service Squadron One. The name of our squadron is not the important thing, the way we do our job is the important thing.

"I want each of you to take a pad and pencil, go into a corner by yourself, communicate with each other as may be necessary, and when we land in Okinawa I want you to be ready to have a conference at which we will discuss the requirements of this organization in ships, staff, personnel in general."

There were a number of questions. Several of them revolved around ammunition, because there weren't any ammo carriers out there.

It just happened that the few months while I was in command of the Service Squadron One on the west coast, I had gone up where the NITRO (one of the ships built as an ammunition ship) was being overhauled. Much to my consternation her overhaul was not progressing as fast as it should have, and I had had to raise a little cain about that. There had been too many changes of plans about the ship. It had gone in and was being given a fairly extensive revamping and overhaul. It was going to be a good ship when it got out, many months later. But you can't fire ammunition from a ship that isn't going to leave the west coast for a number of months.

We had a good bit of discussion on how we were going to cope with the ammunition situation.

When we got to Okinawa and got out aboard the PIEDMONT, which was the repair ship which was to be our flag ship, I found that my old classmate Chief Topper was the skipper of it. Chief was a sort of happy type officer, and he greeted me with open arms, and wanted to know what he could do to make me happy. So I told him that I'd be wanting to hold a conference with my staff, as soon as we had cleaned up and gotten fed and had a chance to unpack a little bit. So he let us use his cabin, they were still working on getting mine ready for me.

We held this conference. Each one stated his needs. Various ones whose areas of responsibility sort of intermingled with or overlapped with the one who was stating the primary need would question or elaborate and maybe some time add a little bit to it.

At the end of this conference, with my staff sitting in, my chief staff officer drafted a dispatch. After we made a few changes in it, I initialled it and we sent it off.

I don't recall all the details. I remember the number of oilers we asked for was seven. We asked for reefers, we asked for ammo ships. We knew that we wouldn't get the ammo ships very quickly, so we asked for AKAs to use as ammo ships.

After we'd finished this and sent it off everybody began to wonder if we'd asked for the moon.

Q: Isn't it difficult, in any sort of a military operation, to estimate with any degree of accuracy ahead of time what you need, because your needs may expand many times what you initially wanted?

Austin: Frankly this is so true.

We didn't know at the time we drew up this dispatch, how long this thing would last or how many forces would become involved.

For example, before it was over we had a British carrier force out there, as well as our own two carrier forces, to cope with. Then all the miscellaneaous ships that are are with them and do odd jobs.

Frankly, I'd had some qualms after we sent this dispatch. I thought maybe we've asked for the moon, and maybe we would have done better to approach this by increments a little more.

As it turned out, we hadn't asked for the moon. We had use for every ship we got, and a little bit more. In fact, we did have to add to our force rather than subtract from it.

The type of ship that we found just invaluable was one of these landing ship docks. You couldn't think of that initially in your logistic requirements. I found that that ship never finished one job before there were two others for it.

We helped the Army move equipment that they couldn't move any other way. At that time, the roads of Japan were not exactly interstate 95.

My staff had also indicated the increment to the various sections that they thought they required. This added up to a staff of about 95. That turned out to be just about where we stabilized.

We had many very nip and tuck situations. For example, we had to comb the thrown away gear, including ammunition, on Guam and other places to meet some demands. We used these little YP boats to bring bits and pieces up from Guam, until we could get them from the states. We used the Japanese economy.

Today you'd probably have a harder time, because there'd be more anti-war demonstrations and that sort of thing.

For example at one time, when the aircraft carriers began to use napalm, we simply just didn't have very many spare drop tanks to use as napalm containers.

Admiral Ewen was one of the task force commanders of one of the carrier groups. He came to me and made an exorbitant demand for drop tanks. I'd known Eddie before, he was senior to me, but I knew him well enough that I could talk straightforwardly to him. I said, "I don't think you need that many." He hit the ceiling. He said, "Why don't you think I need that many?" I said, "Because you can't use them." He said, "What do you mean? Are you telling me how many sorties I can make from my carriers?"

I said, "No Eddie, I'm not telling you how many you can make. But I know how many hours there are in a day, and I know about the average number of sorties per 24 hours that you people make. I have to know these things. If you use nothing to arm your planes with, except napalm tanks, you couldn't use the number you're asking for to be always on hand in the replacement force. In the second place, we just don't have them. We'll get them for you as quickly as we can, and in as great a number as you need."

Eddie wasn't too happy, but he bowed to the inevitable. I went on the Japanese economy, and made a contract for the equivalent of drop tanks, which was just as good for the purpose being served as if they had been manufactured in the States and passed Navy specifications and all. These drop tanks, as I recall, cost around $35 a piece. The drop tanks that they were replacing cost $220, I think it was.

Just to prove my point to my good friend Eddie Ewen, I told him, "Eddie, if we put as many drop tanks in the replenishment force as you are demanding it's going to interfere with your fueling and it's going to interfere with your reprovisioning. These drop tanks take up a lots of volume. They have to be stored topside in most of these ships. You can't take food space in a reefer down in the refrigerator spaces to store your drop tanks. We just can't do that. They have to be top loaded."

"They have lots of top space on those ships," Eddie countered. I said, "All right now, just remember this – if you find that these drop tanks are holding up your replenishment operations I won't be surprised."

When we got the flow of the drop tanks from the Japanese economy, I loaded one echelon of the replenishment force to the exact demands of Admiral Ewen. In so doing, they did have to find every place possible to put these things. They had them on the tankers, reefers, and every ship that was in the replenishment force.

About a week after they'd been up to North Korea with the carrier task force Eddie came in. He said, "Count, how about getting some of those damn tanks off of those ships so we can refuel and get provisions without taking so long? It's an uncomfortable thing to be tied up as long as we are re-provisioning when we've got those damn things on there." He laughed and he was a good sport about it. "You were right, damn it. I didn't realize those damn things would take so much space."

I said, "We could give you more to store in your aircraft carriers." He laughed and said, "Listen, we've got those things hanging from the overhead all over those carriers now."

With the help of the Japanese economy, at $35 a throw, I was able to give them all they wanted. If we'd had to wait for contracts to be let by the Bureau of Ordnance and ship them out – oh boy.

This recalls something that is appropriately in the logistic part of the discussion here.

One day while I was in Sasebo, I received a request from the U. S. Air Force in the area for a large number of what we called 'tiny tims.' I always tried to help our sister services whenever I could. I figured we're fighting the same war, and that's what we should do. So I didn't hesitate, I gave the go signal. We commandeered a train, and loaded it up with the 'tiny tims' they'd asked for.

It took a while to load this whole train with 'tiny tims,' getting them from the ships to shore, and trucking them, and all. Just as the train was pulling out I got an urgent dispatch from the Bureau of Ordnance in Washington, referencing to the request to me for 'tiny tims' and authorizing me to accede to the request on one condition. That was that I receive the equivalent dollar value of the 'tiny tims' turned over to the U. S. Air Force in 100 and 500 pound bombs.

It was a little late, the train was already pulling out. So I let it go.

I was pondering my answer to the Bureau of Ordnance, when in came a dispatch from Admiral Radford, Commander-in-Chief of the Pacific, referencing the request to me for the 'tiny tims,' and the Bureau of Ordnance dictates to me as to the condition under which I could accede to that request. Then it went on to say, "We are fighting one war, we have one enemy. Anyone who can deliver any ammunition against that enemy, you will assist in any way that you can."

Q: You must have been pleased to receive this.

Austin: Yes, I was, and it took me off the hook.

The thing that the Bureau of Ordnance didn't know was that already the Air Force had been acceding to my requests locally for 100 and 500 pound bombs of which they had enormous supplies. Frankly our pipe line on those had sort of run dry.

That's why the fellow in the Chief of the Bureau of Ordnance's Bailiwick, who was responsible for keeping that pipe line flowing, saw this dispatch and hit upon it as one easy way to get him out of a delicate position. He knew the Air Force had these, and so he figured that this would be a good way to get himself off the hook for not having ordered enough of these in time.

It turned out everybody was happy. In my dispatch back to the Bureau of Ordnance I pointed out that I had already received probably more than the dollar value of the 'tiny tims' in these small bombs that the Air Force had given me with no strings attached.

Q: What about the landing at Inchon? Were there any special problems that came up during that time?

Austin: Yes, there definitely were.

Admiral Struble was the commander of the 7th fleet out there. Admiral Struble was very good about cutting me in at an early time on his plans, because he knew that I didn't have warehouses full of stuff. I had to order stuff so that I wouldn't have a lots of it that I couldn't carry around on my back. He was very good, and his staff was very good about cutting me in on advance plans. On the Inchon plan, this was an exception.

One day I received a dispatch from Admiral Struble. He was then in Tokyo, with his flag ship the ROCHESTER. It said, "Come to Tokyo, earliest. Use my plane." His plane was then at Okinawa, and I was in Okinawa harbor.

So I took his plane and got to Tokyo earliest. I was met by Admiral Struble at the gangway, and most enthusiastically escorted below. As I went further and further below, I began to realize that something was cooking. More and more Marines were providing security as we got further and further down towards this conference room.

We sat down in the conference room, and Admiral Struble gave the word to go ahead with the presentation. This was the presentation of the concept of the naval part of the Inchon landing.

When the presentation had been finished Admiral Struble turned to me and said, "Captain, can you support it logistically?" I answered very calmly, "No sir."

Admiral Struble can become spirited, and he became spirited. He wanted to know why I couldn't support it logistically.

I said, "Admiral, the concept of the operation is to mount out of three seperate mounting areas. The ammunition for such an operation would therefore have to be in three separate areas. That ammunition is not now in the Western Pacific. I'm getting a little out on a limb, but I think I can support that operation in every respect, including ammunition, provided you mount out of only one place the ships that have to have ammunition. I have a cargo ship that's already left the west coast, full of ammunition, cargo loaded, but it's not fleet issue loaded. So I've got to get that ship into port, take it's stuff out, and then peddle it around as needed. I can't fleet issue from it. All of one kind of thing is in one hold, and all of another is on top of it, and so on."

He was not happy. He said, "If you're sure of what you're saying, we'd better go see Admiral Joy."

Admiral Joy was the Commander Naval Forces under Mac Arthur for the Far East. We went to see Admiral Joy and he said, "There's only one answer. We've got to be supported logistically. If we can't get support with the present concept, we're going to have to change that concept.

Admiral Struble said, "We can't change it. That's General MacArthur's concept." Admiral Joy said, "We'll have to go see General MacArthur." And so they did.

General MacArthur easily saw the handwriting on the wall and he said, "Change the concept to suit the logistic commander's requirements because we've got to be supported."

So they told me to go ahead and pick my port. I said, "I'd much prefer the closest port to the objective, of the three places that you're mounting from, and that would be Sasebo. It's a good protected harbor. In case of bad weather you can still boat in there longer than in some place like Okinawa. I would prefer Sasebo." They said, "All right, make it Sasebo. Go ahead and move your ships accordingly."

I got a disptach off before I left ComNavFe headquarters, diverting the ship that was in mid-Pacific and go directly to Sasebo.

There were times when I thought I had overcommitted myself, because the weather did deteriorate. We had a typhoon that didn't come directly over Sasebo, but it came close enough that we had very high winds.

The afternoon before the ships were due to sail the next morning for the operation the boating got bad. The senior officer present afloat in Sasebo ordered all boating to stop.

I got in my little boat and went over to see him. I pointed out to him that we still had ammunition to furnish to some of the ships and that I would like permission to continue boating at my own discretion, which he gave. So we continued to boat until about two o'clock in the morning.

At that time, I received a report that the whale boat, of the senior officer present, had swamped while on a trip ashore to deliver a message to ashore authorities. Whale boats are pretty seaworthy craft, and I could see the light at the end of the tunnel by then, so I ordered all boating cesased until daybreak.

We were just able to get the last bullets to the last ships before they sailed the next morning, that's how close it was. I was happy though, when I got the report that all ammo was aboard.

The Inchon landing itself was fairly hastily conceived. I think one of the successes of it was due to the fact that there had been so few people who had known that it was about to take place.

I feel that many of the operations of our forces in southeast Asia have been less productive than they would otherwise have been, mainly becuase too many people get in on the approval of the operation. Therefore too many people know it's about to come off. There are ears listening along that pick this up and it's communicated to the enemy, and so when you go the enemy isn't there anymore.

Q: I suspect that's particularly true about our move with Cambodia.

Austin: I think so. I think it's true about any operation where the local commander is not able to conceive and execute with dispatch, and without having to go too far to too many to get approval of his concept.

The Inchon operation was extremely successful. We had a minimum of losses for as big an operation as that. I think it was partly the boldness of the operation, it was a classic tactical maneuver, it was a bold maneuver.

As you know, the tides in that area are around 31 feet. Unfortunately, one of my fleet tugs got itself high and dry trying to pull off an LST that had waited too long to try to get off the beach. The poor tug, in trying to pull off the LST, swung itself over a shoal spot and pretty soon the shoal spot was a dry spot. The tide went out that fast. So there was a most uncomfortable fleet tug skipper, sitting up there as if a monument to the tides.

Q: He being the sort of a chap who was always trying to help others.

Austin: That's right.

Fortunately, we had other fleet tugs by that time and we were able to get him off with no great damage.

Interview # 13

Vice Admiral Bernard L. Austin, USN, Ret.
Rockville, Md.

by Paul Hopper

June 7, 1970

Mr. Hopper: Would you like to discuss now, Count, some of the concepts of war gaming that were developed while you were President of the Naval War College?

Admiral Austin: When I arrived at my new post as President of the Naval War College, I immediately looked into the war gaming part of the course. A few years earlier I had been asked to come to the War College after my logistic experience in Korea.

A group of the younger staff officers at the college had been shipmates of mine in times gone by. They were anxious to show me how up to date the War College was getting. I had, I'm afraid, made statements in my talk which might be construed to criticize the time lag of the War College in dealing with up coming changes in concepts and preparations of people for modern type situations.

So as a part of their tour that they wanted me to show me how up to date they were, they took me to the war games department. Sure enough, they were playing with little wooden models down on the checkered floor. I asked them,

"What are they doing, the Battle of Jutland?" Strangely enough the answer was, "yes." They were still doing the Battle of Jutland.

I'm not one to say that there isn't much to be learned from the Battle of Jutland, but I think that one has to recognize that what you learn from the Battle of Jutland you can more or less integrate into your more modern fleet operations and formations and that sort of thing without continuing to hammer the Battle of Jutland into the student's mind. I don't think you need to go through the Battle of Jutland play by play in order to get the essential lessons that are to be had from that particular battle.

Q: It's rather like the Army going over the battles of the Civil War over and over again.

Austin: Yes. There seems to be an attraction for these classical battles. I don't say that one should forget them and not synthesize the elements of them to see how they still stand up in later times.

I do think at the time that I was talking to these members of the staff there were new problems, such as how to maintain the fleet at sea a long time without having to make immediate returns to base. This sort of thing, it seemed to me, was more pertinent to the present than to the emphasis that was being placed on the past in this case.

So when I looked over the war gaming department, I was happy to find that the electric simulator had been installed. It was the first of its kind in the world, it was in operation and the students were using it. But I was unhappy to find that it had developed difficulty. The virgin ground which was plowed by the installation of this mechanism had evidently not been prepared well enough for this sensitive machine. It required an environment which called for a little more air conditioning for uninterrupted performance, than had been provided. So we were experiencing considerable difficulty in the operation of the mechanism. Then a fire developed as the result of the lack of proper cooling and that didn't help at all.

After months of trial and tribulation and fighting the matter through the budget process, because as usual the money hadn't been put in the right pocket to take care of this promptly and effectively, we finally got the thing operating on a reliable and continuous basis.

The war gaming staff was very small, but we did increase it to enable them to cope with what I thought would be an expanding requirement.

We began to develop other than student type working. We invited fleet commanders to come in and try out their own war plans on the simulator, bringing their own personnel too for the judgment function of their own war games for their side.

Then we would provide a staff of students or members of our staff, depending upon the nature of the situation, to be the judgment factor contributors on the other side. This was not entirely a new concept with us, it had been tried out before. We nurutred and encouraged people to come and do this and they were very pleased.

The commanders who took the time and expended the effort to bring their staffs up there to learn how to play on this new instrument were highly pleased with the results that they got. In some cases, they changed plans to correct deficiencies which had been shown up by the war games on the simulator.

Then we extended the war gaming to a remote control center. We first tried it out over at Quonset Point. We had the control staff over at Quonset, instead of right in the building with the simulator. Then we extended it to Norfolk, Virginia.

The first to cooperate with us on that basis were the anti-submarine warfare people in the Atlantic. They had quite a good problem to try out on the simulator. Once we got that established, we got it extended as far north as Canada.

We had difficulty finding the money for the leased wires some times to enable us to do this. The benefits derived from these remote control participations was such that we found people willing to put the shoulder to the wheel and help us out with the leased wire costs from their own budgets in some cases.

The entire concept of war gaming, which the War College had always pioneered in, was greatly extended by the introduction of the electronic simulator. It has the capability of estimating damage to ships, flights of airplanes, and that sort of thing, all based on programming.

All computers have limitations of the proper and thorough programming of them. In the case of a computer of this type you pretty well know the range of each weapon, you pretty well know the explosive effect of each weapon. So there isn't too much excuse for poor damage estimate, except in the area of probability of a hit. This, of course, is pretty well established by statistics through many years. So if your computer is meticulously programmed, you get a very excellent estimate of damage from it. Because the computer knows immediately whether or not the target is within range of the ship that is shooting at him, or the plane that is shooting at him.

So the horizon of the art and the spectrum of war gaming were greatly increased by the installation of the electronic simulator.

The War College is now in the process of installing more up to date computer capability. I think when we get this set up in there, it will take another quantum jump. It's just one of those things which you just can't possibly do manually as

13 Austin - 414

well as a computer can do it for you, because you don't have the time to make all of these long involved mathematical computations for each particular situation. The old manual war games recognized that they didn't have the time to sit down with pencil and paper or slide rule at a bunch of long tables and figure these things out. So they did lots of rolling of the dice to see whether one or six hits were made or what. The computer, I think, is a little more sophisticated and a little more accurate

Q: Are there any further observations that you'd like to make Count about experiences you had at the Naval War College.

Austin: The global strategy discussions at the War College, which take place each year just before the graduation of the classes and courses, was one of the most rewarding parts of the year for me. I took a personal interest in the global strategy discussions.

I personally participated in the selection of those to be invited. This was not an easy matter, because you had more nominations than you could ever possibly invite. The staff sorted these out and arranged them by categories. Then we would meet in my office, the Chief of Staff and the officer in charge of the global strategy arrangements and myself, and we would go over these name by name. It took days to do it, an hour or so at a time. We felt that it was important to keep this thing on as fair a basis and as high a level as possible and that it was worth taking this time. I think it was.

The reaction of the civilian participants was such that I got not perfunctory thank-you letters, but some of them were extremely interesting in their perceptive comments and in their very enthusiastic appreciation of the efforts.

One person in particular I remember had reached a very high place in our society and I invited him, the first or second year that I was up there. He wrote me a letter and he started off by saying that he had attended one of the first global strategy discussions. And therefore when he got the invitation to this one, he hesitated. Because the first global strategy discussion that he attended he found the students who participated in the committee meetings to be lacking in breadth of vision, to have what is often referred to as the military mind regarding the solution of complex social and international problems. Frankly he was negatively impressed. But he said, he did accept. And he was surprised to find that the students who participated in the discussion that year were very broadly informed, were very considerate of all factors of the problems. He said it was just, to him, a very gratifying revelation that the War College students were abreast of international problems

13 Austin - 416

and matters to the extent that he found them.

This of course was gratifying but not surprising, because I knew that my immediate predecessor and some of the predecessor's predecessors had been working in this direction.

The War College has always, I believe, encouraged people to think. In the more recent years, I think, it has encouraged them to think more boradly than perhaps they did think in the earlier days at the War College.

I think that this is not only attributable to the policy of the directing staff at the War College, but also to the fact that more and more, as we have approached the present time in history, the international problems of our country have taken on a very complex nature.

It's no longer a matter of whether we'll send Marines into Nicaragua or not send them, because of the military or political situation. We have a very complex determination to make in this day and time, and that is what would be the effect on all the other Latin American countries if we sent Marines into Nicaragua, and what would be the reaction at home, and what would be the budgetary considerations.

In other words, I think that naval officers through the years without going to the Naval War College have become more broadminded in their considerations of the military factor of our national problems. They realize that the military factor must not be studied in isolation from the other factors that enter into the equation.

Generally speaking, we were able to get very eminent people as speakers at these strategy discussions. The participants I think, with practically no exceptions, did feel that it had been worth their time to take a week off and come and address themselves to and be informed on the major national problems and international problems that might be under discussion at that time.

Q: You spoke, Count, of involving the Canadians in some of the problems at the War College. Did you seek to involve the British and the French also?

Austin: We had a course at the War College for naval officers of friendly nations. This course very often included British students and Canadian students. Generally speaking, the course included about 35 different nationalities.

This course was established pursuant to be a staff study, which interestingly enough was made by Commander Colbert, who is now President of the War College, Vice Admiral Colbert. He was then in my shop in the Navy Department in the International Affairs Division.

I became concerned about the problem of providing naval instruction for those friendly nations who wanted to seek naval instruction in our country. We were having requests made and we really didn't have a good answer. We couldn't very well send them to our course without reducing the level of intelligence and classified information that we would have exposed. So I had this Commander Colbert make this staff study. It was favorably received.

In due time Colbert was sent up there. It was Captain Colbert then. That's how long it took the thing to get from concept to execution Captain Colbert went to the War College to establish this course.

In the consideration of the guide lines for it, we had to determine that every student would be able to speak English because with 35 different nationalities it would be impossible to cater to everyone, like they do in the United Nations. We just didn't have that kind of interpretation service, so we had to require that they all speak English.

Different national government concepts of being able to speak English varied a bit. Some poor fellows would arrive there able to say, "Okay." When you got much beyond that, they were in trouble.

They had to listen to their lectures in English. They had to do their writing in English. So it behoved them. The word got around quickly that they better have a fair command of English when they got there.

Of course, to help them out we did have an arrangement with the University of Rhode Island for the teaching of English for all those who wanted voluntarily to participate in the course. This helped lots of them become quite fluent during the year that they stayed there. The combination of the course that was available to them, and the experience in talking with their peers of various nationalities enabled them to leave there with a good command of English.

I feel that that course has been an extremely successful part of the War College.

Some 20 students that have graduated are now, or have been the heads of their navies. That's a good percentage, because the course was only started about 15 years ago.

For example, the student from Great Britain, at the time of the visit of their First Sea Lord to the War College while I was there, was invited to my house for dinner the night that I had dinner for the British Lord. The First Sea Lord was so impressed by this man that when he got me aside later he said, "I want you to write a letter and remind me that I want this young fellow on my staff. I'm very much impressed by him, and I'm very much impressed by the course he's taking. I think he's what I want on my staff." So a couple of years later, the First Sea Lord came back to this country and along came Captain Williams as his aide.

The course was never oriented to propaganda. There was, during my time at the War College, an effort made on the part of the office of the President to twist my arm to inject propaganda into the course. A group was sent up with that purpose in mind. They were briefed by my staff, and they then were received by me. We talked the thing over, pro and con. I pointed out to them that the type of officer that we had there, in the first place was so smart that if we started propagandizing him he would know it right away. It would be counter-productive.

The very best propaganda in the world is no propaganda. Let them observe, let them see how we do things, let them see how we live and treat our wives and that sort of thing. Then let them go home with an honest appraisal of us and the way we train people for our military careers.

I frankly was a little surprised that when the group had finished their study of our situation, they went back and reported to the President that they agreed with me. And that we were accomplishing more in the way we were doing than we might accomplish if we started injecting knowing propaganda into the course, hard selling our way of doing every thing. That would have been the end of the usefullness of that course, if we had bowed to the pressure.

They said, "You've got all the future heads of their services maybe in this country. You've got them all here right under your thumb. Why not pump them full of our concepts? Why it's stupid not to." I said, "It would be stupid to attempt to." And I think I was right.

13 Austin - 421

Just the other night about 9:30, up to my front door drove three cars. We were expecting them because they had called and asked if we'd be at home and could they come out and say hello to us. The occasion for the visit was the presence in Washington of one of our former students in this course from Mexico.

In Mexico you can take leave from your military service to be a member of parliament. He was here as a member of the Mexican parliament and a guest of our Congress.

So he wanted to come out and see me. His wife was along. She had gotten along well with Mrs. Austin in their mutual attempt to study Spanish and English. We had seen them several times in Mexico City when I made visits down there during my term as Chairman of the Inter-American Defense Board. So they wanted to come out and see us.

Along with them came the two other students who happened to be on duty in Washington, who had been with them in Newport. One was Captain Kapsalis from Greece, and the other was Commodore Pak from South Korea. They all brought their wives. We had a jolly reunion and reminisced until midnight.

Practically every place that I went in Latin America, during my service as Chairman of the Inter American Defense Board, my aide while there, designated by the local government, was the senior former student at the Naval War College. In some cases, I learned there had been quite a bit of competition as to who was going to be my aide.

In fact, in Mexico this one who became a member of parliament had had quite a round with another Mexican student. The other Mexican student ranked him a few numbers so he won out. But he and his wife still invited me and my wife to lunch with them while we were there. He told me, " I wanted to be your aide, but this other guy ranked me a little bit, and he pulled rank on me."

That kind of mutual understanding we were able to develop by keeping that course on a very high level, strictly professional.

I remember one night at the height of the Greek-Turkish flare up, the Mexican student that I just referred to had asked my wife and me to dinner. Included in the other guests were the Greek and the Turkish student.

When we arrived, we were a little earlier than the others, we usually arrived promptly, but other nationalities don't arrive promptly, he showed me the guest list. I said, "How did you get the Greek and Turk to come together?"

He said, "Oh, we invited them before this flare up. We know them both very well on a personal basis. I called them both up and told them, since this flare up between their countries if they wanted to reconsider and not come it would be okay. But I hoped they would come. They both said, 'No, they'd come, we like each other."

During the dinner, you would have never known that there was any difficulty between their countries.

So I think, in many instances, a little better understanding between nations was produced during that course, in a small way. But these things have a way of growing.

We had, for example, the Pakistanian and the Indians together. I'm sure that there was at least one line of mutual understanding between them.

Q: Don't you think Count that the mutual understanding and the respect and admiration among military men from all countries is very much the same?

Austin: Yes indeed, very much the same. There is probably more of an understanding between those who are professional military men. In some countries you find that the military are more political than in others.

In our country in the Navy, you don't find much other than a straight professional approach to being a naval officer. This is true in many other countries.

It is more true in the case of the Navy, I believe, and I don't say this in an unkind way, than it is in the case of the Army. I think that applies to our own country and it applies to the smaller countries.

Q: The naval officer is traditionally more internationally minded —

Austin: And he isn't as long in one place ashore, as in a case of an Army fellow who's sent out to command a regiment or division in some part of Brazil, for example. He may be there for quite awhile, and might become quite politically potent in that part of the country.

Generally speaking, that course was a very very successful one.

One other little element I might mention: We initially specified that there should never be but one student from a country in one year.

When the Indonesians wanted to send students to take the course, they wanted to send more than one. I was then President of the War College. The office of CNO contacted me and wanted to know if we couldn't make an exception. I wasn't the one to say, but they wanted my advice.

I said, "My advice is not to make an exception. In the first place, if you allow the Indonesians to send five this year, you won't get any more Indonesians here. They will say, 'We have all we need of their know-how, and so that's that.' Furthermore, there are several other countries who have wanted to send two or three instead of one. You have to treat all alike. When you begin to accept more than one in some of the smaller nations, you are going to lower the level of professional competence that you get. Because some of these smaller nations don't have too many that are that well groomed and educated and endowed. My advice is strongly not to break the barrier, to keep it as one from each country."

13 Austin - 425

And that has been done.

That should do for that subject, I think, Paul.

Q:

There was a hiatus between the time that you were a student at the Imperial Defense College in London and when you came back to this country, before you became President of the Naval War College in Newport. Would you like to comment on that period of your career?

Austin: I believe we covered fairly well the first job that I had when I came back from the Imperial Defense College. That was the logistic job in the western Pacific.

I think we also covered the short period of time that I served on the staff of Admiral Wooldridge, who was then the Joint Chiefs of Staff representative to the planning board of the National Security Council.

My service with Admiral Wooldridge was terminated rather suddenly because the Vice Chief of Naval Operations, Admiral Duncan, called me on the phone and advised me that the impending departure of the Director of the International Affairs Division for a sea job a little earlier than had been expected put me in line to be his successor. He would therefore like me to come up forthwith and assume the duties of the Deputy Director of the International Affairs Division, so that I could get the lay of the land before I took the reins of office.

I had in the meantime been selected for, but not yet promoted to, flag rank. I went up as the Deputy to the Director of the International Affairs Division and his prospective relief.

As Deputy, I noted that the Lieutenant who was the top secret security officer for the division had rather odd concepts of how to handle matters that needed to be taken up with the Director. In other words, I would ask him about something and he would give the answer to the Director and not to me very often.

I am not, I hope and I think, a very suspicious individual. I tend to take people on face value pretty much, but this particular young fellow certainly aroused my suspicions as to his loyalty to the overall cause and to the country. He seemed to overdo his loyalty to one person, the Director of the division.

So I asked ONI to have a security check made on this young fellow. When the Director became knowledgeable of the fact that I had requested this security check, he called me in and expressed great displeasure at my having ordered the security check on one of his favorite employees.

In the meantime, I had received an interim report from ONI. I said, "Admiral, I think you'd better take a look at this interim report. I've just received it and it doesn't look good."

He reluctantly looked at it and then became very unhappy. Because the interim report indicated not only childhood proclivities toward communist associations, but very recent ones and of frequent nature, with actual known communists.

The Director was very upset and said, "Goodness, we'll have to get rid of him." I said, "Yes sir, I agree. I think the quicker the better." He said, "All right, you handle it with BuPers." So I did. They cooperated very promptly and we had the young man out of our office that day.

This, I think, illustrates the fact that: those who are closest to, and who ingratiate themselves most with, the heads of offices and divisions, and bureaus in a democratic form of government some times have ulterior motives. And unfortunately, the high official very often is blinded by the blandishments or the super service of whatever it may be that is ingratiating the subordinate with the head of the organization. Once they get in well with the head of the organization, it's pretty hard to even for the second man in command in the organization to do anything about it without getting bawled out, as I did.

13 Austin - 428

This recalls to mind an incident similar in nature, when I was the Press Relations officer. I gave a party for the departing head of my organization, the Public Relations Division as it was referred to in those days, Commander Lovett. He could not be relieved by his regular chosen relief for a matter of months, and so I was to succeed him as the acting head of the division.

To this party I invited a couple from the office of Naval Intelligence. He was a very personable Lieutenant and his wife was a very charming blonde of German origin.

In those days, the Press Relations office was a part of ONI. This was why we had ONI people at the party. It was part of our organization.

I had been able to get hold of a sufficient amount of contraband alcoholic beverages for those days. So the party became a jolly party.

Towards the end of the jolly party, I received quite a bit of pressure from this very charming wife of this Lieutenant in ONI about getting her husband transferred into the Public Relations division. I chatted along with her, pretending to be more under the influence than I was. I got lots of information about her family back in Germany. Her father was an industrialist in the Ruhr and he had thought that Hitler might be good for the country. She was giving me quite a good line of how to look on the bright side of Hitler's Germany.

\# 13 Austin - 429

When I got home that night, I couldn't quite get out of my mind this conversation with this lady. As I assessed it, it definitely was intended to open the way for her husband to come into my office. I didn't see quite what the objective was, but it made me a little suspicious in view of some of the things she'd said about Hitler and about her family back in Germany.

So I noticed the habits of the officer for a few days before I went around to see the Director of ONI. His habits were that he'd come into my office several times a day, read the ticker tape, chat about what was going on in the world of Public Relations, viz a viz the situation in the world, and what were our legislative plans and all. After observing for a few days, I noticed that he always had a briefcase when he came through the office late in the afternoon to go home. He always had a nice fat briefcase.

I finally went around and saw the Director of ONI. I told him that I had had this conversation with this officer's wife at this party, that it had caused me to dwell upon it a little bit, it was hard to put out of my mind, I couldn't exactly see any motives or anything, but it seemed not a natural conversation. So I suggested that maybe he might want to observe this officer to see if there was anything amiss, in view of the fact that his wife was of German origin and that she did still have immediate family in Germany who seemed to be not unfavorably inclined towards Hitler.

The Director bristled up and said, "That young man is as loyal as anyone. He's my tennis partner."

When I came back about a year and a half later from England when we were in the war, I casually asked what had happened to this Lieutenant. I was informed that he had been cashiered because his wife had been observed to be a daily visitor to the German embassy. They had intercepted her with copies of highly secret documents from ONI.

So again, an incident of one who has gotten very close to a high official because he was a good tennis player, because he was an amiable chap, and yet he had gotten there for a purpose. It's a highly developed technique.

For example, if they wanted to use a girl in a situation of this sort, they'd never pick an ugly one. They'd always pick a very charming one, one who would be a perfect lady, and highly cultured in every way.

But it is a weakness in our system. You don't have to be a 'Joe McCarthy' to add up two and two sometimes and get four. He always got a little more than four. If you'll be honest about it, there are times when you should bring things to the attention of people.

Q: I have often thought that although the period of McCarthy was bad it had certain by-products which were beneficial.

Austin: Some immediate by-products that were of benefit to our nation, but I think the long range by-products were most detrimental to us. Because now a real admitted communist sympathizer can shield himself from any blame by the media, by wrapping himself with the robes of the persecuted.

Just mentioning the Joe McCarthy era has given an immunity to many people who are not loyal to the extent that they wouldn't have had if there'd never been this heightened advertisement of the fact that you can overdo the suspicion of people being disloyal. And some times the suspicion of disloyalty and the right to personal dissent from the majority opinion became pretty close to the same thing.

Q: There's a bit of that cry 'wolf, wolf' too. Many people now feel that because of the period of McCarthyism that it just simply isn't proper to suspect anyone or to feel they could possibly be disloyal.

Austin: That's correct.

Now we've gotten me into the International Affairs Division. This was my first assignment as a flag officer.

The duties of the office, of course, involved advising the Secretary of the Navy and the Chief of Naval Operations on international matters. This included all National Security Council papers.

13 Austin - 432

One of my experiences in that field was with Mr. Robert Anderson. The first encounter with him, I briefed him on a subject. He agreed with what I recommended that he do, and he told me to prepare a memorandum for the Secretary of Defense for his signature along the lines of my recommendation.

When I took it to him to sign, he read it. He was very pleased, but when he got to the penultimate paragraph there he said, "I don't like to say this."

I said, "Mr. Secretary, that is in accord with the recommendation that I made. But I think I see why you don't want to say it in those words. It could be interpreted as your making a judgment in the field in which the Secretary of State is the responsible officer." He said, "That is exactly right. I don't want to say to the Secretary of Defense that I know better about the political implications of this than the Secretary of State." I said, "I will change it."

So I took it back and I changed it to avoid this little quirk. I took it back and he signed it without a qualm.

As I was about to be relieved as the Director of the International Affairs Division, my successor was to be Admiral Smedberg. He'd been my Deputy as an understudy preparatory to relieving me.

I told him one day, "Smeddy, it's about time you had personal dealing with the Secretary on some National Security Council papers. Suppose you go down and brief him today."

So Smeddy went down and briefed him. He came back and wrote the memorandum to the Secretary of Defense in response to what he had understood to be their meeting of minds. He came back after taking it down to the Secretary and he was very puzzled. He said, "He wouldn't sign it."

I took it and I said, "Smeddy, I saw this before you went down. I was afraid the Secretary wouldn't sign it. In view of the urgency of this matter time wise, I didn't suggest that you rephrase it. This is the sentence, that if you will change it, I think he'll sign it."

I called in our secretary, Donna, and dictated that sentence over again. I said, "Just do the thing over with that sentence this way."

Smeddy looked at me and said, "Do you think that's all right?" I said, "Yes, Smeddy."

So he went down again and he came back all smiles, he said, "He signed it. All he read was that one little bit. How did you know this?"

I said, "Smeddy, when you work for a man like Mr. Anderson you learn his desires, his ways of expressing himself, and how he thinks. Mr. Anderson is a very religiously proper individual. He does not ever want to encroach on anyone else's area of responsibility, or even intimate that he in encroaching on his area of responsibility."

Here I have again jumped to the end of my tour, without giving you anything in the middle.

In the job there, it was interesting many times for me to go to a CNO briefing and find that everyone around the table was recommending opposition for a course of action based mainly on the fact that it was a course of action proposed by either one of the other services or the State Department. I never could accept this as a valid reason for opposing the course of action. So quite often I found myself in opposition to everybody else around the table. Some times these things were decided against me, and I guess some times I was wrong.

One time I remember, Admiral Fechteler was the CNO at the time I believe, I listened to all the other briefers then I said, "Admiral I have to advise you to Consider ——." And I gave him my line

He said, "You sound like you've got some good points there Count." Then all of the others started hammering away at my points.

Admiral Duncan, he was a pretty wise Vice Chief, sat there through all of this discussion. He let them tear me to shreds. Finally when it looked like the pack was going to really get me Admiral Duncan said, "You know, Count's right. The others haven't given one valid reason. He's given plenty of good valid reasons why we should do it the way he recommended. The others are all biased because it's not invented in the Navy Department. I recommend to you that you follow Count's advice.

Much as we like to think that we've gotten away from bias and parochialism, it's a hard thing to get away from. Being objective is very difficult. This is one of the reasons why when I was the Director of the Joint Staff I strongly recommended, without success I might add, that the Joint Chiefs of Staff all be required to have their Principal offices alongside of the chairman and be briefed by the Joint Staff first on every item of the agenda rather than getting bias from their service staffs before they heard other people's views. I still think that would be a step in the right direction.

I recognize that no chief is ever going to want to give up control over his service, which is his by virtue of being the senior officer of his service. But the law does provide that he have a Vice Chief of equal rank with himself, who shall take over from him the detailed duties of his office so that he can give his primary effort to being a member of the Joint

13 Austin - 436

Chiefs of Staff. They really do not do it. As long as they keep their offices up in their respective bailiwicks, instead of bringing them down in the joint arena, it will not work as well as it should.

During this time, we had a number of interesting developments. This was after the Korean fracas.

We developed, during that time as I've already told you, the concept for the establishment of the course at the Naval War College for the foreign officers of friendly nations.

We developed a very orderly and systematic way of keeping ourselves in readiness to give prompt advice in international matters. We did this partly by means of preparing black books on each area of responsibility. The organization of the International Affairs Division was such as to mesh with the State Department organization. So we were organized on a regional basis. Each of these regional sub-offices kept what they called the black book.

The black book just had the pertinent things, like copies of treaties and background information that was generated day in and day out about that particular region. Of course, it started out with the latest intelligence estimate on that area and then superimposed on that things like copies of treaties, etc. etc.

One day I received a frantic call from CNO. He was down in the JCS meeting room. He said, Count, "Have you got a copy of such and such a treaty?" I said, "No, sir, we don't have a copy of it. But I think I have the NEW YORK TIMES version of it in my black book." He said, "Well, get it down here as quick as you can."

Sure enough, I got the black book for that area and it had the text of the treaty as printed in the NEW YORK TIMES. So the JCS used the NEW YORK TIMES text of the treaty, as included in the black book, as the authoritative version of the treaty for the purpose of their study of the particular incident and problem that they had on the table at that time.

In many other instances, the CNO and the DCNO would find it useful to call down and say, "How about letting me have your black book on such and such a nation."

It did have, in nicely arranged form, readily available pertinent information. Of course, they were highly classified because they also had the latest national security policy in respect to that region, and that sort of thing.

Q: Very different type of reference

Incidentally I was going to ask you Count, how did the International Affairs Division of the Navy and it's comparable divisions in the other services mesh back into ISA?

Austin: The ISA organization of course made less viable many of the State Department's and military service channels of communication, which had been previously established and which were working very well.

Actually at times, I felt that perhaps ISA was not performing overall as well as the individual departmental organizations had previously performed because they tied in perhaps at a higher level with the State, but I'm not sure they had the working level tie-ins that we used to have.

Of course, many of the functions of the International Affairs Division of the separate military departments were taken over by the ISA organization in Defense. They were taken over by them, because there was a commonality and it provided one interface instead of several interfaces. Of course, you always had the single interface of the Joint Chiefs organization.

Generally speaking, I found that ISA and my shop worked together well, harmoniously. We were able to help them, I think, at times. If anything, I think that if they had leaned more on help from the services it might have been better, because we had accumulated a certain amount of know-how and background in these divisions which I think very well could have been used some times.

13   Austin - 439

ISA has to, in some way, be able to tap the information sources in the individual military departments in order to speak with any authority about military capabilities, limitations, and that sort of thing. It should be a coordinating function.

13   Austin - 440
through 444

These pages were eliminated in the re-typing process as they were a duplication.

Interview # 14

Vice Admiral Bernard L. Austin, USN, Ret.
Rockville, Maryland

by Paul Hopper
June 17, 1970

Mr. Hopper: Count, as I recall in the last interview you were discussing the relationship of the naval officers of International Affairs with ISA in the Department of Defense. Have you further comment?

Admiral Austin: During the period of service as the Director of the Joint Staff, I think I learned more than at any other time in my career about the importance of face to face solutions to problems between organizational entities who did not have a common source of information regarding the problem at hand.

It was so distressing to me, as a military man, to see the Joint Chiefs at times in all sincerity at great odds on a matter of great importance to the military security of our country.

I honestly believe that the decision which was taken at a later date to require all officers to have duty in a joint job before being eligible for selection to flag or general rank was a good decision.

When you serve in the Joints Staff or on a joint staff of some joint commander, you get a different viewpoint. It isn't that you lose any loyalty to basic concepts of your service or of your early upbringing. But in the first place, you learn that men of the other services also are interested in the security of our country. And that your service doesn't have any monopoly on patriotism, or devotion to duty, or intelligent foresight as far as weapon systems are concerned, or sole responsibility.

During my service as the Director of the Joints Staff, several of the senior people in the Secretary of Defense's office learned that if they came to me on an informal basis they could get information which was needed on an urgent basis without sending to the Chiefs a formal demand for such information. Of course, this put me in a delicate position a number of times.

I didn't make any secret of my activity. I, in fact, very frequently informed the Chiefs of requests and of the answer that I had given.

I always made quite clear to the Deputy Secretary of Defense, or this or that or the other who might seek some quick information from the Joint Staff, that this was only a staff bit of information and had not received the blessing of the Joint Chiefs of Staff.

I remember one time the Deputy for Personnel came down. He made a request that I really didn't feel I could in all conscience give him the answer to, because it was a request for more of an opinion than for facts. So I told him, "I can tell you my own view on that, but I don't think it's fair to even get anything from the Joint Staff on that because it's an opinion. The Joint Staff should not express opinions on important personnel programs or policies. This is something which should come only from the Chiefs themselves."

He was a very knowledgeable, interesting, and nice sort of person. He said, "I see your point, but gosh it would help me if I could get this right away. I've got to go up to Congress. If I could just tell them that the Joint Chiefs of Staff think this way or that way, it would help me a heck of a lot." I said, "Well, I appreciate that. If you wish to do it, I will take a request from you for this opinion and submit it to the Chiefs on an urgent basis and give you as quick an answer as possible." He said, "No, I think that it would take too long."

Actually lots of people got the impression that it took longer to get something through the Joint Chiefs than was the case.

I recall in one instance where an emergency situation had arisen in which the United States was asked to furnish the logistic support for a relief situation. There was no great military significance to what was going to promptly be done, but in view of the fact that they were using JCS assets naturally the Chiefs were asked to provide the airplanes and so forth so as not to discobobolate any capabilities that they might have that the State Department may not know about.

So I received an advanced notice by telephone early in the morning. I went up to see the chairman of the Joint Chiefs and he said, "This is something we'll have to act on very fast. You call a meeting of the Chiefs right away. In the meantime, have your staff draw up the necessary dispatches to get the planes moving. Assume that the Chiefs will go along with this."

So by the time the Chiefs met, all they had to do was look at the dispatches that we laid before them and give their nod, and the planes were on their way. This was all done in the matter of about an hour. Of course, the people on the State Department side of the river there were flabbergasted by the speed with which we had acted. But it can be done.

Frankly I think that if my pet solution to JCS difficulties had ever been accepted, and the Chiefs had offices right down alongside of the chairman, many things could be handled in a much more timely and much more proper way than under the present arrangement.

The general training that an officer gets in one of these joint jobs, I think, stands him in very good stead whether he's ever selected for flag rank or general officer rank either. Because if he goes out, because he's not selected for flag or general rank, to look for a job in the civilian part of our society, the broader view that he will have had as a result of serving on a joint staff will stand him in very good stead.

Q: I feel equally that way. Many of the officers that I've interviewed from time to time do have joint staff training. I always give them a few more credit marks.

Austin: They will probably fit into more jobs and be a little bit more generally useful to the organization that they go to.

Q: They adapt better to civilian type work.

Austin: Now Paul, do you want me to say anything more about the service on the Joint Staff as the director, or do you want me to shift to something else? Of course, the experiences on that staff for a full tour of duty are innumerable.

Q: I think it would be interesting, Count, to include some more episodes of this same type which illustrate the way the Joint Staff worked and the relationships, not only to each of the individual services but to ISA and the extent to which it had relationships with the State Department.

Austin: I might go into the interface between State Department and the Joint Chiefs of Staff.

When I first went to the job, the Joint Chiefs were having a monthly meeting with officers from the State Department. Mr. Murphy was usually the head of the State Department delegation. He was the JCS contact man in the State Department, and a very understanding and wonderful person. Mr. Merchant was another. Of course, they always brought with them their experts, depending upon the agenda items to be discussed.

Then, of course, there were meetings other than those regularly scheduled meetings, when a situation came up that either the State Department or the Joint Chiefs felt should be discussed face to face between them. They would ask for a meeting, and it was always granted regardless of which asked for it. It was made convenient to hold it.

These meetings did much to bring about a better understanding between the military considerations and the political considerations in the political-military problems, but very often at these meetings it would become clear that each side had been briefed from such different viewpoints that it was very difficult for them to bridge the gap between their original concepts before coming to the table.

The Joint Chiefs told me to go into this matter and to see what I could do to establish a working interface between the State Department and the Joint Chiefs of Staff at a lower level than Chiefs themselves and Ambassador Murphy's level.

So I had a meeting with Chip Bohlen, who was the head of the policy planning staff at the State Department. He and I rolled up our sleeves and went into this problem in a very meaningful way. The result was a recommendation, which I submitted to the Chiefs, that we exchange officers between the Joints Staff and the State Department, and that we also establish a regular direct relationship between the Director of the Staff and the head of the policy planning staff in State.

The Chiefs balked at this. They weren't ready to go that far. They agreed to the establishment of the line between the head of the policy planning staff and the director of the staff. And they authorized me to take any members of the staff with me to these meetings. It was specified that these meetings were to be without commitment on either side merely for the prupose of trying to pave the way for a meeting of minds on problems that were common to the two organizations.

I think that these meetings did in fact pave the way a great deal, because they certainly brought the meeting of minds between the Joints Staff and the policy planning staff on such things as for example, the Marshall plan. I was actually a member of the inter-agency Marshall plan planning group. The full recommendation, I think, would have been better, but the time was not right.

When I would come back from one of these meetings, I would see that, through the proper channels, all of the Chiefs were informed of the pertinent points that were raised, and the views that were expressed. Although the meeting had no binding effect on anyone, it at least did enable us to meet around a table and to exchange views without having to take a biased view, in a friendly and uninhibited atmosphere.

At a later time, when I was down here on a trip from Newport, Buz Wheeler was then the director of the Joints Staff, he learned that I was in the building and asked me to come down and see him.

He said, "Count, I recall that you tried to get the Chiefs to agree to exchange of officers with the State Department and they turned you down. Do you still feel that that would be a good thing?"

I said, "Yes, I do. The time just wasn't right for it then, Buz. I think now you'd have a better chance of getting it accepted by the Chiefs. I think we've gone a long way since then."

He said, "Well, I'm on the verge of making that recommendation. Before I did, I wanted your slant on it. I knew that you had made quite a study of it, and had argued the points before the Chiefs. So I wanted to see if you still felt the way you expressed yourself at that time."

I said, "Yes, I do, and even more so. I think it's even more important now than it was then."

So the proposal was made and it was accepted at that time, and there is now an exchange of officers between the two organizations.

Q: Incidentally Count, I think that subsequent to that time there was put into effect an arrangement whereby more than one officer or civilian from ISA would go to the State Department and spend a period of two to three years and a State Department comparable employee would go to ISA.

Austin: That's what I meant by an exchange.

The present President of the Naval War College was one of those exchange officers. He was over in the State Department and subsequently was sent over to the White House, I believe, as a sort of an aide to one of their people over there in the political-military field.

I do feel that the fears that prevented an earlier acceptance of this were not as well founded as was the need for a better and closer interface. After all, the security angle is some times overdone. If an officer is in high repute in the State Department, he should be just as acceptable from the security angle as an officer who wears stars or bars.

The day to day working relationship between the Joint Staff and the staffs of the service chiefs was something that I gave much consideration to. I always encouraged officers of the staff, when they first reported on board. I encouraged them to know as much as they could about what was available in their department and where to get it and who to go to. I also made it quite clear to them that they were no longer wearing the suit of their service, they were wearing a joint suit. And I expected them to shed any service bias or any concept that they were in any way an agent for their service.

Some people, at first were a little shocked by this and didn't take to it too kindly. But I found, in the long run, they all felt it was the only way to work. After all, you can't do a good job if you have divided loyalties worrying you all the time. And if you're doing a good and conscientious job on a Joint Staff, there may be those in your parent service who will criticize you, in fact there will be. But I think in the long run, they will respect you more for being able to be objective and to do a good job and to shed credit on the service, rather than the other way around.

I regret to say that the only officer that I ever had to really have up and threaten to send out of the Staff was a naval officer. He was a very enthusiastic naval aviator, he was a brilliant officer, but he was on a project that he thought should go all naval aviation and he was not being quite as objective as he should be.

I had a presentation made to me by this group. They had differed on a very fundamental point, in fact it was holding up their study. After I heard all the arguments, I agreed with the Air Force chap who was the head of the group. This just made the naval officer feel very very badly.

He came back to me, after the group had departed, and he said that I had just pulled the rug out from under him.

I said, "No, I don't agree with you. I put you in the position of having to make your case instead of just expecting that I'll support you because you wear a blue suit. Your case was not good, it wouldn't stand up in court. If you come up here with a good case, I'll support you. If you don't, I won't. In the second place, you stop being an agent for the Navy, or you'll stop being a member of this joint organization."

It was pretty tough for him to take this aboard, but he did. And he turned out to be a good officer. In fact, he went back to the Joints Staff for a subsequent tour of duty.

The duties that I had as an operations deputy for the Navy gave me an insight into the joint arena from a different angle. I think we've covered some of that.

Did I tell you about the time that we had the joint strategic objectives plan all approved, except for one thing, and that was the definition of 'limited war'?

Q: No sir.

Austin: That's an interesting one and it illustrates the point that when in a joint arena even one of the parties does not wish to arrive at a solution to a problem, it is very difficult to do so.

In this case, the operations deputies had set up the deputies of the operation's deputies to go into the detailed analysis of this plan. The officer that I had designated was a Rear Admiral named Miller. He was a very knowledgeable chap, and a very fine officer. He was my assistant, he was the assistant Chief of Naval Operations for plans and policies, which made him my deputy.

I was the senior operations deputy at that time. I had urged them to all assign to this group someone they could deputize to use his own judgement so he wouldn't have to go back and ask them so much. So they had all assigned pretty smart people to this group.

The group had really done a commendable job. They started out with something like 35 splits, and they had reduced it to this one split. The split was on the definition of 'limited war'.

Finally the deputies to the OpDeps reported to us that they could not reconcile this one thing, but they had a meeting of minds on the JSOP on everything else.

We called an OpDeps meeting to face this problem. The operations deputies all came down with their definitions to 'limited war.'

In the workings of the Joints Staff and the Joint Chiefs, when a service has a view which is different from that which is printed in the 'green' as it were, which is the committee print that comes out of the staff effort and it's printed in the green, if there be a difference of opinion from the green the service view is expressed in what is called a 'purple.' This is simply because the reproduction facilities of most of the services, at that time, produced white paper with purple mimeograph.

When we met on this problem, all of the OpDeps had 'purples.' And we argued, and we cajoled and we tried to reach a meeting of minds. We finally ran out of time and scheduled another meeting for the next day.

Then we went through the same process, each bringing down a new 'purple' to try to bridge the gap which had been manifested by the dissertation and the arguments of the previous day.

So at the end of that long session, we still had no agreement. So I said, "Gentlemen, we are going to try to reach an agreement on this thing. It's silly to get the Joint Chiefs in on something like this." So we scheduled another meeting.

At that meeting I led off by saying that I had read all of the last 'purples' of all of the services. And that I was prepared to accept, of course, the Navy 'purple' or the Army 'purple' or the Marine Corps 'purple' or the definition of 'limited war' as set forth in the Air Force dictionary.

The OpDeps looked at each other. The Army OpDep and the Marine OpDep said that was a fair enough proposition and they would go along with that and they would accept any of those four.

I asked the operations deputy of the Air Force how he viewed this proposition. He said, "I will only accept the phraseology of the Air Force's last 'purple.' The definition in the dictionary is out of date."

I said, "The definition in the dictionary was published over the signature of General Nathan Twining. That was only a matter of a short time ago, because General Nathan Twining is the Chairman of the Chiefs right now."

He was a little embarrassed, but he adamantly refused to go along with the acceptance of his own service's dictionary enunciation of what constituted 'limited war.'

I do not know, but I strongly suspect, that he had been told not to let that paper get up as an agreed paper. Therefore, he was to drag his feet on this. I'm only conjecturing this, but why else would one do so on a matter which really after all didn't make that much difference.

Q: Incidentally Count, speaking of the Joint Chiefs of Staff in arriving at decisions, must they be unanimous or can it be a divided decision?

Austin: When their decisions are not unanimous, there is sent forward by the chairman the dissenting view of the dissenter or dissenters. Some times, I regret to say, there have gone forward four different views. It could even be five, if the chairman didn't agree with any of them.

I observed, either as director of the staff or as an operations deputy, enough to have a pretty broad view, I think, of the type of men who get to be heads of their service and therefore members of the Joint Chiefs. I would say that they are all highly capable, highly intelligent, highly motivated, patriotic citizens, as well as professional competent individuals in their particular services. Therefore, I feel that most of the difficulties which have been referred to as inner-service rivalries have stemmed from the fact that there are so many problems that must be faced by the Chiefs. Their average agenda is 13 items, and some of them are very involved things.

So they have to depend to a large degree on their service staffs to brief them on the pertinent facts that affect each problem, or that bear on each problem. If your service staff is highly competent, highly motivated, dedicated, you'll get a good briefing and an objective briefing. But if your service staff contains people who are steeped in narrow concepts, you may have withheld information at the briefings and you may get a lopsided briefing. You may even get some times a briefing that is so phrased as to deceive.

I recall one time, General Curt LeMay was acting Chief of his service, he used a set of figures at the JCS table which had been given to him by his staff and those figures were literally correct. Mr. Gates was then Secretary of Defense, and he was sitting in on this meeting because it was a highly controversial matter.

I was an operations deputy, at the time, for the Navy. I was allowed by my chief to speak to this problem. When I called to General LeMay's attention that these figures, though literally correct, were most deceptive in view of the fact that they dealt only in megatonage and not in numbers of delivery capabilities, General LeMay saw the point. And so did the Secretary of Defense.

This is one time when the figure that was given at the service briefing, which was intended to give a sort of distorted picture, was technically and literally correct.

This is very much like the advertisements that you some times see on television. They give one impression, you can't sue them, technically they haven't violated the law of verity, but they have distorted it to the limit of the law.

Q: Like the old saying that: 'figures don't lie, but liars figure.'

Austin: Yes.

Actually I think that the average Chief realizes that there is a certain amount of lack of appreciation of the other sides views. I have even heard the Chiefs speak to their service staffs and tell them that what they're giving them won't stand up in court. In other words, it won't stand up to the cross fire at the JCS table.

I had a very difficult time with the staff of the CNO at the time that I was the operations deputy there because Admiral Burke, at that time, had been the CNO for so long and he had gotten around him so many people that were devotedly loyal to his concepts. Frankly a few were there because they followed those concepts and always told him what he wanted to hear.

I found that it was most difficult for me to get some parts of the staff to make an objective study and to come forward with an objective briefing. More often than not when they would bring forward their briefing sheet to me, preparatory to the next day taking it to the CNO briefing for the JCS meeting, I would have to send them back to the drawing board.

I'd say, "Gentlemen, this won't stand up in a joint arena. It just doesn't have enough basic logic." "But that's what Admiral Burke said last year."

I'd say, "Yes, but things have changed in this year. Admiral Burke can't go down there and convince the other Chiefs that this is the way it should be simply with the argument that, 'this is what Admiral Burke said last year,' because they don't give too much of a continental darn what he said last year, this year, or the year before. Because they are only going to bow to logic and to fact. Now go back to the drawing board and come forward with some proof that this should be the position, not just a statement that this is what Admiral Burke said last year."

This caused my tour there at times to be rather difficult, because I was dealing with lots of people who I think in some cases began to wonder if I weren't too doggone joint in my view, and to question my loyalty to my service.

Q: I believe some time before Count you suggested that you had always thought the Chiefs individually would receive a less biased point of view in their breifings, at least a more objective one, if they were briefed by the entire Joint Staff, instead of being briefed by their individual services.

Austin: I certainly do, Paul. This is not to say that some times there is information in the individual services which has not gotten down to and been fully assessed by the Joint Staff. Therefore, I would suggest that if they were briefed first by the Joint Staff that they then have access to any briefings by, not only their own service, but any of the services. I think this would really smoke out the biased viewpoint chaps and lay the facts on the table. When you lay the facts on the table, most high principled people will judge them pretty fairly.

As I was saying just a minute ago, I think that at times there were a few who questioned my Navy loyalty. And in fact one day Admiral Burke, at a JCS briefing, when I had had to take a position which was not the position of his experts on this subject, he said to me not entirely in jest, "Count, you're too damm joint in your views."

After that meeting, I stayed behind and I asked Admiral Burke for a few minutes in his office alone. At that time, I told him that if he ever embarrassed me before my people again in that manner that he would have to find himself another operations deputy. I felt that my usefulness would not continue, if he gave substance to the whisperings of a few that I was not being as diligent in my putting forward of the Navy's best foot as I should be to be the operations deputy for the Navy.

There were times, of course, when I went to a JCS OpDeps meeting when I had to argue like heck for something that I personally didn't believe in, because I had been instructed by my chief that those were his views. And therefore, I couldn't very well undercut him by agreeing to something which was not his view at the JCS meeting.

I did my best, if I had a strong feeling to the contrary, to convince him that he shouldn't hold those views or that he should modify those views. But in all loyalty to the chief that I was serving in the service that I was representing, I had to let him determine what that service's position was to be, if he had taken it out of my hands. In some cases, that was the case.

I don't think anyone can point to a case where I was disloyal to the naval service. And I am quite confident that they can never point to a case where I was disloyal to my country. If there were a choice, I'd rather be disloyal to a service than to my country.

Q: You have covered nicely your tour as Director of the Joint Staff and your tour as head of the International Affairs Division of the Navy Department, and also your experiences as President of the Naval War College.

Could we go back now and have you relate some of your experiences during the time that you were commander of cruiser division number two?

Austin: Command of cruiser division number two was my first sea assignment as a flag officer. I went to that immediately after completion of my tour as director of the International Affairs Division in the Navy Department.

As you know, that cruiser division was in the Atlantic. It was excellent training for me, as a 'make you learn' type young flag officer. I was very fortunate in that I was given command of the Midshipmen's cruise, during the year that I had the job.

This cruise took us to Quebec. If you've ever navigated the St. Lawrence at the foggy time of the year, you know some of the problems incident to that section of the River.

I had aboard a group of civilian guests of the Secretary of the Navy. We had a very successful visit to Quebec. The Canadians were extremely hospitable and killed us with kindness.

14   Austin - 466

The U. S. Consul General there was a very fine chap, whom I've met a number of times since, as a matter of fact. He also did his job for the Midshipmen and all in a very commendable manner.

We left Quebec all spirits high, everyone had had a wonderful time. I invited the Secretary of the Navy's guests to be my guests at dinner in my cabin that night as we were going down the River.

Due to the visibility being very poor, I had stayed up on my flag bridge until just before I had to do down to welcome my guests in the cabin for dinner. I noticed that the visibility was not good and getting worse all the time as night came on.

So I got down below and we were chatting along at dinner. The dinner was going very nicely. The chef had done himself proud. Everybody was in a good mood. When all of a sudden, I felt this crash.

I excused myself very abruptly and dashed up to the bridge just in time to see this little British freighter right across the bow of the PITTSBURG. The poor commanding officer, of course, his first impulse was to back clear. I said, "No, wait a minute Captain. Slow, but don't back. Because if you back, that thing may sink. Hold your bow in there until you know whether or not he will float if you take your bow out. Reduce your speed."

Of course, the Captain of the little British freighter was very excited about that time and he was yelling. My main concern immediately was whether or not there was any loss of life, and if so were there people in need of medical attention. We finally got the word from the Captain of the steamer that luckily there had been no loss of life and that he needed no medical assistance.

When we were sure that it was safe to disengage, the PITTSBURG very slowly backed away and the little steamer was able to still navigate. So he went off to the side of the river and anchored.

I called my staff into session and I said, "Now I want the Chief of Staff to go over and invite the Captain of the little freighter to come on board for an investigation of just what happened."

The Chief of Staff went over and came back. He said, "No, the Captain wouldn't leave his ship." I said, "We'll find out if he's agreeable to having an investigation on his ship." No, he wasn't agreeable to that. In other words, he wasn't talking.

Q: He realized that he was at fault.

Austin: Actually he was. He had been coming up the river in the opposite direction, and then had cut right across the bow of the PITTSBURG, who was on his proper side of the river.

Due to being as close as ~~you are~~ *he was*, the radar didn't show it in time. It was the old human eyeball that first detected that he was coming across the course of the PITTSBURG.

Of course, I had to have a thorough investigation of it. I regret to say, as so often happens when you have an investigation, you find somebody who didn't do something he should have done. The thing that the Captain hadn't done that he should have done was to have started sounding his whistle at intervals as specified by the inland rules before the visibility got so bad that he couldn't see far enough to avoid such a collision.

But the actual handling of his ship was done in a very shipshape fashion. He came out smelling like a rose, except for this one thing. The investigation had to point a finger at him for that.

It's the old old story, if there hadn't been a collision probably it never would have been noticed that he hadn't been sounding his whistle.

Q: Unusual too, because the British are normally quite conscientious about the rules.

Austin: Yes. This skipper had radar. He had heard a whistle which he was avoiding, but in so doing he came right across the bow of the PITTSBURG.

Of course, the damage to the PITTSBURG was nil. This was not a repetition of the time that she lost her bow, which was a previous situation.

Q: Did the United States pay compensation of some kind to him, or was that ruled out?

Austin: I frankly don't know what the Admiralty decision in the case was.

Now with cruiser division number two, we did a tour in the Mediterranean. While in the Med, I had the good luck to be in command of an amphibious exercise conducted there. But I was unlucky enough to have it in very very bad weather. Bad weather and amphibious exercises don't mix too well.

The situation was one of those border line ones. It was rough weather, but it wasn't quite rough enough in my opinion to give up the exercise.

The commander of the amphibious group was a very good friend of mine. He was so reluctant to launch his boats that I finally had to cruise up into the area to see for myself whether or not the water there was too rough to launch boats. Because he kept telling me he couldn't launch his boats, the water was too rough.

I did steam up into the area and, in my opinion, the launching was not too difficult. So I ordered him to launch his boats. He, of course, came back with the usual reclaimer that it would be on my head if anybody was hurt. Luckily, no one was hurt.

It was a good bit of training in rough weather conditions. If you avoid all training under rough weather conditions, then what kind of an amphibious force have you got?

Q: How are you going to operate in rough weather if you have no experience dealing with it?

Austin: That's correct.

I'm afraid that situation didn't help this particular Captain, who was the amphibious group commander there. I'm afraid it didn't help him to get selected for flag rank. He balked on this occasion.

I still have a high regard for him. He was just being a good conscientious over-cautious fellow with his people. I didn't criticize him for that.

I'm afraid when the analysis of the exercise was made and the dispatches were read by the people who did the analysis, they probably didn't feel that he had been as quick in getting his people ashore as he should have been. And that he shouldn't have had to have a prod from the force commander. (I was acting as the task force commander there.)

14 Austin - 471

Q: Incidentally Count, did you see the movie called MEDITERRANEAN HOLIDAY?

Austin: No, I haven't seen it.

Q: It's a delightful picture. It's purely a tourist sort of a picture. It was based on a practice cruise of a contingent of Norwegian naval cadets to the Mediterranean. It was MC'd, you might say, by Burl Ives. It was a good life.

Austin: There was the pleasant part of a Mediterranean cruise. The Riviera was high on the priority list to be visited by any group of ships in the Med at that time. I was fortunate enough to get my outfit there for the usual liberty ashore.

I got up for a golf game. I remember I was quite surprised to see girl caddies. This was a very long 18-hole course that we were playing on this particular day. I'm afraid that we weren't the easiest foursome to caddie for. There were several balls that went into the rough, and the caddies were pretty good at being right on them. But when we finished, the girl who was caddying for me said this was her third 18 for the day. I was so tuckered that I wondered whether I could have done 18 holes three times that day or not. So she got a good tip.

The experience of being a cruiser division commander depends largely on the breaks that you get. As to whether or not you are in a spot to get command of a Midshipmen's squadron or command of an amphibious exercise or command what they call springboard exercise down in the southern waters. Otherwise, it's pretty routine. You almost feel like you're a passenger riding lots of the time. When you get the breaks as I did, it can be quite interesting.

I was just coming back from Cuban waters with a very good size task force that had been down for Springboard exercises ---

Q: What is 'springboard?'

Austin: Springboard is a training underway program which is designed to maximize the use of different types in inner-type training. You get them together in a place like Guantanamo Bay. Nobody is concentrating on anything except training for a couple weeks or ten days or whatever the period may be that you can devote to this. It gets in a maximum amount of training. You can use the airplanes from the carriers to two targets for some of the boys to shoot at.

Q: Your resources must be quite varied in a training exercise of that type.

Austin: Yes. You have submarines to play target for the destroyers, and that sort of thing.

I was on my way back from this Springboard exercise, when I received a message from the Chief of Bureau of Personnel, Admiral Holloway. Which in effect said, "I would be happy to know that I was to be left in command of my cruiser division an extra length of time and that I would go to the Mediterranean for another tour of duty over there."

So as soon as I got into Norfolk I called my wife, who was then living in our house in Wardour in Annapolis. I told her that I would look for an apartment. I had about five weeks before I'd be shoving off again. So I'd look for an apartment for that time, for her to get herself packed, and come on down.

I had just gotten my last pair of socks stowed in the new apartment, when my wife called me to the telephone. She said, "It's Admiral Holloway."

Admiral Holloway said, "Count, how soon can you be all packed ready to go to Paris?" I said, "I thought you were going to leave me in my job for another tour in the Mediterranean." He said, "Yes, that's right, we were. But now we're not. How soon can you be on your way?"

Fortunately, I'd sub-let this apartment from a friend who was exceedingly nice. I got my check back from him when I departed, without asking for it. He was very kind.

You don't always strike that kind of a deal. That was one of the few times that I had change of orders and it didn't cost me a month's rent.

Q: Before we get into that Count, I think perhaps we'd better sign off today. Then we'll have another full tape, and we can finish up loose ends in your tour of duty with the NATO organization, and also your experiences with the Inter-American Joint Defense Board, and whatever else you want to cover.

Austin: We haven't covered very much of the second fleet tour either. We might get that in.

Interview # 15

Vice Admiral Bernard L. Austin, USN, Ret.   by Paul Hopper
Rockville, Maryland   September 5, 1970

Mr. Hopper: Count, I believe we had agreed at our last session that you might begin this interview with the discussion of your being Commander of the Striking Force for NATO. Would you like to proceed?

Admiral Austin: Yes Paul. The tour of duty to which you refer was that in which I was the Commander of the Second Fleet with my U. S. hat on, and the Commander of the Striking Fleet Atlantic with my NATO hat on.

The two Fleets were the same, except that the Striking Force Atlantic included the Second U. S. Fleet and those units assigned in those days by both the French and the British. The British contribution was usually more than the French, because the French concentrated on the Mediterranean more than on the Atlantic at that time, as far as their NATO contribution was concerned.

I recall one exercise that we held with Striking Fleet Atlantic. The British had one carrier and several cruisers and destroyers in the Force.

I think the British Admiral was a little surprised when I turned over Tactical Command to him, during one phase of the operation. He was, I think, as delighted as surprised.

I had many indirect upchecks from British sources about it. Evidently they were highly pleased that their senior officer in the Striking Fleet would be given an opportunity to do what he would have to do in case, shall we say, the throw of the dice in battle caused the Commander Striking Fleet Atlantic to be a casualty.

He ran the job very confidently, I might say. And no one criticized me for having done it. I think it was done many times thereafter, the ice had been broken.

The exercises, of course, as Commander Striking Fleet Atlantic, and training were mainly focused on enabling the different nationalities to work together as a team. Of course the scenario of the various exercises involved opposition to probable NATO opponents. Some of them were quite interesting. I don't think it's necessary to go into that, you can imagine the nature of them. But they did provide good training for the national unit in their own services as well as in a combined international force.

Now back to my job as the Commander of the Second Fleet. At the time that I was Commander of the Second Fleet, electronic warfare was a bit in it's infancy.

I carried out exercises which involved a higher degree of electronic silence than ships had been accustomed to. This meant that if they weren't able to listen well, they felt a little blinded. So I had many reports of down equipment.

Instead of giving them hell, which is one of the Commander's courses of actions, I decided that the situation required more than just censure of the individuals in command.

Q: Could I ask you to illuminate a bit further there Count? When you speak of electronic silence, precisely what does that mean? It obviously doesn't mean total silence. It means that some electronic noise, conversation, communications get through. Could you distinguish there as to what it means?

Austin: By electronic silence I mean, you do not send out any electro-magnetic transmission from your equipment. You can listen to other electro-magnetic transmission from other sources, without sending them yourself. Just like one can listen without talking. In fact, one listens better when one isn't talking. By the same token, when you do deny ships the ability to pump out their radar impulses and see what's out there, you heighten the keenness of their ability to listen.

But as I was saying, the situation was rather disturbing to me. I had a very excellent young officer as my Staff electronics expert. So I called the Chief of Staff and the electronics expert in, and discussed with them my concept for correcting the situation.

It was simply that we would form a Second Fleet Staff electronics team, which would visit any ship that requested the team's visit to help them get their electronic gear on the line and perking properly.

After discussing it, we decided it was a good idea, and I had the necessary Fleet notice prepared. Immediately we had lots of business. People didn't feel that we were spying on them because we made it, 'on request.'

But if they didn't request help and then came out with down equipment, then the Commanding Officer came over to see me. So there was a little carrot and stick in this.

We got the curve of competence to maneuver complex formations of many ships, without emendating electronic transmissions, to a much higher state than it was at the beginning of this little teamwork proposition.

When I left the Fleet, I will have to admit, it wasn't at the level that I would have liked to see it. But it was so much better that there was definitely light at the end of the tunnel.

During this time there was a proposal in the Joint Chiefs of Staff Organization by the Chief of Staff of the Air Force that a war game be set up which would test the ability of a fleet at sea to survive. SAC was to attack it and sink it, of course. It was my job to prepare for this exercise.

Admiral Wright was the Commander-in-Chief Atlantic at that time, my immediate superior on the U. S. side. He called me and told me about the forthcoming test and the fact that he wanted me to take charge and get the Fleet ready for the exercise. I was to make sure that ships not under my immediate Command also were ready for the exercise. And he said he would send me something in writing on it.

The next day I got about a five page directive from him, signed in the proper form and everything. I read it and then I re-read it.

Then I called in my Chief of Staff and had him read it. His reaction was the same as mine, although I had not told him what mine was. He said, "My God Admiral, he's given you all the responsibility for this damm thing and he's given you no authority to do anything about it without asking his staff every time you do anything." I said, "Well Dan, that's the way it reads to me. Send in my writer."

I dictated a less than one page directive from the Commander-in-Chief Atlantic to the Commander Second Fleet, subject - preparation for this exercise. I took my dictated memorandum and the five page job that I had gotten up to CinCLant Fleet, and I saw Admiral Wright.

I said, "Sir, you have sent me a directive. I feel that it is my duty to tell you that with that directive we will come out with very little accomplishment between now and the date set for this exercise." (Or tentative date set for it, they changed it a couple times as these things usually do happen. They involve so many forces that to get them all at one time is a real job.)

Admiral Wright said, "What's wrong with it?" And I told him. I was specific. I pointed out the requirements to wait for decisions from his staff about my proposals and all. I said, "Admiral we'll just spin our wheels between now and that exercise, if this is the way things are done. I suggest that you give consideration to giving me this directive." And I showed him the directive which I had written.

He said, "I don't see anything wrong with that. But I'd better let my experts see it." I said, "Well sir, why don't you call them in and let them see it while I am here, so I can answer any criticism." "Yes, that's a good idea." So he sent for his experts.

They immediately jumped on it. They said, "Why this authorizes him to go directly to CNO over your head." I said, "Yes sir, it does, Admiral. After all, if I am to run this by delegated authority, why should I bother you every time I want to get a little piece of equipment on a ship to make it able to do it's part in this exercise?" He said, "I think you're right."

So I answered all of their objections, and he reached over and got his pen and signed it. So we were in business.

I had been relieved as Commander of the Fleet before the exercise ever came off, but we were in a lots better position than we would have been had I tried to operate under the directive that his staff had drawn up for him to sign.

This is not an isolated case. I'm afraid that too often staffs tend to try to keep in their hands more control of more situations than they are capable of handling.

They like to give orders to somebody else and put the ONUS on him if something doesn't pan out all right. But they aren't quite ready to give him the tools with which to do the job that they have given him. So I think that is not an exceptional situation, but more or less difficult.

Q: I think a staff is much more inclined to do that than the Commander himself is.

Austin: Very definitely, that's been my experience at least.

While Commander of the Second Fleet I had a rather unique experience in that I was told by Admiral Wright to conduct a combined Sixth Fleet - Second Fleet exercise, because I was the senior of the two Fleet Commanders. The Sixth Fleet, as you know, is in the Mediterranean and the Second Fleet is in the Atlantic.

So I started to make the necessary plans for this operation, and then there was a flareup from the NATO Commander. He didn't want the Sixth Fleet participating in U. S. combined exercise which would take them out of their assigned area in his area of responsibility.

So for awhile it looked as though the exercise was going to be cancelled. But then only a few weeks before the scheduled date for this exercise, I was given a dispatch which said that the exercise was on again and to get the planning going.

15 Austin - 482

It happened that the Commander of the Sixth Fleet was a classmate of mine, who was a very cooperative individual. And so I sent him a dispatch right away and I, of course, gave him the information in the dispatch to me in case he hadn't gotten it yet. I told him that I was sending my Chief Planner and Planning Staff to his flag ship the next morning, and that I would appreciate all that he could do to expedite the joint planning of this operation.

I think my willingness to go to him instead of, "Send your planning staff to my flag ship earliest," or something like that, probably caused his natural willingness to cooperate to be a little greater than it would have been otherwise. I had a most warm and cooperative message back from him, thanking me for my message and my initiative and all, and sending my people to him, and assuring me that he would see that his people cooperated one hundred percent.

So we got the show on the road by the time it was scheduled, but it was not an easy exercise to plan. Because one of the conditions on which SACEUR had agreed to the Sixth Fleet's participation was that under no circumstances should the exercise take the Sixth Fleet out of the Mediterranean. So we had to get quite a few clearances for overflights of nations that were going to have to be overflown if we conducted an exercise between the Atlantic Fleet and a Mediterranean Fleet at the same time.

Q: Did you take your Atlantic ships into the Mediterranean?

Austin: Yes, I did.

So we were able, by the skin of our teeth, to get all of these clearances and arrangements made in time and the operation came off on schedule. We didn't have any repercussions from it, and the exercise was a real success, especially from the Second Fleet viewpoint. Because according to all the data, we won the inter-fleet contest.

It was gratifying to me, in that it showed me that my training in my Fleet was certainly not inferior to that of the Sixth Fleet in the Mediterranean.

Q: Then the Sixth Fleet was larger, wasn't it?

Austin: No, it wasn't. I think I had the edge on them.

Actually one of the main jobs of the Second Fleet Commander was to train the elements that were going to relieve in the Sixth Fleet. I had had word from a number of the Commanding Officers of ships that were trained by us and sent to the Med and then came back to us for another training period which indicated that they felt more highly trained when they left the Second Fleet than they did after they'd been spinning around the anchor off the Riviera in the Mediterranean.

They said that the conditions in the Mediterranean just didn't conduce to quite as high a state of training as they were able to get during their training period in the Second Fleet.

Of course this was an area in which I was greatly interested because it was my responsibility to see that the Sixth Fleet got well-trained units when they got them.

One of the other things that I was greatly interested in as Second Fleet Commander was the "permanency" of assigned units in the Fleet. Because I was quite concerned about my responsibilities for taking a group of ships that had never worked together and going into battle with them.

I had a little experience with this in the South Pacific during the war. The first time I had all the ships of my Division together we went into a night battle.

So I tried to keep some control over ships, even when they were in the Navy Yard. Not that I was trying to grab power or anything, but I felt as soon as they said good-bye to a Commander that his instructions after that weren't very impressive to them. But if they knew they were still under his administrative wing, maybe they might be a little more responsive to things that they could do even while repairing their ships to get ready for electronic silence and that sort of thing.

So we did make some progress in that direction.

The rotation of ships through the fleet was still higher than I wanted, but I had to be practical and I had to recognize that their were other factors than my desires.

I would notice that when I would get a new group of ships we'd spend several days just learning how to work together without danger to each other. It was quite interesting though to see the rate at which they could improve, when you put them through their paces with consideration for their limitations and consideration for their Commanding Officer's time on the bridge and all that sort of thing. They were as anxious, as it were, to get on the step as you were to get them on the step. So if you just gave them the chance and worked them hard enough, but not too hard, it was amazing how fast they could get into the groove.

Personnel was one of the areas in which I felt great concern, and I started with my own Staff. I think I told you already about the case of the nine Ensigns that I had on the Staff. I had each one up and had a cup of coffee with him —

Q: One of them wrote your biography.

Austin: That's right.

I think I've told you that, so I won't repeat that.

Generally speaking, at this time we had a fairly high level of competence among our people.

One of the big problems frankly was the scarcity of what we called critical specialists. Very often a man would get back from a Mediterranean deployment and due to the scarcity of personnel in his rate, the Personnel Officer of the Atlantic Fleet would order him to the ship across the dock that was just getting ready to go to the Mediterranean. This, of course, didn't make him happy.

I pondered this situation and did all I could, within the confines of the policies of the Bureau of Personnel, to correct it. But I was still considering this when I went to my next assignment, which was as Deputy CNO for Plans and Policy.

So one day I called the Chief of Naval Personnel into my office as he passed and I said, "I want you to look at the proposal I have here for you."

The proposal was substantially this - have for each three ships of the same class four crews. Schedule those crews to schooling at the home port of those ships. And schedule them to deployment, not on a hap-hazard basis, but on a rotational basis. After a crew had been at school for say three months, then it could be expected to deploy for a period. Then it came back from that deployment and it would go into navy yard or whatever the ship was scheduled for, until it was relieved by the relief crew.

In this way a man would be able to determine even a year ahead whether he'd be able to be home for Sally's wedding on a certain date, whether he could plan to take his family for a little outing in the mountains during the time that he had his leave, because he'd know when he was going to get his leave. He was going to get his leave when he wasn't deployed.

The Chief of Naval Personnel looked at this proposal. He said, "Count, I've got trouble enough now keeping one crew on one ship. I can't even consider this thing. Please don't submit this."

Well I did submit it, because I felt it should be submitted. And I later, when I went up as President of the Naval War College, had research done on this. The research indicated that for the first couple of years you would have a costly program, but that after the first couple of years you would begin to reap the benefits of the program in raising the level of competence of your personnel in the fleet. Because you would have a higher shipping over rate, because people would have fewer wives demanding that they get out as soon as they could. You would therefore have a higher shipping over rate, and you would be using more efficiently the time not deployed in the schools that were located at the point of home porting.

Of course this would have cost money to get those schools established at those ports. But in most cases your schools of East Coast ships are all in the Norfolk area anyhow.

Of course to make a scheme like that work properly, you should have some assurance that the housing for your personnel in the area of their home porting will be reasonable enough and attractive enough to cause them to have their families there instead of back in North Carolina with the family and whatnot.

This program was never adopted. But the Polaris submarine people have a similar thing, in that they have two crews for every ship, the blue and the gold crew concept.

I don't think you need that much for destroyers because they aren't under the water as long. They could stand longer deployments and longer tours of duty with shorter periods of rest.

I still think with the complexity of equipment increasing, we're going to have to do something like this in order to have the degree of competence, the degree of expertise to operate that equipment at it's peak effectiveness.

Q: That would seem to me like an eminently sensible arrangement Count. I can see where obviously you could not do that during hostilities, where you would have to improvise and use all kinds of makeshift arrangements. It seems to me that during peace time that some such system of rotating your crews, as you say, giving them increased competence, and permitting a chap to know a year ahead or a year and a half ahead where he's going to be would very definitely make the service more attractive.

Austin: I think so, Paul.

Of course, it was not intended as a war time measure. In war time one has to grit one's teeth, and do what I did in World War II. I was away over five years from my family then. So you take it, when there's a war on. Most people are willing to do what is necessary.

But in time of peace, very few men have wives who are willing to let them have a second Med deployment when they expected to have them home. It's these dashed expectations that kill you, as far as personnel reenlisting is concerned.

Think of the wife and family that expected that electronics technician, who was just back from a Med cruise, to be home or at least within striking distance for a while. His ship was going in the navy yard or whatever. He'd be where they could see him once in awhile, be where he could take care of all the problems that had accumulated during his absence. And then a phone call, and he's away again. Wives don't like that. And the statistics show that we have a married Navy today, not a bachelor Navy.

I think probably I've said enough about the Second Fleet and Striking Fleet Atlantic tour. Shall I move on to the Inter-American Defense Board tour?

After I left the job as Deputy for Plans and Policy in the Navy Department, I went as you know to President of the Naval War College for four years. At the end of that four years, I was approaching the age for retirement for age.

The Chief of Naval Personnel requested that I request retirement a few months earlier than my birth date, as it were, in order to accept an international job for which the Joint Chiefs had recommended me. That was the job of Chairman of the Inter-American Defense Board.

I had heard lots about that Board, not all of it complimentary. I had an Ambassador assigned to my Staff as my political advisor, as it were. He had had considerable experience in the Latin America area. In fact, he had been the Assistant Secretary of State for Latin American Affairs just shortly prior to coming to the job at the College.

I called him in and I asked him some very pertinent questions. I said, "You know me pretty well. Would I be happy in your estimation, in the job of Chairman of the Inter-American Defense Board?" I asked him several other more pertinent questions than that, but that was the broad area that I wanted to explore. I wanted his estimate of the job as far as my estimated capabilities and inclinations were concerned.

He said, "Well Admiral, I think you would now, because I think there's a challenge there now. I know you wouldn't be happy to just go and have a job which was pleasant and sociable and not have something to do. But I certainly believe that at this juncture there is a job to be done there. I think I would say - yes, you should take it."

I asked the Chief of Naval Personnel for more information on the job. So he wrote and told me that he had looked into it quite a bit because he had thought he might get it himself. He gave me his estimate of the job.

His estimate didn't impress me as much as that of the State Department's expert did. Smedberg thought it would be about a half-day job a day, that had been his estimate.

At that time there had been a friend of mine in the more wealthy part of the community of Newport who had been trying to get me to accept directorship in a few corporations in which he was interested. I had fended him off on the basis that I didn't feel that an active duty officer should be dividing his attention between the commercial world and his military duties.

So as soon as he learned about my forthcoming retirement, he hit me again out at the Clambake Club. He said, "Now this puts a different complexion on this situation. How about it now?"

I said, "I'm going to an international job the day after I retire from the Navy. I'll go to that job, I'll look it over, and I will then let you know as to whether or not I feel that I can conscientiously do that job and also serve as a director of a commercial corporation."

I came down here and was retired on July 31st, 1964. On August 1, 1964, I reported to the Joint Chiefs of Staff as Chairman of the Inter-American Defense Board in Washington.

After I had been there for about six weeks, I wrote my friend a letter. I told him, "I can't conscientiously accept any responsibilities other than my primary one as Chairman of this Board. Because there's a job to be done here that will take all the time and effort that I've got and maybe a little more."

In the meantime, I had requested of the Judge Advocate of the Navy an opinion as to whether or not my service on the board of directors of a company would in any way conflict with my interest as a military man in an international job. His opinion had been that that was perfectly legal, perfectly all right, provided my service on the directorship jobs was done on my own time. Take leave to go to directors meetings and that sort of thing.

I thereby turned down my opportunity to become a man of industry. But I have found since then that I wouldn't change my decision.

I found that the Inter-American Defense Board was a little in the doldrums. They were spinning their wheels pretty much, there was lots of frustration. I think that I gave them the leadership which enabled them at long last to face up to the problem of communist subversion within the countries of the hemisphere. Up to this time this had worried them, but they wouldn't face it.

The planning paper that we produced didn't get through until the eve of my being relieved three years later. It wasn't a perfect plan and it didn't stop subversion in the little countries of Latin America. But it at least crossed the bridge, it crossed the Rubican, as far as facing up to the problem and acknowledging that it did exist. And that there was an area in which all could cooperate and help each to identify, and to reduce the probability of communist subversion in their countries.

I had many veryclose associations with many very fine gentlemen in that job. I, of course, traveled to all the countries of Latin America during the job. I was received by the Head of State in each case, and of course always by the Minister of Defense because he was the one that I was representing as Chairman of the Board.

The Inter-American Defense Board is not an integral part of the Organization of American States. I think this is unfortunate. During my time there I unsuccessfully attempted to get it under the OAS, where I think any military organization should be. It should be under the political entity that is the head of the whole organization.

But when the Board was formed the Mexican government successfully opposed having it a part of the Organization of American States.

They set it up as a separate agency, responsible only to the individual Secretaries of Defense and Heads of States of the twenty-one separate members. This makes for a situation that will not promote progress, because any one of the twenty-one states can throw a monkey wrench into the cartwheels.

Q: I was going to ask you Count if you knew what the basis of objections that the Mexican government brought up against including it under the American States Organization.

Austin: Frankly Paul, the reason at the time of it's establishment and to this day is the fear of a military coup.

In all of these countries there have been many military coups. There is still the haunting fear that if you put the Inter-American Defense Board in the Organization of American States, it would take over the Organization of American States. Because it would become impatient with certain developments on the political side and it would usurp the political power.

I don't think this is very logical. I think though that it is a natural fear that has received emphasis from events even of recent times.

We almost succeeded in getting a resolution through the meeting of the Inter-American States in Rio de Janerio during the time that I was President of the Board. The meeting to prepare for the meeting at Rio was held in Panama. And the U. S. representative to that meeting was lukewarm about getting this item on the agenda.

I was happy that the Inter-American Defense Board, knowing of the meeting in Panama and the subsequent meeting to be held in Rio, did pass a resolution calling upon all the Ministers of Defense of the States represented on the Board to take the necessary steps to bring the Board under the wing of the OAS.

But I called up one day to check on the U. S. progress in this direction, and found that the paper that was going through the JCS was not scheduled to be on the agenda even until the eve of the meeting in Panama. I knew that this would be too late. The position papers would already be drawn up in State, and this would be given the back burner position if the Joint Chiefs did not express an interest in it.

So I asked my former Chief of Staff, who was then the Op-Dep in the Navy Department, to see what he could do about getting this on an earlier agenda. He called me back and said, "It's being put on a clear by hand basis, and the Chiefs should vote on it today."

They did, and they sent a very nice memorandum to the Secreatry of State, taking a very strong position in favor of the incorporation of the Board into the Organization of American States, and pointing out their reasons for so recommending.

Then the State Department sent it's blessing on the Chiefs position paper to their representative in Panama. But he claimed that it was too late to do anything about it. He made an effort, but claimed that the Mexicans had everybody lined up against it and that time had passed for bringing this up.

So it was not on the agenda when we went to Rio, but the Argentine delegation felt very strongly about this. They felt at Panama it had not been pushed properly, and so they submitted the resolution at the meeting in Rio.

Mr. Bunker was the Acting Chief of our delegation after Mr. Rusk departed from the meeting. It was at that time that this resolution came up. Mr. Rusk came down for the opening, and the usual first few days, and then he left when the shirt sleeves got rolled up, and they got down to brass tacks.

I went around to see Mr. Bunker and I told him my reasons for wanting to see this go through. He listened very attentively and said that he would give it consideration, but that he didn't think the U. S. would take a very agressive part in this.

And they didn't, and it didn't pass.

The speeches made against it are the basis for my answer to your question a little bit ago. They were emotional, they were not supportable by facts in many cases, they alleged things that were not in the resolution.

The young Argentine Ambassador who presented the resolution did a beautiful job. And was most restrained in his rebuttal of these emotional tirades against it. He and I became very close friends after that.

I went to him after the meeting and complimented him on his restrained and gentlemanly efforts in behalf of the resolution. He and I were good friends when he came back to Washington as Ambassador here. We had several social tete-a-tetes at his Embassy and at my house.

But it still is not under the OAS. And so on that particular program I failed, Paul.

Q: You certainly haven't failed in many of your programs that you set out to accomplish, Count.

Perhaps my logic of rationality isn't sound but it would seem to me, as you've indicated, that if the Inter-American Defense Board was actually under the Organization of American States that there would be less likelihood of coups succeeding in various countries. Because if you had the two working closer together they would be known to be in support of the existing government.

Austin: I agree with you, although several of my friends who were members of the Board during my Presidency --- (I let the word 'presidency' slip because to the Latin the chairman of an organization is "El Presidente" of the organization. And there being more Latin members of the organization than U. S. members, I was called "Presidente" more often than Chairman.

Q: Incidentally, are the Canadians members?

Austin: No, they are not. They were invited, and they did not come. They do send observers to some meetings, but they have stayed out.

Q: Being members of the British Empire.

Austin: That's right.

They have toyed with the idea. And I think that there's a definite inclination to get in, but it has never received the approval of the government.

Several of my friends of those days, who were members of the delegation of their countries, are now the heads of their governments.

I do believe that, generally speaking, the military people that come to the Board, either before becoming the dictator of their country of after, are men of high caliber. They're men of high ideals. They are men well-educated. They are men who not always come from the old first families of the land. Many of them today came up the hard way from the poorer families, and just by the gratuitous circumstances that enabled them to get an education they made their way up on their merit.

15   Austin -499

One such man, who was not a member of the Board but whom I got to know very well, was the Minister of Defense of Mexico. He was an old Indian, a brilliant old gentleman, and a very impressive man. But he'd come up the hard way in the Mexican army and he was the Minister of Defense there.

There comes to mind, for example, the President of Brazil at the present time. Or the head of the Brazilian government would be more accurate. His name is General De Medichi.

DeMedichi is a very restrained, brilliant man, who knows a great deal about the needs of his country. I know this from having had many personal conversations with him. Yet he is the head man in a junta in his country.

I feel that De Medichi's service in this country on the Inter-American Defense Board gave him a slant on the way the military are sub-servient to the political will of the people in this country, which will conduce toward his earlier return of power to the people in his country if he can convince himself that this will be in the best interest of his country under the circumstances in that country.

And I think this is true of a number of those who have been through the Inter-American Defense Board. I talked to them in a very confidential way. My door was always open to anyone who wanted to come and talk to me. And they did.

One of the times that I was most unhappy as a result of their visits was right after the Dominican Affair.

15   Austin - 500

That morning as soon as I got to my office there was a line outside of my door. The first one that came in said, and tears were literally running down his cheek. He said, "Why didn't your Presidente let us know in time to be helpful? I've been on the phone with my Presidente during the night, and he is a most unhappy man. If they had only told you and you had told us on a confidential basis to inform our countries, they would feel so much better about it. Now my Presidente is going to have to oppose the United States in the OAS. This makes him unhappy, and it makes me very unhappy. I know you had to do what you did, but you did it against your promise that the United States would not unilaterally interfere in the affairs of any of our countries. If we had only been told. Not asked, but just told before we learned it from other sources."

This was the gist of the unhappiness complaint that I received from practically every visitor that day. It was a regretable thing that the President was not able to be properly advised.

Even if he'd called the Ambassadors to the OAS to come to the White House, they would have come. They didn't have to have a meeting of the OAS and wait for the ponderous machinery to work. But if he had only given them an invitation to come to the White House for a confidential disclosure, I'll venture to say everyone would have been there, and told them that our troops were going in at such and such a time. And that this was being done to protect their Embassies as well as our own. And give them a briefing

#15 Austin - 501

on the situation as reported to him. Then they could go back to their Embassies, get off a dispatch to their Chief of State, and he would at least feel cut in. And then when the thing came up in the OAS, we wouldn't have had some people balking just because their feelings were hurt.

Q: My friend, Tom Mann, I think is largely responsible for that episode.

Austin: I have found the memorandum for the record which I was looking for. I wanted to read this to you to illustrate one thing.

Whatever effectiveness I had as Chairman of the Inter-American Defense Board, I'm sure was in part due to the fact that I was an honest Chairman. I was not a U. S. agent, I was not anything that I did not pretend to be. I did not accept dictates from U. S. sources, any more than I accepted dictates from Mexican, Uruguayan, Brazilian, or any other sources. And I think the members all knew this. But for the most part I was able to do this with the complete cooperation of U. S. officials. The Joint Chiefs of Staff never tried to twist my arm to promote their position. They had a delegation at the Board and they used it for that purpose.

There was however one case that stands out, of attempted arm twisting. This came from someone in your old bailiwick of ISA.

I will read this memorandum for the record. It was classified at the time, but the classification was by me. And although at the time it was classified, I think that in the context of this oral history it does not warrant classification.

15 Austin - 502

It's a memorandum to the Chairman of the Joint Chiefs of Staff. Subject: Conversation by phone with Mr. X, Deputy Assistant Secretary of Defense International Security Affairs. Then there's enclosure one, copy of memorandum for record of subject conversation, and enclosure two, copy of Inter-American Defense Board minutes of a secret part of session ___, document ___. (That's why it had to be classified, because it had minutes of a secret part of a session. I will not read that in here.)

"As indicated in enclosure one, the Deputy Assistant Secretary of Defense for ISA called me this date and made a request that I review the minutes of the session held on 9 March 1967, with a view to considering their amendment to delete from the statement of the Peruvian delegate objectional parts of his expressed opinion.

"The opinions to which Mr. X referred are critical of the United States policies in Latin America. But the delegate was giving what he considered to be the real basic reasons for the Argentine proposal regarding the institutionalization of the Inter-American Defense Board to fail to receive the necessary support in Buenos Aires.

"I am reporting this matter to the Joint Chiefs of Staff in order that they may be informed in the premise in the event that this matter is raised in regular channels.'

"This is the only instance during my Chairmanship of the Inter-American Defense Board when an official of the U.S. government has made a request of me as an international officer to deviate from the code of ethics which I consider to be essential for a proper performance of an international job such as the one I hold.

"In my opinion to have acted as requested would not only have been unethical, but would have jeopardized the effectiveness of all U. S. officers in international positions by putting them in the light of political control by U. S. authorities."

The memorandum for the record which that covering memo refers to is as follows ---

After writing this I submitted it to a Brigadier General in the Air Force who stood by my desk during the entire conversation, because we were due at a meeting in the Pan-American building forthwith. I had asked him if he wanted to ride with me, and he had come to go with me. So I was really on the verge of leaving when his phone call came in.

"At about 9:16 hours this date Mr. X called me by phone. He first expressed his regrets that he would not be able to attend the twenty-fifth anniversary celebration of the Board's establishment.

"He then addressed himself to a second subject by asking if I had read the minutes of the secret part of the Inter-American Defense Board meeting of 9 March 1967. I replied in a sense that I read everything which crosses my desk, but that some things about which I am already familiar I do not read verbatim.

"He then said that he invited my attention to those minutes to which he had referred, and requested that I ammend them by deleting the opinion expressed by the Peruvian Chief of delegation.

"I informed Mr. X that it would be quite inappropriate for me, an international officer, to accept such a request and to act upon it. I explained that as Chairman of the Board I am an international officer on loan for that duty. I also explained that the minutes of the Board are subject to amendment only by the action of the Board's council.

"He reiterated his request that I review the minutes to which he had referred, with a view to amending them as requested.

"I again told Mr. X that he obviously did not understand the nature of our organization, that I, as its Chairman, could not properly change the record of a Chief of a delegation's statement of his own opinions, even though those opinions may not be considered correct and may be even objectional to some.

"Mr. X then expressed the view that I should not as Chairman of the Board have allowed such expressions of opinions, which were mainly political, to be made.

"I asked Mr. X if he had read my statement as Chairman during the meeting in question, explaining why I had not called the delegate out of order.

"Mr. X said he had read the statement, but that he still considered that I had erred in not calling the delegate out of order.

"I then replied to the effect that it is at times quite difficult to draw a fine line between the political and non-political parts of a political-military problem. I explained that the delegate in question was expressing his own opinion as to why the Argentine proposal to correct the organization difficulties of the Inter-American Defense Board had not been successful at Buenos Aires. I explained that I felt that the delegate not only had a right to express his opinion regarding a matter of such direct interest to the Board, but that the other members of the Board had a right to be allowed to hear the Peruvian delegate's views on the subject which had been reported on earlier in the session in question.

"Mr. X then expressed his shock that such statements as contained in the reference minutes should be made in the Inter-American Defense Board. His words, though well chosen, were quite critical of my performance of my duties as Chairman on this occasion.

"He said that he had been called by Mr. Y's office in the State Department, and that he again requested that I review the minutes to consider the desirability of amending them as requested.

"I indicated to Mr. X that I felt that he was putting pressure on me to do something inconsistent with my concept of what is appropriate for an officer in an international job to do.

15   Austin - 506

"He immediately denied that he was putting any pressure on me and said again, "I am only requesting that you review the minutes in question, and have them amended so as to remove the derogatory remarks, particularly those that speak about the head of the government of Peru."

"At this point I reassured Mr. X that I would review the minutes but that I could not review as requested with a view to unilaterally changing them.

"In view of the lapse of time I informed Mr. X that I was already ten minutes late in starting for the twenty-fifth anniversary meeting of the Board at the Pan-American Union Building, and that I hoped that he would understand if I asked that we discussed this no further at this time.

"He readily agreed to discontinue our discussion, again reiterating his original request."

Q: I'm really surprised I've known X a long time. I knew him when he headed up the   section of ISA. That seems to me to be presumption beyond reason.
Austin: He was being pressured by Mr. Y.
When I took this to the Chairman of the Joint Chiefs of Staff by hand, I called him up and asked him if I could have a minute of his time. He said, "Why sure, come on over."

15   Austin - 507

When I went in and he read this, I asked him to read first the minutes of the secret part of the session. Which I have not read, because I don't feel that I can declassify them. The covering memorandum and my memorandum of conversation were not in fact secret but the facts that they had attached to them, secret minutes, I classified them secret too.

I asked him to first read the remarks of the Peruvian delegate in the minutes in enclosure two. And then read my memorandum of the record of conversation. And then read my memorandum to him showing why I was submitting this.

He did this in that order. When he finished reading the minutes of the meeting he looked up at me and said, "Well there are things there that we may not like to hear, but I'm afraid he's right. Even if he weren't right, he has a perfect right to express his opinion. Nothing further will come of this. I'll put it in my drawer here and keep it in case anything should come up."

I said, "Oh no Mr. Chairman, I don't agree with you that nothing further will come of this. I suggest that it's highly probable that your Chief of the U. S. delegation will receive similar pressure in the very near future. Mr. X was acting under pressure from Mr. Y in the State Department. He indicated this to me over the phone in more ways than one.

"I don't think Mr. Y's going to let this drop, at just making a demarche through Mr. X. He will go through other channels to try to get accomplished what he wants. And that is to expunge from the record things that put him in a bad light.

Q: How could you do that Count though, without a vote of consent with the members of the Board?

Austin: You can't, and a man in Y's position should know that.

I got home well after six o'clock, because I had left the Pentagon about five-thirty. My wife met me at the door, she said, "Goodness, there's been a General trying to get hold of you for the last hour and a half. He said he tried to get you before you left your office at the Pentagon, and he missed you there. He's really anxious to talk to you about something."

I said, "I think I know who it is." I waited a few minutes and sure enough the phone rang again. It was the General who was the Head of the U. S. delegation at that time.

I had seen him at the meeting at the Pan-American Building at the twenty-fifth anniversary ceremony of the IADB. And I had told him very briefly that Mr. X had called me, and had expressed his concern and alarm about what the Peruvian delegate had said, and that he had indicated that Mr. Y had been made very unhappy by it and that he wanted it out of the record.

So I said, "I tell you this because I suspect that you may be approached in view of my refusal to accede to the request."

He led off in his phone conversation by saying, "You predicted correctly. I have been called by Mr. Y. And Mr. Y has demanded of me that I take steps as Chief of the U. S. delegation to have those remarks expunged from the record."

I said, "As I left General Wheeler's office, he made this statement, "If the Chief of the U. S. delegation is approached on this subject, tell him to see me before he does anything." So you're informed of General Wheeler's wish to see you before you do anything."

So he went down to See General Wheeler and told him about it. General Wheeler told him as Chairman of the Joint Chiefs of Staff not to comply with said request.

Buz Wheeler called me and told me that the Chief of the U. S. delegation had come to him and what he had instructed him to do. He said, "I think that's it.

I said, "No, sir, that won't be the end of it. There will be further attempt to bring pressure to bear, and there will probably be a request that I be kicked out of my job."

He said, "Oh, they couldn't do that. You haven't done anything wrong. You protected your country against making a faux pas that would make it a laughing stock in international circles. You haven't done anything wrong."

15 Austin - 510

I said, "Sir, I cannot escape the feeling from the conversation that I had with Mr. X and his insistence about this, and his repeated referral to the unhappiness of Mr. Y and all, I suspect that they will do what I have suggested they will do."

Q: Was Mr. Y then Assistant Secretary for Latin American Affairs?

Austin: Yes.

A few days later a letter was submitted to Mr. Rusk, which castigated me as being disloyal, un-American, and everything else, and unfit to hold my job. But in going to Mr. Rusk it had to pass through someone's hands who had the good judgment to call the Pentagon and ask a few pertinent questions about this particular episode. When he learned about the episode from another angle, he didn't think that Mr. Rusk should sign this letter. The letter was addressed to Mr. McNamara.

So when that letter was refused a much tamer one came up which did not call me names, but informed the Secretary of Defense of the incident and stated State's views thereon.

That letter was signed by Mr. Rusk.

NOTE: Page 511 was eliminated by Admiral Austin - considered redundant.

Interview # 16

Vice Admiral Bernard L. Austin, USN, Ret.
Rockville, Maryland
by Paul Hopper
January 16, 1971

Mr. Hopper: Admiral as I recall at our last session it was agreed in ending up the memoir that perhaps we'd go back over some specific points that Dr. Mason had indicated information was particularly desired upon, in connection with the Nimitz biography. Would you like to comment further on some of those?

Admiral Austin: One of those points was the reaction of Admiral Nimitz to Admiral Halsey's run to the north at the time that the Japanese fleet units debouched from San Bernardino.

I thought I had covered this, but at the risk of repetition I will give you my recollection of this again.

On the morning in question Admiral Nimitz buzzed me quite early. I went into his office, he was obviously a little concerned. He asked me if there were any dispatches that he hadn't seen regarding the situation off the Phillipines.

I told him that I knew of none. I said, "Will you tell me what in particular you are looking for."

He said, "I'm very concerned because nothing that I have seen indicates that Admiral Halsey has left San Bernardino guarded against the Japanese units coming through there and getting our ships off Leyte."

I said, "Well Admiral, that is an unclear point in dispatches and several other people are wondering about the same thing." He said, "If anything comes in, let me know right away." I said, "Aye aye sir."

I went out and made a double check with all sources, and found that there was no indication that San Bernadino had been left properly guarded.

The interval between the first call to his office and the second was not very long. I went in again, and he asked again if anything had shown up to clarify the situation about San Bernadino. I told him that unfortunately there wasn't anything to clarify it. He thanked me, I went out, and he buzzed me again shortly. This happened quite a number of times.

So finally I suggested that he ask Admiral Halsey if he had left San Bernadino guarded. I said, "That's what you want to know, why don't you just ask him?"

He thought for a moment and then he gave me the answer which I expected. And that was that he did not wish to send any dispatch which would directly or indirectly influence the responsible tactical commander in the tactical use of his forces.

I knew that he was very strong on this principle. That's why it took so long for me to get the courage to suggest that he ask a simple question.

The next time he buzzed me, he was up pacing the floor. And Admiral Nimitz was not one to pace the floor. He faced many problems calmly and without any outward manifestation of the difficulties that he was having mentally coping with the situation. But on this occasion, he was pacing up and down.

So I knew that this was an index of a very high order of perturbation on the part of the Fleet Admiral.

So I suggest this time, "Admiral couldn't you just ask Admiral Halsey the simple question — where is Task Force 34?" Because if he left San Bernadino guarded, he left Task Force 34 to guard it. They would be guarding against the coming out of the Japanese battleships.

He thought for a minute and he said, "That's all right. Go out and write that up. That's a good idea."

So I went out and I had my yeoman write out the dispatch as I dictated. It simply said, "Where is Task Force 34? From Fleet Admiral Nimitz to Commander Third Fleet."

When this got down to the coding room however — it seems that Fleet Admirals are not the only ones who worry about situations that may place our forces in jeopardy. Because a young Ensign down there who had to do the coding for this message had gotten himself sufficiently perturbed that he forgot the rules about padding of messages of a short nature. And he padded the message with words that could be easily inferred to be a part of the text.

So the message went out something like, "All the world would like to know where is Task Force 34." This evidently caused Admiral Halsey unhappiness.

I don't think in my own mind that he should have for one moment entertained the thought that Admiral Nimitz was getting sarcastic with him. He, of course, had to take the message as it came and didn't realize that it had been added to by an Ensign.

Admiral Halsey immediately proceeded to send part of his force back to San Bernadino, but it was too late. The cat was out and the mice were stirring.

I think I told you about the press release on our encounter with the Japanese forces that came out of there. I'm pretty sure I covered that.

It was written by an officer, shall we say, who was naval air minded to the extent that evidently the fact that destroyers did interpose themselves between battleships and carriers was not noticed too much by him, but the fact that a few shells went all the way through the little carriers did make an impresson on him.

It was a bad time for the little carriers. They didn't have enough speed to get away from those battleships. They didn't have enough ammunition and planes to stop them. And so they were in a bad way. Their hulls weren't much thicker than a destroyer's hull. So it was a bad situation.

It could have been far worse, if the Japanese Admiral had not turned back. Why he turned back of course only he knows. But I think he thought it was a trap. It was too obvious a situation. He just had ships to shoot at everywhere that were good easy targets to sink. I think he just thought, "Oh boy, the Americans are trying to pull me into a trap."

Admiral Halsey was going north on pretty good intelligence that he was going to be able to come to grips with and sink very valuable units of the Japanese fleet. Shall we say, it's a matter of judgement.

He interpreted the reports which he had received from his air reconnaissance as indicating that the Japanese were not going to come out at San Bernadino. Actually I think one of his airplanes had reported that they had turned around and were heading the other way.

The fact was they were there, he knew they were there. Even if they reversed course for awhile, they could turn around again.

The considerations that caused him to go north with everything, instead of leaving part of his force there to guard San Bernadino, would be interesting to explore with someone like

Admiral Carney who might know just what the considerations were. Because I wasn't there, I don't know what his considerations were.

We all know that certain axioms of warfare are impressed upon you as you're brought up in the Navy. One is that it's not always safe to divide your force in little pieces.

Of course there was, as you know, an old battleship force that was part of the Leyte Gulf covering force. But they had, unfortunately, gotten pretty low on ammunition, and they weren't a match, even so, for these new Japanese ships.

So I'm sure that in an analysis of the situation later Admiral Halsey regretted leaving San Bernardino Strait unguarded.

I don't believe that you can, shall we say, gamble on the hundred to one shot when you are in effect gambling with the success or failure of a whole operation.

Q: His was part of the whole operation, was it not?

Austin: He was the covering force for the overall Leyte operation.

The Leyte operation had, as I previously said, its own old battleships and destroyers and jeep carriers to cover the landing, and to act as the immediate covering force for the vulnerable ships like transports and cargo ships that were involved in the operation.

But the sort of strategic covering task was that of Admiral Halsey. In the case of the Japanese forces which came through San Bernardino, that was part of his task to see that they didn't interfere with those landing forces.

Q: Halsey was inclined to be a little impulsive compared to Nimitz.

Austin: I don't know that I'd like to use the word 'impulsive.'

Admiral Halsey was the colorful type of leader. He inspired a very high order of esprit in his forces. He seemed to be willing to take chances, where in many cases they were well justified. But he was not the deliberate and thorough analyzer that Admiral Spruance was.

Admiral Nimitz, I think, recognized this. But he felt that he needed both types in that particular part of the war. And he was quite happy with Admiral Halsey. But I think he slept better when Admiral Spruance was at sea.

Admiral Spruance was more or less asked what he'd like when he came ashore. He said, "I would rather be President of the War College than to have any other assignment."

Q: Being a full Admiral, did he not revert to two-star rank?

Austin: I don't know that he had to revert. At that time I don't think the numbers game was quite as tight as it later became.

He never was Fleet Admiral, as you know. This was one thing that caused Admiral Nimitz a lingering unhappiness. Admiral Nimitz said to me on several occasions that he was still going to do anything he could to get Admiral Spruance his recognition as a five-star Admiral. But Admiral Spruance never got it.

It was one of those things - so many for the Army, so many for the Navy, so many for the Air Force.

Q: Speaking of Japanese ships, Count - how good were they? I always knew the Japanese had battleships larger than ours but I have often wondered if they were as effective, given comparable handling.

Austin: Paul, I think that one would have to say that the Japanese ships and their armament up to the point of technical development that they had reached were first rate. Their torpedoes frankly were better than ours.

We had an advantage on them in radar. I think we had some advantage over them in communication.

But their ships were very modern, very well built, and their personnel were very well trained. So they were not, shall we say, a paper navy. They were a very formidable outfit.

I think that our great losses in and around Guadalcanal during those early days was proof of it.

Their naval aviators were extremely good, both at night and daytime. Their gunners seemed to do pretty well both at night and daytime. But we did have an edge on them in radar.

I think that one of the obvious poor uses of their naval forces was the way they used their submarines. I think this was dictated by the fact that they had so many outposts that they had to keep in touch with, the submarine was the best thing to keep a trickle of supplies going into these places with men and information. They were using their miliatary submarines as cargo submarines in many instances.

So frankly our people in the Pacific were far more casual about the anti-submarine alertness than were those in the Atlantic. I know because I went from the Atlantic to the Pacific, and the difference was marked.

The reason for it was that nobody ever got sunk by a Japanese submarine, until they did. You remember we lost the cruiser, the INDIANAPOLIS, to a Japanese submarine. Of course after that happened, people took a little more precaution against loss of their ships by submarines.

The Captain of the INDIANAPOLIS was doing what most everybody else out there was doing, saying that, "A good straight course was all right when you're that far away from Japan."

He was a nice man. I only knew him very briefly, but I formed a very high opinion of him. I can tell you this - that loss of his ship etched itself on his consciousness. I talked with him as he came through Pearl and I felt very sorry for him.

But there was no other alternative other than to have the investigation. He, of course, being the Captain, got the brunt of it. That's the way those things go.

Q: Was our naval aviation superior to the Japanese? I've been told our naval aviators functioned more effectively as a part of the naval team effort than did the Japanese.

Austin: I think our naval aviators deserve a good bit of credit. The times when our naval aviation was pitted against Japanese naval aviation we showed up very well.

We had some might intrepid naval aviators in that theater. I say that with considerable feeling because several of them shot down Japanese planes that might otherwise have shot down my ship.

So it's one of those things that I don't think you can say that it was entirely due to the edge that our naval aviators had over the Japanese, but that certainly was I think a factor.

I do think that we probably overall used our naval forces a little bit more skillfully from a strategic and tactical viewpoint.

Q: Wouldn't you say too that we made better use of what we had in a given situation?

Austin: I think that enters into how you use your forces.

If you undertake something - it's kind of like in a poker game. If you undertake to boost the pot and make it big when you have the second best hand, that's not good planning. Of course you always think you have the best hand.

There is the same element of doubt always in war, because what the enemy has you have to determine in a large degree from your intelligence sources and your books that you've kept on the known losses that you've had.

So I think that when one tries to set the index of expertise of two opposing forces, such as the Japanese and ourselves in that war, there are so many factors that enter into it that you can't pin it down to any one, two, three, or four to any great degree of certainty. Because if these things could be done over, in the light of known quantities instead of unknown, I'm sure, for example, we wouldn't have lost the ships that we lost incident to those Japanese ships coming through San Bernardino. Because I'm sure that Task Force 34 would have been sitting there waiting for them, and would have let them have a pretty good salvo right as they got in the most vulnerable point of their turn out of the Strait.

Q: Being inferior to the Japanese after Pearl Harbor in ship strength I presume we had to husband our resources in every way possible.

Austin: We were, and we had to play it close to the belt. I think, frankly, that in the long run that was a blessing in disguise.

Q: Isn't it remarkable though, giving the devil its due, that the Japanese, taking into account small country and limited resources, were able to conquer as vast an area as they did in such a short time and to prolong the war for four years?

Austin: I think the Japanese are very, very industrious people who will always find their way in the sun.

I was greatly impressed when I was in Korea, in the Korean fracas, in my exposure to the Japanese people at that time. By being the Logistics Commander out there, I had to have business dealings with them as well as social dealings.

You just simply have to take your hat off to a people who are willing to work as assiduously and as long as they do each day, and with the minimum of fringe benefits. And they maintain a degree of morale that's very high, with very little to make them happy. Just a clean little floor to put a straw mat on and a few sips of sake once in awhile and a little string music, and they're perfectly happy.

Our people seem to require a great deal more to inspire them to endeavor. I think the Japanese are probably as industrious as any race of people that I've ever come in contact with.

Q: The Japanese have a wonderful knack of seeing and expressing beauty in simple terms, for example, their lovely gardens, simple but elegant interiors and exquisite flower arrangements.

Austin: Yes, the Japanese have developed this to a high point. They can get great happiness out of little garden spots that they have cultivated. They don't have to have a dozen American beauty roses in a vase. They can take one rose out of a garden and with a few little sprigs can make it just as artistic and pleasing to them, and to most people with artistic appreciation, as you can do with a dozen American beauty roses with very long stems.

Tokyo, of course, is so much like any other great city in the world today. It's overcrowded, undernourished, ecologically repulsive, and all that sort of thing. But there are beautiful parts of Japan still.

Q: Shall we go on to Nimitz's conversation with Roosevelt as to the strategy involved in taking the Marianas as a prelude to the conquest of Japan?

Austin: I think the next one was - the question I think was posed in the context of the Nimitz dinner table conversation about that. I was not present at the dinner table when the President and Admiral Nimitz were talking this over.

But as you know, the Marianas had figured very largely in Admiral King's assessment of the strategy of the Pacific for a long long time. He was of the opinion that the Marianas were more or less the key to the conquering of Japan. They afforded bases for the B-29s. They were only 1350 miles from Japan. They cut the Jap lines of communication, which was one stepping stone out to their bases farther south. They were close enough together to have mutually supporting air bases.

The taking of the Marianas had been approved by Roosevelt and Churchill on the conclusion of the Cairo conference, and a tentative date had even been set for taking them, which was October 1, 1944.

Then I think the success in the strike against Truk added to the argument that you didn't need to take everything down there before you got up farther north. You left the others to wither on the vines.

If you could take the Marianas and cut the sort of communications link to places like Truk, after you'd given it the blow that we did give it in the strike on Truk, you just let it wither on the vine.

There was a JCS directive that came out on 12 March 1944 that ordered Admiral Nimitz to seize the Marianas. On 15 June they developed the B-29 bases and made facilities there.

Now just what was said between Admiral Nimitz and President Roosevelt, as I say, I don't know. But I know all these things that I've mentioned were considerations that Admiral Nimitz sort of evaluated from time to time and I'm sure that the conversation probably included some of them.

Q: To follow up on that, Count, is this third point of the differences in fighting style as between the soldiers and marines ---

Austin: As you know, the Marines and the U. S. Army had different philosophies about fighting. They both had the same objective, and that was to win the objective given to them. But as demonstrated on Tarawa, the Marines were inclined to drive ahead and accept high losses for a short period of time in order to gain an objective and avoid a long drawn out string of losses. I don't intend to get into the pros and cons of the two philosophies but the two philosophies did, shall we say, exist.

Admiral Nimitz was a great person to promote harmony and happiness within his family. He didn't like controversy within his family of officers. And so it distressed him a bit to have this difference of philosophy between the Marines and the Army brought to a cataclysmic climax between the two General Smiths.

General Ralph Smith, as you will recall, I believe his Division was the 27th National Guard Division. I think the 27th came from New York. Some people said that the 27th was officered by people who were some times more politically influential than militarily competent, and all that sort of thing.

I don't know what the proper assessment of that is, and I don't intend to attempt it. But I did have the pleasure of meeting Ralph Smith the very day that he returned, having been relieved of his command by General How"lling Mad" Smith.

There was a couple in Honolulu who had a lovely place to which they invited various people that they thought might need a little rest and recreation. On this particular week-end I and Ralph Smith were among those invited to the *beach cottage*. Charlie Lockwood, of submarine fame, was one of the others I recall invited for the week-end. The famous Shakespearean actor, Sir Lawrence Olivier, was another one. I don't know how he got invited because he certainly didn't have war fatigue.

During the week-end I saw a fair amount of General Smith. I naturally didn't mention the Smith-Smith controversy, nor did he, nor did anyone. It wasn't mentioned the whole week-end. It was obvious the man was trying to forget a little bit, and was trying to really relax. He was a charming man.

From all that I know of the situation, I think he did probably as well as any General could have done with the assets that he had at his command.

But it is a fact that the Marines were moving their front faster than General Ralph Smith's Division was moving its front. The result was that the Marines were being exposed to flanking attacks and behind their line by the Japanese, because the 27th Division wasn't keeping up with them.

Evidently General "Howling Mad" Smith felt that this was a situation that could not be tolerated, and he did what I'm sure his conscience dictated. He held the top man responsible, and relieved him of command on the field of battle.

This of course caused quite a flurry in the Army High Command. General Richardson of course came over to see Admiral Nimitz about it. I'm sure General Richardson was receiving dispatches from his senior in Washington. The boat was rocked quite a bit by this incident.

General "Howling Mad" Smith, as he was affectionately called by Marines, was a very able, a very forceful commander, no doubt about it. But when Admiral Nimitz assessed all the factors, he was not too happy with General Marine Corps Smith's decision to relieve General Ralph Smith on the field of battle.

When he wrote up his fitness report on General "Howling Mad" Smith for that period, he called me in and personally assigned me the sad task of showing the report to General Smith. I did so and when General Smith finished reading it, tears rolled down his cheeks and he said in effect, "It wouldn't hurt from anybody but Admiral Nimitz." You could tell it was a tremendous shock to him.

What Admiral Nimitz had said in the report I can't divulge, it wouldn't be ethical. But it was not derogatory, it simply expressed Admiral Nimitz's unhappiness that General Smith had found it necessary to do this under the circumstances, and pointed out the imperative nature of cooperation with our sister services in the front line.

As General "Howling Mad" Smith interpreted, it was Admiral Nimitz's judgment that he had erred in this matter. And he felt that he had done right, of course, or he wouldn't have done it. I'm sure he searched his soul before he did it.

So I guess that covers that point.

Q: You covered that point very well.

Do you have anything to say about Admiral Nimitz's assessment of strategic value of Iwo Jima and Okinawa?

Austin: Iwo Jima and Okinawa were both frightfully difficult operations, as you recall. But I think Admiral Nimitz thought, difficult as they were, it was a necessity to take them.

Iwo Jima, of course, gave the B-29s, based on Okinawa, the necessary fighter support both going and coming.

The Okinawa campaign was commanded by General Buchner, who lost his life, as a matter of fact. It went on and on and on. They really had to be dug out.

They were getting so close to the heart of the Japanese Empire, that they were simply standing to the last man.

The calculations logistically had not taken into account quite so long an assault. There was one time there when we were supplying mortar shells by air, that's how tight it was getting.

And that's the time when the Marine General got caught trying to send out the plane load of whiskey that I told you about. He labeled this as combat front line equipment. One of my very able young officers at the terminal saw one of the cases drop and leak, so he stopped the loading and came up and saw me about it. We sent a few cases of whiskey on that plane, and mainly mortar shells.

Q: I suppose Okinawa was the hopping point for our close up bombing of Japan.

Austin: It was to be the stepping off point.

Q: Another point Dr. Mason inquired about was the damage to Halsey's fleet from typhoons and in general the problems typhoons caused our naval operations in the Pacific.

Austin: Yes, I have quite a bit of knowledge of that.

As you know the typhoon reporting system in the board reaches of the Pacific, especially during war when part of the area is under control of the enemy, is not perfect. So the meteorologist on the flag ship of the Fleet Commander had quite a responsibility.

Even when you're getting reports from land stations, it's not always easy to determine with certainty the path that a typhoon is going to continue on for the next 24 to 36 hours.

Admiral Halsey's meteorologist I think lacked the fundamental ability to assess the data that he had and then advise a safe course. The first encounter with the typhoon was I believe just before they were going to refuel the next day. Under certain circumstances you know many ships have to reballast to get ready to fuel

A meteorologist who knows from the data that he's getting locally and anything he can get from the
or any other place by radio and from other ships at sea, he should take into account how vulnerable those ships are when they pump out their ballast

I know that Admiral Nimitz was greatly distressed by the damage sustained and the loses sustained. We lost ships.

Q: Where did this occur?

Austin: I forget the exact position in the Pacific there, but it was incident to Admiral Halsey's operation while he had the Fleet at sea. I forget the exact location.

Q:

Austin: Incidentally, I had a little typhoon experience out there myself on a few occasions. I might briefly run into that.

I was the senior officer present at Okinawa during the Korean fracas. This was essentially during a peace time condition. We were getting reports from many places that you wouldn't get them from in war time. And the more I plotted these things the more I was in a quandary as to just whether I should go east or whether I should go west.

Of course if you went west, you were in a bad situation, because you were getting in shallow water. That China Sea is not as deep as the broad Pacific.

I plotted all the known typhoons that we had record of in books on board and the paths. And I studied the path that this one had made up to this point. Then we began to get non-concurring reports from the aero-reconnaissance of this thing.

So it was boiling on towards Okinawa, the place where we were sitting. I had a fair number of ships. They weren't all under my Command, but as the senior officer present they were. I was responsible.

I delayed my decision until I could delay it no longer with safety. Then I made my best guess on the best information that I had at that time. It wasn't a guess that took me completely clear of rough water, but it did turn out to be a correct guess. Because although we were buffetted about quite a bit, we didn't lose a man and we didn't lose a ship.

But my flag ship Captain got very unhappy. The PIEDMONT was my flag ship. The Captain of the PIEDMONT was my classmate, a very fine fellow named Topper. Old Topper would come over ever so often and say to me, I was up on the bridge all the time, he'd come over to me in my flag part of the bridge and say, "Commodore, I think we ought to do something." I'd say, "Well Captain Topper, what would you suggest?" He'd say, "Well I can go faster."

You see he was trying to get farther away from the path of this storm. I said, "Yes, I know you can. But you know that ten knot *reefer* back there can't go even a smidgen faster. He's going all he can right now. We're going to have to stick with him."

He'd pace for awhile and then he'd come back, "Commodore, I think we ought to do something." We'd go through the same process

But we managed to get clear. It was rough, but we were safe all the time and we didn't lose anybody or any ship.

Admiral Radford was at that time the Commander-in-Chief of the Pacific. And he laughingly told me when I came back through *Pearl* on my way from that assignment, he said, "You caused my staff an awful lots of perturbation when that typhoon was heading for Okinawa. They kept coming in pestering me to order you to get your ships underway and get out of there. I wasn't as worried as they were, I knew you'd do what you should when the time came. So I wouldn't let them send you any dispatches telling you what to do. But it certainly was not very clear whether you should go east or west. How did you make up your mind?"

I said, "Well, sir, by waiting to the last minute. And then taking the course that the information at that time seemed to indicate was best."

Then the other time was one I think I told you about when we were loading ammunition up in Sasebo. The typhoon didn't come right over, we were in the edge of it. I consulted with an old Japanese pilot. I asked him how long he had been in Sasebo. He'd been there a long, long time.

I said, "How many typhoons have you seen?" "Oh, a good many." I said, "What is your experience of ships leaving here to get clear of them?" "Very bad, sir, very bad. With all islands off the entrance, we have had many ships that left here to run out of the way of typhoons and came to grief on them."

I said, "I notice you have pretty good anchorage buoys." "Oh yes, we take great pride. They are very good, well anchored." I said, "Have you ever known of a ship to be lost that was tied to one of those buoys?" "No, I've never known of a ship to suffer storm damage at buoy, but it must be only one ship to one buoy."

So after talking with the old pilot, I made my decision. I ordered everybody that was doubled up in buoys to single up, in other words, one ship, one buoy. We had a battleship in there at the time, and we had a carrier. We had quite a few ships that were fast ships that could run from a storm. But as the old fellow had said, I kind of felt that they were better off right in there because Sasebo is very well protected by high rims of mountains all around practically. There's just a gap to come in.

Suffice it to say that we turned out to be all right. The ships were a little anxious at times. They tugged at their moorings but nobody got any damage.

Q: If you didn't have enough buoys for all the ships, I presum you had to tie more than one ship to a buoy even though it was customary to have a buoy for each vessel?

Austin: That's right.

Q: Is it appropriate to say something about plans for the actual landings in Japan? Had you been personally involved in their development?

Austin: Of course I was not a part of the planning staff but Admiral Sherman discussed it with me in the privacy of our room.

I think it would have been a tremendous undertaking if we'd had to do it, and I think it would have involved a considerable loss of life.

Q: As I recall casualty estimates ran into the hundreds of thousands.

Austin: You would have been dealing with a people with their backs to the wall willing to sacrifice their very life if necessary to protect the Emperor in their homeland. And it would have been a long and bitter struggle as on Okinawa, only on a greater scale.

Q:

Austin: There're always differences of opinions among honest men, I think, who are courageous enough to express those differences. There certainly were things that were not as far advanced as they would have been for the invasion if, it had actually come off. For example, I'll give you one thing —

I was not the one in charge of logistics on Admiral Nimitz's staff at all, I was not that senior. But I was in charge of administration, to the extent that I controlled air lifts and that sort of thing.

One day one of the people from General Leahy's office, he was the logistician on Admiral Nimitz's staff, an Army Major General at that time, came down to me with an urgent request for sending an enormous amount of military vehicle tires to Okinawa by air.

I said, "My goodness, this will just buy up all the air lift we've got for a long time. What's the urgency of this?" They said, "This has got to get out. It's equipment for the invasion of Japan." I said, "What's been happening to this requirement all these weeks that it hasn't already been shipped out there?" There was lots of humming and hawing.

So to make a long story short, I looked at the routing slip and the dates on it. It had been kicking around up in General Levy's bailiwick between his five one-star level chaps for a matter of a couple months. So I took the thing and went up to see Levy himself. He was a very able individual.

I said, "General I'd love to give you the air lift for this, but I think it would only be encouraging your people in putting off until tomorrow what should be done today. I can get these on a fast cargo ship, top loaded, that's going to Okinawa. I don't think that they'll be urgently needed out there for reequiping vehicles for this invasion quite that fast." He smiled and said, "I agree with you, put them on the ship." And that's what we did.

That gives you one little illustration of how things were shaping up for that invasion. It was taking a tremendous amount of reequiping and repairing and getting everything in tip top shape for the final push. It was going to be an awfully difficult invasion.

And I think if you'd had an invasion of Japan, you'd have had a more difficult aftermath than we did.

When they of their own volition decided to throw in the sponge then they felt a moral obligation to put their shoulders to the wheel and cooperate.

I think if we'd invaded and gone through the tremendous amount of killing that would have been necessary to beat them down, it would have been just like on Okinawa.

Q: I've always thought that Truman made the right decision.

Austin: I think so, under the circumstances. It was a difficult decision to make. It did unveil the powers of the atomic weapon.

Q: In a way though it might have been better not to have revealed the bomb, if we could have kept it secret and if, as seemed apparent, Japan was seeking surrender terms before the bomb was dropped.

Austin: This is an interesting thing to discuss, because one never knows. If this had not been unveiled at this time, it was known to be, so when would it have been unveiled. And what would the consequences have been, if it had been unveiled at a time when instead of having a handful, people had big arsenals full of them.

Q: I am frequently amazed at the professed concern of our politicians regarding our development of germ warfare capability. After all it is no more unethical to develop ability to conduct biological warfare when you know that your potential enemies are doing it than it is to keep abreast in nuclear weapons.

Austin: Not at all. And it some times frightens me a little bit that some of our public men highlight these things that are if not obviously against our own national interest, certainly not in that interest.

I was somewhat amused the other day about the Okinawans. They parade and demonstrate about the existence of these gases on their island. Then when the Army tries to take them off the island, they parade and try to stop them from taking them off. I'm not sure where they're getting their motivations from.

Q: I think a factor which often rubs people the wrong, and I suspect it is the case in Okinawa, is the disparity in living standards between our military and the people of the country where our forces are stationed.

Austin: I feel that you're right there. I had a fairly good exposure to Okinawa during the Korean unpleasantness, because my main base was there for awhile, until we moved up to Sasebo.

One of the things that I thought was being overdone was the great contrast between the living facilities of the people stationed there and the Okinawans. This is something that's difficult to deal with, because you are dealing with your own people. You can't always accept the living practices and standards of the local people for your people, but you don't have to overemphasize the difference.

Q: I don't imagine that you, Count, ever make a point of your rank under any circumstances.

Austin: I felt complimented several times during my recent trip to Switzerland and Austria to be accosted by one of the local people asking to be directed to some place, because they thought that I was a native. That's a real compliment. My German is just nil.

Q: I bet you didn't let them know that you were a retired naval officer of three-star rank.

Getting back to Mason's questions, did the supply train concept originate with Admiral Nimitz or did it develop of necessity through various persons working on the problem?

Austin: I don't think there's anything so special on that.

It was an extension of things that developed in the Fleet before Pearl Harbor. Admiral Calhoun was Admiral Nimitz's Service Force Commander out there. Admiral Nimitz was very fond of Admiral Calhoun as an individual, and I think made suggestions to him from time to time in other than an official way.

But it was something that so many people had to do with that - for example, there was a fellow called Scrappy Kessing, who was given the job of developing one of the advanced bases and did a very good job of it. There were so many people that contributed.

Admiral Nimitz, of course, had graduated from the Naval War College. On one occasion when I had him there while I was President of the College, he paid great tribute to what he'd learned as a student at the Naval War College.

He said in effect that every decision that he made in the Pacific could be said to have been influenced by what he learned at the Naval War College. He said that the only thing that hadn't been developed at the Naval War College that he had to face was the kamakazi attacks. He said other than that the decisions that he made were definitely helped by his having studied the theoretical situations while a student at the War College.

So I think that he had the necessary breadth of background study of fleet operations before he became the Commander out there. Then he had lots of good people to help him. He was a methodical individual, as you know.

So the first thing that occurs to a very methodical military man is if you don't have the logistics you don't go very far

Q: He knew what was needed to be done and passed the problem to people able to solve it.

Austin: That's right. And he had a lot of able people on his staff to cater to his expressed desires.

Q: After you left the Inter-American Defense Board, you more or less completely retired from the naval service.

Austin: Yes. I retired but was called back to active duty when the SCORPION sank. I conducted that investigation and submitted our report. Then later they found photographs of the wreckage and so we were called back into service to examine the photographs, of which there were many.

So actually my date of final retirement from that temporary assignment was 19 December 1969, just in time for Christmas.

Q: You certainly have had a wonderful career, Count. You can look back on it with much pleasure and great satisfaction.

Austin: I was tempted at an early age to get out of the service, at the time that my family was developing financial requirements, the Congress reduced our pay 15% and froze pay for promotions. This resulted in my receiving inadequate pay to meet those requirements.

I was offered a very tempting job with a brokerage concern. They offered to start me with a salary of about an Admiral's at that time, and guaranteed me a five year contract.

But I've never regretted in any way that I didn't get out of the service. I love it, and I think of all the big organizations, it's among the best.

I'm ready to recognize that all big organizations have weak points and their fallacies. But I think the Navy has done pretty well through the years as a big organization, with a little bit of heart as well as an eye on the ball. I'm happy to have served my country through it.

Q:

Austin: Paul, I don't think that many of us could endure what we have to endure in the Armed Services and take the risks that we take in wars if we didn't feel that in so doing we were contributing to the security and the future happy development of our country

Q: That's what makes me a little apphrensive Count at the present time, seeing the attitude that so many of our young people have.

This has been most pleasant and satisfying, and certainly a stimulating experience in having these sessions with you. I'm sure that your memoir will be a real contribution to this phase of naval history and the history of our time. Thank you.

INDEX

for Interviews with

VICE ADMIRAL BERNARD L. AUSTIN, USN (RET.)

ABC Conference, 120

Ammon, RADM Wm. B., 92

Anderson, The Hon. Robert, 432-434

Astor, Lady Nancy, 116-118

Austin, B. L., school, 1-3; student army training, 2-3; appointment to Naval Academy, 4-6; youthful enterprise, 7-8; hunting, 8-10; fishing, 11; high school, 13-14; sports, 14; marriage, 17; "Count," nickname, 19-20; home town, 1, 13; made Captain, 267-268; Commodore rank, 317-319

Bailey, Admiral Sir Sidney, 99-101

Baker Island - naval operation, 244-45

Berry, RADM Robert Wallace, 72 ff

Boiler Tube incident, 213-216

Bougainville Engagement, 251-260

Brooklyn, USS, 174-5

Brynes, Hon. James: appointment to the Naval Academy, 4-6

Buka Engagement, 261-265

Bunker, The Hon. Ellsworth, 496

Burke, Admiral Arleigh, 196, 198-201; 204-205; 215, 261-265; 461-463

Burton Island - Ice breaker, 391

Bush, Stone Elkin, 18

Calhoun, Admiral Wm. L., 309-310

Capon Springs, Va., 71

Central Intelligence Agency, 322, ff

Chandler, Vice Admiral Alvin Duke, 372

Churchill, The Hon. Winston, 87-89, 99

Citadel, The, 12

Civilian Control of military, comment on, 180-183; illustration, 188; 189-190

Cliveden set, 115

Colbert, Vice Admiral Richard, 417-418, 453

Combat Information Center - DD's, 217

Coordinating Committee - Secretariat of State, War, Navy: Austin serves as Navy member, 316, 325-329

Cruiser command, question of for Austin, 383-386

Cruiser Division #2, 465; amphibious exercises, 469-471; midshipman cruise, 465-469

Cuban quarantine - student reaction, Naval War College, 191-192

De Medici, Gen. - Brazilian President, 499

Denebrink, Vice Admiral Francis C. 392, 394

Denfeld, Admiral Louis, 64, 143, 164-5, 366

Destroyer Training Program - young officers: genesis of, 153-157

Dominican Republic - U. S. intervention, 499-501

Dora, Chief, 28-29; chief petty officer on R boat, 28, 76-78, 81-82, 83, 85

Dorchester Hotel - London, 96

Drake, Capt. Waldo, 278-283

Dulles, Hon. John Foster, Secy. of State: 181, requests CV to Buenos Aires, 181-2

Duncan, Admiral Donald, 434-435

Edwards, Admiral Richard S., 307-308

Eisenhower, President Dwight D., 330-332

Ewen, Vice Admiral Edward C., 399, 400-401

Fedala - North African invasion, 206-27

Foote USS - DD, 157-158; commissioning of, 158-9; departure, 160-161; training program, 162-4, subsequent Training, 165; patrol duties and problems, 166-170

Forrestal, The Hon. James, 309-310

Fox, Lt. Gen. Alonzo Patrick, 186-188

Gates, Secretary Thomas, 204

Ghormley, Vice Admiral Robert Lee, 87ff, 93-94, 96-97, 99-103, 115, 120-121, 125, 127, 129, 358-359

Godbold, Asa, paper and laundry business, 7-8

Goodenough, Comdr. Michael, 102-104, 107

Gray, The Hon. Gordon, 357-377

Gruenther, Gen. Alfred M., 105-107, 110, 371

Guam - communications cable, 296

Gunther, John - author, 128, 131, 133

Haines, Capt. Gordon W., 238-240

Halifax, Vicount, 116

Hallas, George: athletic officer, Nimitz staff, 312-313

Haynsworth, Comdr. Wm. McCall, Jr. (Max), 210-212

Hazlett, Capt. E. E., Jr. (Swede), 135

Hitchcock, Comdr. - Assistant N. A. for Air, London, 91-93

Holloway, Admiral James L., Jr., 473

Imperial Defense College: 362, question of Austin's appointment, 362-367; contrasted with National War College, 374-375

Inchon Landing - plans for, 404, 408

Indianapolis, 520

Intelligence organizations - discussion of polic, 357-360

Inter-American Defense Board, 490; effort to get under OAS, 493-497

International Affairs Division - Navy Department, 425-439

ISA - Department of Defense, 437-439

Japanese Mandated Islands, 100

Japanese naval units - comments on, 519-520

Johnson, The Hon. Louis, 370

Joint Chiefs of Staff: Manner of discharging responsibility, 193-196; informal requests for information, 446-447; illustration of speed in decision making, 448; memo to from Chairman, Inter-American Defense Board, 502 ff; interface with State Department, 450-453

Joint Staff (of Joint Chiefs) Director, 330-336, 340; virtue of duty on a joint staff, 445; relations with staffs of service chiefs, 454-455

Joint Staff problems (of Joint Chiefs), 454-455, 463, difficulties with unanimity, 456, 462; question of service loyalties, 463-464

Joy, Admiral Charles Turner, 405

JSOP - Joint Strategic Objectives Plan, 355

Kauffman, Vice Admiral James L., 272-273

Kirk, Admiral Alan G., 90-91, 97

Kluckhohn, Frank Louis, New York Times correspondent, 63-64

Knox, Secretary Frank, 125

Kolombangara - operations around, 248

Kwajalein, 269

Labor problems: American, 218-222; Australian, 222-223

Lamar, Capt. H. A., 290-294

Leahy, Fleet Admiral Wm., 55 ff, Leahy and the atomic bomb, 66-68

Leavey, Major Gen. Edmond H., on Nimitz staff, 536

LeMay, General Curtis, 460

London clubs, 99

Londonderry-Greenock Mission - USS Woolsey, 207-209

Lovett, RADM B. B., 69 ff

MacArthur, General Douglas, 406

McCarthy, Senator Jos., 430-431

McMorris, Vice Admiral Charles H., 294-295, 298-299, 300, 302, 314-315

McNarney, Gen. Joseph T., 132

Mercer, Rear Admiral Preston V., 273-275, 383

Merrill, Vice Admiral Aaron S., 247

Military services - unity in overall effort: discussion of, 197-205, illustration of Austin argument for, 198-202

Miller, Rear Admiral George H., 456

Miller, Rear Admiral Harold B. (Min), 281-283

Missile ships - first use, 269

Missouri - BB, 387

Mountbatten, Admiral Lord Louis, 107-109

National Security Council - Navy member, 343-353

NATO Striking Force Command, 475 ff. (See also, 2nd Fleet Command)

NATO - study of future naval forces, 110-112

Naval War College, 376-380; concepts of war gaming, 409-414; global strategy discussions, 414-417; course for officers of friendly nations, 417-425

New York – BB, first duty, 26, 32-33

Nimitz, Fleet Admiral Chester W., 125-126, 274-278, 280-282, 286, 292, 295, 297, 300, 311, 314; strategy involved in taking Marianas, 524-525; deals with friction between army-marines, 526-529; strategic value of Iwo Jima and Okinawa, 529; supply train, 540; tribute to Naval War College, p. 541; Task Force 34, 512 ff

Nimitz Staff: personnel recommendations, 275-276; direction of mail, 277-278; public relations, 278-283; insubordination problem, 300-302; decisions, 283-289; 302-304; relaxation of censorship, 306-308; award giving ceremony, 311-312

Norstad, Gen. Lauris, 112-113

Ofstie, Vice Admiral Ralph A., 228

Piedmont – repair ship, 397, 533

Pitcher, Major Gen. Ollie, 336-339

Pittsburg, 466-469

Portugal – wait for passage there, 128-133

Potomac: President yacht, 53-54

Press relations officer, 55-60

Radford, Admiral Arthur, 223-226, 227-244, 392-393, 402, 533-534

Retirement of military men: remarks on, 67

Rockefeller, The Hon. Nelson, 355-356

Royall, The Hon. Kenneth C., 326-327

Rusk, The Hon. Dean, 510.

Sasebo, 406, 534

Schuyler, Gen. Cortlandt van R., 111-113

Scorpion - SS: investigation of sinking, 542

Second Fleet Command (See also NATO Striking Force Command):
exercises involving electronic silence, 477; exercise with SAC, 478-480; exercise with Sixth Fleet, 481-483; training units, 483-484; scarcity of specialists, 486; personnel proposals, 487-489

Selfridge - DD, 247

Service Force, Western Pacific: Austin organizes, 392, 394-399, 402

Service Squadron 1, 388-392

Sherman, Admiral Forrest P., 298, 304, 320-321, 383, 393

Slessor, Sir Jack, 370

Small Staff - discussion of, 353-357

Smedberg, Vice Admiral Wm. R., III, 432-434, 491

Smiley, Lady, 122-124

Smuts, Prime Minister Jan Christian, 368-369

Sowers, Rear Admiral Sydney, 320-322, 351-353

Spare parts - electronic parts for ships, 246-247

Springboard - training underway program, 472-473

Spruance, Admiral Raymond Ames, 518-519

Squalus - DD, 60-62

Stark, Admiral Harold R., 90, 100, 125, 128-129

Struble, Admiral Arthur D., 404-405

Student Army Training Corps, 2-3

Submarines: SS school, 40-41; duty on R-6, 42-43; incident of sump tank, 46-48; incident of electronic spares, 50-51; R-10, 76 ff; Kingston valves, 77-78; assigned SS duty instead of DD, 135

Sundowners, 230-235; examples, 238-240

Symington, The Hon. Stuart, 326

Taylor, Gen. Maxwell, 196

Theleen, Capt. David, 40-41

Thorne, Lt. Comdr. Oakleigh, 290

Thorp, Capt. Pinkie, SS commander, 45

Thunderbirds - Air Force show, 182

Topper, Capt. James Russell, 533

Torpedo School - Newport, R. I., 37-39

Towers, Admiral John H., 297

Truman, President Harry S., 352

Turner, Admiral R. K., 271-272

Twining, General Nathan, 336-337, 458

Typhoons in the Pacific - comments on, 530

Walkie-talkie, use in battle, 269-270

Watkins, Rear Admiral Frank, 385-387

Weiser, Bud, 18-19

Wentworth, Capt. Martin, 126-127

Westmoreland, Gen. Wm. C., 3

Wheeler, Gen. Earle G. (Buz), 452-453, 509

Wier, Lt. Henry, 139-140, 147

Winant, Ambassador John, 121-122

Windsor Castle, 123-124

Woodson, Capt., 53-56

Woodward, Admiral, 58-59

Wooldridge, Admiral Edmund Tyler, 320, 347-348, 363

Woolsey, USS - DD, condition of, 134; 136-138, 144-145; morale on board, 146; sinking of German SS, 147; commendation, 147; additional stories, 173 ff; The Exec - Lt. Wallace, USNR, 147-149; experiences in, North Africa, U.K., 205-212

Wright, Admiral Jerauld, 479-480

Yeager, Vice Admiral Howard A., 365